The Dachshund Handbook

BY

LINDA WHITWAM

ISBN: 979-8692955456

Recommended by

The Dachshund Breed Council
Health Committee

Author's Notes

The Dachshund Handbook is written in British English with British spellings, except where Americans have been quoted, when the original US English and spellings have been preserved.

The term *Standard* has been used to differentiate the larger type of Dachshund from the Miniature.

I have alternated between *he* and *she* in chapters to make this book as relevant as possible to all owners.

This book has been printed in black and white to make it affordable for new owners. The **Full Colour Dachshund Handbook** is also available from Amazon.

I am deeply grateful to the passionate breeders, owners and canine experts for sharing their extensive knowledge and love for the incomparable Dachshund. This book, the 18th in The Canine Handbook series, would not have been possible without you.

Specialist Contributors

THE DACHSHUND BREED COUNCIL

MELISSA M. SWORAB

IAN SEATH

LISA COLE

PAULINE CHEESEMAN

KRISTIN CIHOS-WILLIAMS

Major Contributors

Special thanks to (in alphabetical order): Bastiaan Smit and Judith Smit Haffmans, Brenna Carlisle and Laura Potash, Hannah Norton, Judith Carruthers, Kristin Cihos-Williams, Lisa Cole, Lisa Lindfield, Marianne McCullough, Melissa and Mark Sworab, Pame Bates, Pauline Cheeseman, Sandra and Karl Robertson, Dr Sara Skiwski, Stefanie and Steve Millington, Sue and Ian Seath.

(Breeders' details appear at the back of the book)

Table of Contents

1. Meet the Dachshund

The Dachshund has been a popular breed for decades – Waldi the Dachshund was the mascot for the Munich Olympic Games back in 1972 - but never more so than today. This fiercely loyal dog with the heart of a lion has captured hearts and minds in countries around the world.

Dachshunds have established themselves as a firm family favourite and love snuggling up with their beloved humans. But don't expect a lapdog; you're getting a pure hound on short legs! Nobody has told the Dachshund he's small, and he approaches the world with the attitude of a much bigger dog.

Treat him with respect, teach him some manners and exercise him regularly. You will be rewarded with THE most loyal and affectionate friend, and a lifelong companion second to none.

A Lot of Dog in a Small Package

There are hundreds of breeds registered with the Kennel Clubs and all of them are different – but there's something extra special about the Dachshund.

For a start there's the breed's appearance. Line up 100 non-dog lovers, show them a variety of breeds and every one would instantly recognise the Dachshund. The short legs and long body are unique. So is the breed's personality, which is why many owners won't consider any other dog once they've had a Dachshund.

The breed has to suffer many nicknames - not all of them flattering: Sausage Dog, Wiener, Weens, Weenie, Teckel, Dachel, Daxie, Dashie, Doxie, Doxin, Dotsun dog - and even Datsun, which I always thought was a car. His unusual shape has made him a cartoonist's dream and the butt of countless jokes.

Yes, the Dachshund is comical, both in both personality and shape - *"Half a dog high and a dog-and-a-half long!"* - but there really is so much more to this dog than his amusement factor.

This noble breed was originally developed as a scent hound. His job was to track badgers, rabbits and other animals into their subterranean lairs, then to fearlessly hold his ground, barking loudly to alert his master above ground.

If you've ever seen a badger close up, you'll understand why the Dachshund has a reputation for bravery and tenacity (determination, never giving up).

Badgers are powerful animals that can grow to twice the size of a Standard Dachshund. They have long, sharp teeth and claws and, if cornered, will fight to the death. A dog needs bucketloads of courage to face down a trapped badger.

Dachshunds have lively, intelligent minds that love a challenge and, like all hounds, they are feisty (spunky in the US) and independent-minded - some would say stubborn! - as well as creative thinkers.

These traits are genetic, bred into them over decades to enable them to hunt alone or in pairs at a distance from their masters. They also still love burrowing - so pat the bedcovers or cushions very carefully before sitting down.

These long-lived dogs approach life from their own unique viewpoint - don't expect yours to jump to your every command, nor be easily housetrained. Although they are intelligent, they first have to be persuaded that it's in their own interests to co-operate, often with some form of bribery!

Most Dachshunds display symptoms of "Big Dog Syndrome." In their minds, they're six-feet tall and a match for anything and anyone. This can sometimes lead to rashness and taking on more than they can handle, so monitor their food intake, exercise, swim time, play time and interaction with new dogs – especially big ones.

They are often noisy with a big, booming bark that sounds like it's coming from a Great Dane. They are extremely alert, can hear a pin drop at 50 paces and make excellent watch dogs. Whether they then greet your visitors with licks or suspicion often depends on how socialised they are.

Well-socialised Dachshunds make super family pets, form deep bonds with children and get on well with other animals in the home, especially other Dachshunds.

Start training early and get your dog used to other people, animals and environments. Under-socialised Dachshunds can be territorial, suspicious of new people and dogs, possessive of food and toys, or nuisance barkers.

Pictured is the beautiful Miniature Long-Haired Ruby (Kenmar's Calm Before the Storm), aged one, bred by Marianne McCullough. Photo by owner Meghan Poort.

Although they may get on very well with your pet cat, once they are out and about, it can be a different story. Coupled with their incredible sense of smell, many Dachshunds also have a strong prey drive and will chase anything small and moving - including the kids!

Teaching the Recall is very important, as Dachshunds love running free off the lead (leash) and you want yours to come back.

Back at home, the Dachshund loves nothing more than digging up your beautiful lawn or garden with his strong paddle-like paws - this breed is hard-wired to dig!

 Set aside plenty of time to devote to your Dachshund during the first few months of his life. These are not low-maintenance dogs as far as temperament goes. Moulding your Dachshund into the dog you want him to become requires time and effort, with oodles of repetition and patience.

But the rewards are more than worth it. Dachshunds are the most affectionate and loyal of dogs. Many will form the deepest bond with one person, while some will attach themselves to the whole family. They like to stick close to you; really close. If you've a tiny Mini puppy, don't wear shoes in the house, as they are likely to get under your feet without you noticing.

This is not a breed to leave alone for long hours; they love being involved in whatever's going on and crave companionship – from humans or other dogs at home.

They are surprisingly sensitive and can pick up on moods. They may come for a cuddle if you are sad or crying, and be cock-a-hoop with energy when you are playing and laughing. They don't respond well to shouting or aggression, and trying to force them to do anything will have the opposite effect - patience and encouragement are what's needed for training and housetraining.

The Dachshund is no lapdog, but he does love playing games and snuggling up on the couch or bed with you - even IN bed, if allowed. Once built, that bond he has with you is unbreakable. These are the most loyal of dogs and extremely affectionate; they are snuggle bugs par excellence.

Different Varieties

There is a Dachshund to suit everybody; they come in an impressive range of sizes, coat types and colours. In North America and the UK, there are two sizes: **Standard** and **Miniature**. (Standards are normally just referred to by their coat type). They weigh 20lb to 26lb in the UK, and anything from 16lb to 32lb in the US. Miniatures are much smaller, with adults weighing just 10lb or 11lb.

In their native Germany and other countries, there is an even smaller size called a **Kaninchenteckel,** or "Rabbit Dachshund." Officially, there is no such thing as a "Teacup" or "Toy" Dachshund. They are not accepted by the Kennel Clubs and often have structural health problems.

In America, **"Tweenies"** is a nickname used to describe dogs weighing 12lb to 15lb as adults, so in between a Miniature and a Standard.

Then there are three coat types:

- ❧ Smooth
- ❧ Wire
- ❧ Long

and numerous coat colours and patterns - see **Chapter 14. Grooming** for more information.

Although all types of Dachshunds share a lot of traits, there are some differences between them. Standard Dachshunds generally have a higher "drive," which requires more exercise and mental challenges. Some Minis can be a little timid if they have not been introduced to lots of other people and experiences.

There is some discussion as to the different temperaments of the three coat types. A big generalisation would be to say that the Wires are the most like Terriers, which is not surprising as they have Terrier ancestry. Noisy and wanting to be in the thick of things, they approach life full-on.

Longs are perhaps the most gentle, laid-back and least suspicious of the three, again not surprising. The friendly, tail-wagging Spaniel was introduced into the Dachshund DNA to create the Long coat.

The Smooths are the one-and-only original Dachshund. Deeply affectionate with their owners, some also have a reputation for being a bit bossy and territorial.

Only The Dachshund...!

The Dachshund is unique. He'll make you laugh, and he could well make you cry when you're trying to train him! But whatever life throws at you, your Dachshund will be there for you through thick and thin.

Fourteen UK and American Dachshund breeders with hundreds of years of combined experience have added their expertise to this book. It's fair to say they know a thing or two about the breed. Here they share some personal anecdotes that epitomise the one and only Dachshund, a breed like no other.

Hannah Norton (Standard and Mini Smooths): "We had a stud dog come to visit. Instead of getting out of the car, he stepped on the central locking button and locked himself in! The owner had to get a lift home to get the spare key and travel back again to let him out. The entire time he was in the car he barked at us...typical Dachshund! We encouraged him to step on the button again, but all he managed to do was to switch the hazard lights on... our neighbours were not impressed!

"Mine love digging under duvets and blankets; they absolutely love to be underneath bedding. It's adorable, I always have one or two under my duvet at night."

Pictured is Hannah's son, Jackson, with seven-week-old Pikachu.

Melissa (Mini Longs): "I've had them stand on the window controls and roll the window down in the back seat while I was driving down the highway! So, it's not safe to leave them in the car - even for a minute - because they can lock you out or roll down a window while you aren't looking."

Judith Carruthers (Standard Wires): "Dachshunds are so funny and ours make us laugh every day. They each have their quirks: one refuses to go out in the morning and always has to be lifted outdoors, another thinks her place is on top of a crate, not in it!

"They're adept at cuddling under blankets. You can't see them.... just their shapes. They are also clever at attracting eye contact... once they do, they can be quite vocal and it's almost like they're "talking" to you and teaching you their language. They are very clever and can be quite manipulative....in a quirky way!"

Brenna Carlisle (Standard Longs): "My Wilbur is obsessed with wash clothes - clean or dirty. He loves to lay and roll on them. He has taught all the other dogs in the house his "addiction" and they all do it now! We have to put up them somewhere high or he will get them out!"

Lisa Lindfield: "My dogs like to move their bedding and drag it off into other rooms, or even into the garden when it's sunny, and lay on it on the patio. They are sun worshippers and love being warm, whatever time of year it is. They love heat and snuggling next to people 24/7....... or hiding under anything warm, like a duvet, piles of freshly-folded laundry in the laundry basket, or burrowing into a discarded jumper, etc.

"They also like to hide toys all over the place and enjoy "surprising themselves" (I think this is the hunter trait in Dachshunds). They can hide toys under bedding, behind doors, in the garden, in my laundry basket, down the side of the sofa, etc. As for cushions, pillows, padded dog beds or toys, they love pulling out the stuffing, and my home often resembles a snow scene!

"One of mine is obsessed with the hosepipe and goes nuts when I attempt to water the garden. She loves being squirted and soaked.... but will fake a wee outside if it's raining, and wee inside the house instead!"

Melissa added a couple more anecdotes: "I once spent two hours getting one of my Longhairs, GCH Rabows Strange Fruit of Paladin ROM, ready for a show. She was bred from an imported dog, so it took a very long time to blow dry her thick UK coat. As I briefly turned around to let someone in the house, I heard a splash...she had jumped in the swimming pool!

"Some can climb under a fence in 10 minutes or climb over it in two - or squeeze between three-inch fence rails. Most are very loyal. Once, when I stepped away to take a phone call, I came back to find an empty backyard. I screamed: "GET BACK HERE, RIGHT NOW!!" and all nine of them came running back through the loose picket on the fence.

"Well, all except Sadie (*pictured*). She was older and a little more stubborn in her advancing years, and was following a stray cat down the road at the time. Fortunately, she moved slowly, so I was able to catch up to her!"

Ian Seath (Standard Wires and Mini Smooths): "Ours get off the sofa at 9.55 pm, stare at my wife Sue and demand a biscuit."

Bastiaan Smit (Standard Wires): "Each of them has their own specific funny habits. One likes to be cuddled like a baby, he lays on his back in your arms and gives kisses when you ask for one – not licks! They are always looking for attention, they drive you crazy with their staring and directing you to the lead for a walk. They also guide you to the food bin for an extra treat.

"When we open the door, they should wait for the call "Out!" and then shoot outside – but only one does, the other four have already bolted! Dachshunds are personalities who speak to you."

Stefanie Millington: "Whenever my Dachshunds encounter something for the very first time, they poke at it really quickly with their noses, like a child pokes something it doesn't know; my other dogs don't do it. But my Dachshunds aren't frightened of anything, they are very forward and bold. They are excellent hunters, very much to the dismay of pigeons, rabbits, mice and any other feathery or furry things in our garden..."

Lisa Cole: "In long grass or snow they have to make little leaps to go forward, which causes their ears to flap; it's so funny. They poke you and other dogs with their noses when playing. They are sneaky and silent, and will steal food, drink your tea and you have no idea how they did it, as you didn't even see them move. They even talk to you; they make little grumbles and talk."

Sandra Robertson (Mini Smooths): "My girl Tiffany is so funny. Whenever she hears me get the car keys, she beats me to the front door, then rolls on her back and plays dead because she wants to come. If the front door is open, she plays dead on the drive!

"How on earth can we leave her behind with all the effort she puts in? The thing is, my other two are now getting very interested in how Tiffany is getting out more than they are...it won't be long before they catch on."

Sandra tells a story that highlights the affectionate nature of the Dachshund: "This year our Chihuahua Leo passed away at 16 years. He got on very well with our two Dachshunds, and even though the Daxies had each other, they really missed Leo. Leo had his own cushion and they had theirs, but after he died, they decided they would start sleeping on his cushion.

"They were both quite withdrawn for a week or so, looking very lost and sad. It was quite heart-breaking to see them. They were both missing Leo very deeply, even down to belly scratch. The Daxies normally rolled over for a belly rub, whereas Leo would just snuggle under my hand to say: "Scratch, please." He would even pull my hands down to his belly to give him a scratch. One of my Daxies, Copper, now does exactly the same.

"They are so loving and comforting. If I'm upset, they both come sit on my lap or at my side. When my dear brother passed away unexpectedly, it was such a shock. But my Daxies never left my side, when I cried, they washed away my tears. They definitely knew I was heartbroken and the love from them was tremendous. It gave me a lot of comfort."

Pame Bates: "Rose always lays next to me or near my feet, whatever I am doing. She is Mom's dog. She is reserved and regal and has discriminating tastes as to who she warms to. Pearl and Frisbee, on the other hand, are gregarious and love to play ball and show off.

"Pearl is the quickest and is ball-obsessed. We have tried every game to hide the ball from her, even ones she has never played with before, and she always finds them, and goes nuts if they are put up too high for her to reach." *(Library photo).*

"Bonton is such a lover, he wants people and petting more than anything in the world. Sela is our monster baby, she chews shoes and gets inside to munch them.

"All of the dogs are unique and fun. We have a circus every evening: the dogs all run in circles playing for about 10 minutes, everyone joins in; it's the last burst of energy before bedtime!"

Pauline Cheeseman: "They all have their own little ways: if Frankie likes you, she grabs hold of the bottom of your trousers and shakes it. Cassie kicks like a donkey with her back legs when she's playing!

"Bonnie chews the others' ears until they are like wet cloths. And when you stroke her in her sleep, Darcie groans and squeaks like a teddy bear that growls when you turn it upside down. Annie is just ball and toy-obsessed, but if no-one throws the ball, she goes and hides it under the curtain, turns away then pounces on it! She plays by herself for ages – well, until she pushes in under the sofa or cupboard."

Pauline tells us of her first Dachshund, Frankie: "Frankie was my daughter's black and tan Miniature Smooth. At that time, I had Great Danes and had taken on a very traumatised one, Amara, who had been physically abused. She had been in seven homes in three years, and was so fearful that she'd completely shut down.

"I dog-sat Frankie while my daughter was working. Well, she was the only living creature Amara trusted. Frankie would curl up on top of her and walk next to her front legs whenever she moved. If Amara hesitated, Frankie leaned on her front leg to reassure her.

"When my daughter came to take her home each night, Frankie found it harder and harder to leave - she was howling, barking and wouldn't settle until she came back the next morning to settle Amara. So, Frankie moved in with us, and I witnessed a dog help another like no other. They were inseparable - Frankie even laid curled up on top of Amara when we had to put Amara to sleep.

"Frankie went on to have her own puppies and fostered many orphans of various breeds, from Pugs to kittens! She helped every one of my bitches whelp over the years, and every single one of them let her be with them in the whelping box. I've never seen that happen before and don't think I'll ever see it again.

"I now have her daughter, Frankie the 2ⁿᵈ, **pictured aged 11**. She looks just like her. Yes, Frankie is the boss of the house, but in the same quiet peaceful way as her Mum."

Dachshund Heritage

The exact origins of the Dachshund are shrouded in the mists of time; various types of long-eared, short-legged hounds have been around for centuries. We do know that the Dachshund was originally developed to track badgers in Europe, and his name is German - *Dachs* means badger and *Hund* is dog. He's known as the *Dackel* or *Teckel* in Germany.

The original breed was larger than today's Standard, weighing 30lb to 40lb, and originally came in straight and crooked-legged varieties (the modern Dachshund is descended from the latter). These early dogs were not unlike French Basset Hounds, although canine historians have variously suggested that Terriers, Pointers, Bloodhounds and even Pinschers have been involved in their make-up.

Whichever breeds were involved, today all types of Dachshund classed as a dwarf breed dogs. Their short legs are the result of a genetic mutation which has been selected for in breeding - although the modern Dachshund's legs should not be bowed like those of his distant ancestors.

This 1888 illustration shows Mr. F. Barclay Hanbury's Dachshund "Fritz." Imported by Mr. Schuller from the Royal Kennels, Stuttgart.

The Dachshund might look unusual, but he was bred to be ideally suited to the task of hunting badgers. He's long and low to the ground, ideal for getting into burrows - with a long, straightish tail, so he could be pulled out if he got stuck!

His long, droopy ears trap the scent for his incredible sense of smell, and his front feet are two like two mechanical shovels. Housed in that deep chest is a big pair of lungs, giving him stamina and a loud bark, while his loose skin reduces snags and injury when burrowing in tight spaces.

The original Dachshunds were black and tan, red or brown, although dapple was already known by 1900. As experimentation with the breed continued, two distinct sizes emerged: the Standard, which hunted badgers and even wild boar, and the smaller (now Miniature) variety, for hunting rabbits and vermin.

Dachshunds arrived in Britain from mainland Europe in around 1850 and quickly rose to prominence, thanks in no small part to Queen Victoria, who was introduced to them by her German husband, Prince Albert.

In 1879, the famous canine author Stonehenge wrote: "The Dachshund is perhaps one of the most ancient forms of the domesticated dog. The fact is that he has for centuries represented an isolated class between the hound and the terrier, without being more nearly connected with the one than the other.

"His obstinate, independent character, and his incapacity to be trained or broken to anything beyond his inborn, game-like disposition, are quite unrivalled among all other races of the dog.

"Regarding his frame, he differs from the hound, not only by his crooked fore legs and small size, but by the most refined modification of all parts of his body, according to his chief task - to work underground. It is not possible to imagine a more favourable frame for an "earth dog" than the real dachshund type."

Stonehenge goes on to describe the character of 19th Century Dachshunds, much of which is still true over 100 years later: "In hunting above ground the dachshund follows more the track than the general scent (witterung) of the game; therefore he follows rather slowly, but surely, and with the nose pretty close to the ground.

"His noise in barking is very loud, far sounding, and of surprising depth for a dog of so small a frame; but, in giving tongue while hunting, he pours forth from time to time short, shrill notes, which are quickened as the scent gets hotter, and, at sight of the game the notes are often resolved into an indescribable scream, as if the dog were being punished in a most cruel manner.

"Though not a pack hound, the dachshund will soon learn to run in couples; and two or three of these couples, when acquainted with one another or forming a little family, will hunt pretty well together. They do not frighten their game so much as the larger hounds and, when frequently used, they will learn to stay when arrived at the line of the shooters, not by obedience to their master, but because they are intelligent enough as to see that it is quite useless to run longer after the game.

"For tracking wounded deer or a roebuck a dachshund may be used when no bloodhound is to be had; but they must be accustomed to collar and line for this purpose, and then they are rather troublesome to lead in rough ground or coverts.

"They retrieve better by running free or slipped, but must carry a bell, for they are apt to keep silence when they find their game dead; and, beginning to lick at the wound where the ball has gone into the body, they will slowly advance to tearing and to eating their prey.

"Dachshunds are very headstrong and difficult to keep under command; and, as they are at the same time very sensitive to chastisement, it is next to impossible to force them to do anything against their will. Many good badger dogs have been made cowards for their whole life by one severe whipping.

"They must be taken as they are - with all their faults, as well as their virtues. When treated always kindly, the dachshund is very faithful to his master, and not only a useful, but a most amusing dog - a very humourist among the canine family.

"In spite of his small frame, he has always an air of consequence and independence about him; but, at the same time, he is very inquisitive, and always ready to interfere with things with which he has no concern. He seems to have an antipathy to large dogs, and, if they object to be domineered over, the dachshund will certainly quarrel with them. When his blood is up, he will care neither for blows nor for wounds, and is often bitten dreadfully in such encounters.

"Therefore, dachshunds should not be kept in kennels with larger dogs. When kept in houses and accustomed to children, they will make good pets, for they are clean, intelligent, and watchful, without being noisy, though often snappish with strangers."

"The Book Of Dogs - An Intimate Study Of Mankind's Best Friend" (1919)" describes their hunting methods: "The dachshund, or badger dog, combines to a high degree the qualities of the hound and the terrier, and probably both of these were used in his development, but where he got his crumpled legs is less apparent. He is the favourite dog of Germany, where his special work is to enter a badger hole and hold the attention of the animal until it can be dug out."

"...To follow this fierce, belligerent, and really dangerous animal (badger) into his burrow and drag him out requires a dog of great courage and tenacity, not to mention peculiar design. His (the Dachshund's) long body, short legs, and large, out-turned fore feet subject him to much ridicule, and it is often said that in Germany he is sold by the yard.

"In disposition they combine to an unusual degree the virtues of their respective ancestors, having the affectionate, companionable qualities of the hound and the tenacity, courage, and self-reliance of the terrier."

The Wire-Haireds and Long-Haireds had already started to appear in Britain by the late 19th century. The Cocker Spaniel, with its long, wavy coat and sweet disposition, was involved in the development of the Longs, and Terriers were introduced to create the Wires, the last of the three coat types. According to Stonehenge, the first Dachshunds were imported into America in the late 1860s. These mid to late 1800s were exciting times in the dog world. It was an era of great canine experimentation, particularly in England, and the birth of the conformation dog show.

Interestingly, Dachshunds were first recognised and exhibited as a separate breed at the Crystal Palace Dog Show, London, in 1873 – several years before they were first shown in Germany. And the English Dachshund Club was founded in 1881, some seven years prior to the formation of Deutscher Teckelklub in Germany.

Admitted to the AKC Stud Book in 1885, the breed's popularity in America was immediate and enduring.

In 2020, a Wire-Haired Dachshund called Maisie, *pictured,* (Ch Silvae Trademark), achieved the ultimate accolade by winning Best in Show at Crufts, the world's biggest and oldest dog show.

Photo of Maisie, owned by Kim and Duncan McCalmont, winning Crufts by Elena Matselik.

Today, the Dachshund is one of the most popular breeds in dog-loving countries across the globe, and it can only be a matter of time before one wins Westminster Dog Show in the US.

A firm favourite with celebrities and their cameras, there are 12 million photos of Dachshunds on Instagram alone! Because of this and other high-profile exposure, the Miniature has a somewhat unfair reputation as a "handbag dog" - but underneath he's still a noble hound.

Once a hound, always a hound.

Sources:

- "The Dogs Of Great Britain, America, And Other Countries. Their Breeding, Training, and Management in Health and Disease," 1879, by John Henry Walsh (Stonehenge)
- "British Dogs: Their Varieties, History, Characteristics, Breeding, Management, And Exhibition," by Hugh Dalziel
- "All About Dogs - A Book For Doggy People," 1900, by Charles Henry Lane
- "Dogs Of All Nations," 1915, by W. E. Mason
- "The Book Of Dogs - An Intimate Study Of Mankind's Best Friend," 1919, by Harold Baynes & Louis Agassiz Fuertes
- Wikipedia
- Chest of Books www.chestofbooks.com

....

A Final Few Words...

And finally, we asked our breeders to sum up their Dachshunds in a few words:

- 🐾 Courageous, outgoing, loyal, fun
- 🐾 Loving, stubborn, happy, sausages
- 🐾 Hunter, personality, explorer, obedient
- 🐾 Funny, feisty, affectionate, game
- 🐾 Courageous to the point of rashness!
- 🐾 Endearing, loving, super cute
- 🐾 Determined, bonded, bold
- 🐾 Funny, loving, beautiful, loyal
- 🐾 Cheerleaders of the canine world!
- 🐾 Small (Minis), loving and, most of all, very loyal
- 🐾 Courageous, loyal, clever, stubborn
- 🐾 Courageous, faithful and addictive
- 🐾 Best dog breed ever

Read on to learn how to understand, train and take best care of your Dachshund for the rest of his or her life, and how to successfully build a deep bond that will become one of the most important things in your life - and certainly his or hers.

....

2. Breed Standard

The Breed Standard is a blueprint not only for the ideal appearance of each breed, but also for character and temperament, how the dog moves and what colours are acceptable. In other words, it ensures that a Dachshund looks and acts like a Dachshund. Good breeders strive to breed their dogs as close as possible to this ideal list of attributes.

If you are looking to buy a puppy, familiarise yourself with the Breed Standard and have a good look at the mother and father - or at least the mother. Your puppy will take after his or her parents. Avoid Dachshunds with over-elongated backs, which can cause spine issues and unsound movement, and sore or watery eyes.

The Breed Standard is laid down by the breed societies. In the UK it's the Kennel Club, and in the USA it's the AKC (American Kennel Club) that keeps the register of pedigree or purebred dogs. Dogs entered in conformation shows run under Kennel Club and AKC rules are judged against the Breed Standard.

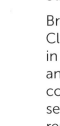

Breeders approved by the Kennel Clubs agree to produce puppies in line with the Breed Standard and maintain certain welfare conditions. Responsible breeders select only the finest dogs for reproduction, based on the health, looks and temperament of the parents and their ancestors.

Dachshunds are scent hounds originally bred to hunt badgers, and all types are classed in the *Hound Group* by the Kennel Clubs. The Kennel Club says this about the Hound Group: "Breeds originally used for hunting either by scent or by sight. The scent hounds include the Beagle and Bloodhound and the sight hounds such breeds as the Whippet and Greyhound. Many of them enjoy a significant amount of exercise and can be described as dignified, aloof but trustworthy companions."

Points of Concern

In 2014 the UK Kennel Club launched its **Breed Watch Fit For Purpose** campaign. It identified potential faults that could lead to health issues. There are three categories:

1 Breeds with no current points of concern reported

2 Breeds with Breed Watch points of concern

3 Breeds where some dogs have visible conditions or exaggerations that can cause pain or discomfort

All Dachshunds are classed in Category 2. The Kennel club says: "Particular points of concern for individual breeds may include features not specifically highlighted in the breed standard, including current issues. In some breeds, features may be listed which, if exaggerated, might potentially affect the breed in the future." The two Points of Concern for the Dachshund, added in 2020, are:

🐾 Incorrect hindquarter/unsound movement

🐾 **Sore eyes or excessive tearing**

The UK's Dachshund Breed Council is trying to discourage show judges from rewarding Dachshunds with too-short legs and too-deep chests. They say: "By definition, the Dachshund is an "exaggerated" breed; the genes for dwarfism cause the breed's characteristic short legs.

"The Breed Standard's use of the word *"low"* relates to this dwarfism; the breed is <u>low to ground at the withers compared with a non-dwarf breed.</u> Low to ground does not mean lack of ground clearance and the standard specifically requires *"body sufficiently clear of the ground to allow free movement."*

The UK and USA Breed Standards differ when it comes to colour. Double dapple is unacceptable and pied, tricolour and the dilute colours isabella (fawn) and blue are highly undesirable in the UK.

··

UK Breed Standard

This is the Kennel Club's description of the Dachshund: "Originating in Germany where he is known as the Teckel (badger dog) the Dachshund is still used for both tracking wounded game such as deer, and for going to ground after badger or rabbits.

"In his native country there are three sizes: standard, miniature and Kaninchen (rabbit dog) all defined by measuring the circumference of the chest. In the UK there are two sizes with miniatures preferably weighing under 5 kilograms. There are three coat types in each variety: the Smooth haired, the Long haired and the Wire haired and the six varieties all share the same breed standard, divided by size and coat." And here is the Breed Standard:

General Appearance - Moderately long and low with no exaggeration, compact, well-muscled body, with enough ground clearance to allow free movement. Heights at the withers should be half the length of the body, measured from breastbone to the rear of thigh. Bold, defiant carriage of head and intelligent expression.

Characteristics - Intelligent, lively, courageous to the point of rashness, obedient. Especially suited to going to ground because of low build, very strong forequarters and forelegs. Long, strong jaw, and immense power of bite and hold. Excellent nose, persevering hunter and tracker. Essential that functional build is retained to ensure working ability.

Temperament - Faithful, versatile and good tempered.

Head and Skull - Long, appearing conical when seen from above; from side tapering uniformly to tip of nose. Skull only slightly arched. Neither too broad nor too narrow, sloping gradually without prominent stop into slightly arched muzzle. Length from tip of nose to eyes equal to length from eyes to occiput.

In Wire haired, particularly, ridges over eyes strongly prominent, giving appearance of slightly

broader skull. Lips well stretched, neatly covering lower jaw. Strong jaw bones not too square or snipy, but opening wide.

Eyes - Medium size, almond-shaped, set obliquely. Dark except in chocolates, where they can be lighter. In dapples one or both 'wall' eyes permissible. **Ears -** Set high, and not too far forward. Broad, of moderate length, and well rounded (not pointed or folded). Forward edge touching

cheek. Mobile, and when at attention back of ear directed forward and outward. **Mouth -** Teeth strongly developed, powerful canine teeth fitting closely. Jaws strong, with a perfect, regular and complete scissor bite, i.e. upper teeth closely overlapping lower teeth and set square to the jaws. Complete dentition important.

Neck - Long, muscular, clean with no dewlap, slightly arched, running in graceful lines into shoulders, carried proudly forward.

Forequarters - Shoulder blades long, broad, and placed firmly and obliquely (45 degrees to the horizontal) upon very robust rib cage. Upper arm the same length as shoulder blade, set at 90 degrees to it, very strong, and covered with hard, supple muscles. Upper arm lies close to ribs, but able to move freely. Forearm short and strong in bone, inclining slightly inwards; when seen in profile moderately straight, must not bend forward or knuckle over, which indicates unsoundness. Correctly placed foreleg should cover the lowest point of the keel.

Body - Moderately long and full muscled. Sloping shoulders, back reasonably level, blending harmoniously between withers and slightly arched loin. Loin short and strong. Breast bone strong, and so prominent that a depression appears on either side of it in front. When viewed from front, thorax full and oval; when viewed from side or above, full volumed, so allowing by its ample capacity complete development of heart and lungs. Well ribbed up, underline gradually merging into line of abdomen. Body sufficiently clear of ground to allow free movement.

Hindquarters - Rump full, broad and strong, pliant muscles. Croup long, full, robustly muscled, only slightly sloping towards tail. Pelvis strong, set obliquely and not too short. Upper thigh set at right angles to pelvis, strong and of good length. Lower thigh short, set at right angles to upper thigh and well-muscled. Legs when seen behind set well apart, straight, and parallel.

Feet - Front feet full, broad, deep, close knit, straight or very slightly turned out. Hindfeet smaller and narrower. Toes close together, with a decided arch to each toe, strong regularly placed nails, thick and firm pads. Dog must stand true, i.e. equally on all parts of the foot.

Tail - Continues line of spine, but slightly curved, without kinks or twists, not carried too high, or touching ground when at rest.

Gait/Movement - Should be free and flowing. Stride should be long, with the drive coming from the hindquarters when viewed from the side. Viewed from in front or behind, the legs and feet should move parallel to each other with the distance apart being the width of the shoulder and hip joints respectively.

Coat - *Smooth Haired:* Dense, short and smooth. Hair on underside of tail coarse in texture. Skin loose and supple, but fitting closely all over without dewlap and little or no wrinkle.
Long Haired: Soft and straight, or only slightly waved; longest under neck, on underparts of body, and behind legs, where it forms abundant feathering, on tail where it forms a flag. Outside of ears

well feathered. Coat flat, and not obscuring outline. Too much hair on feet undesirable.

Wire Haired: With exception of jaw, eyebrows, chin and ears, the whole body should be covered with a short, straight, harsh coat with dense undercoat, beard on the chin, eyebrows bushy, but hair on ears almost smooth. Legs and feet well but neatly furnished with harsh coat.

Colour - All colours permitted but no white permissible, save for a small patch on chest which is permitted but not desirable. The dapple pattern is expressed as lighter coloured areas contrasting with the darker base. Neither the light nor the dark colour should predominate. Double dapple (where varying amounts of white occur all over the body in addition to the dapple pattern) is unacceptable. Pied, tricolour and the dilute colours isabella and blue are highly undesirable. Nose and nails black in all colours except chocolate/tan and chocolate dapple where they are brown.

Size - Ideal weight: 9-12 kgs (20-26 lbs).
Miniature ideal weight; 4.5kgs (10lbs). Desired maximum weight 5kgs (11lbs). Exhibits which appear thin and undernourished should be severely penalised.

Faults - Any departure from the foregoing points should be considered a fault and the seriousness with which the fault should be regarded should be in exact proportion to its degree and its effect upon the health and welfare of the dog and on the dog's ability to perform its traditional work.

Note - Male animals should have two apparently normal testicles fully descended into the scrotum.

*Note for prospective puppy buyers: Size – the Kennel Club Breed Standard is a guide and description of the ideal for the breed; the Size as described does not imply that a dog will match the measurements given (height or weight). A dog might be larger or smaller than the Size measurements stated in the Breed Standard.

US Breed Standard

The AKC describes the Dachshund temperament as: "Friendly, Curious, Spunky," and adds: "The famously long, low silhouette, ever-alert expression, and bold, vivacious personality of the Dachshund have made him a superstar of the canine kingdom. Dachshunds come in two sizes and in three coat types of various colors and patterns.

"The word "icon" is terribly overworked, but the Dachshund — with his unmistakable long-backed body, little legs, and big personality — is truly an icon of purebred dogdom. Dachshunds can be standard-sized (usually 16 to 32 pounds) or miniature (11 pounds or under), and come in one of three coat types: smooth, wirehaired, or longhaired.

"Dachshunds aren't built for distance running, leaping, or strenuous swimming, but otherwise these tireless hounds are game for anything. Smart and vigilant, with a big-dog bark, they make fine watchdogs. Bred to be an independent hunter of dangerous prey, they can be brave to the point of rashness, and a bit stubborn, but their endearing nature and unique look has won millions of hearts the world over." Here is the full and very detailed AKC Breed Standard:

General Appearance: Low to ground, long in body and short of leg, with robust muscular development; the skin is elastic and pliable without excessive wrinkling. Appearing neither crippled, awkward, nor cramped in his capacity for movement, the Dachshund is well-balanced with bold and confident head carriage and intelligent, alert facial expression. His hunting spirit, good nose,

loud tongue and distinctive build make him well-suited for below-ground work and for beating the bush. His keen nose gives him an advantage over most other breeds for trailing.

NOTE: Inasmuch as the Dachshund is a hunting dog, scars from honorable wounds shall not be considered a fault.

Size, Proportion, Substance: Bred and shown in two sizes, standard and miniature; miniatures are not a separate classification but compete in a class division for "11 pounds and under at 12 months of age and older." Weight of the standard size is usually between 16 and 32 pounds.

Head: Viewed from above or from the side, the head tapers uniformly to the tip of the nose. The **eyes** are of medium size, almond-shaped and dark-rimmed, with an energetic, pleasant expression; not piercing; very dark in color. The bridge bones over the eyes are strongly prominent. Wall eyes, except in the case of dappled dogs, are a serious fault.

The **ears** are set near the top of the head, not too far forward, of moderate length, rounded, not narrow, pointed, or folded. Their carriage, when animated, is with the forward edge just touching the cheek so that the ears frame the face. The **skull** is slightly arched, neither too broad nor too narrow, and slopes gradually with little perceptible stop into the finely-formed, slightly arched **muzzle,** giving a Roman appearance. Lips are tightly stretched, well covering the lower jaw. Nostrils well open. Jaws opening wide and hinged well back of the eyes, with strongly developed bones and teeth. **Teeth -** Powerful canine teeth; teeth fit closely together in a scissors bite. An even bite is a minor fault. Any other deviation is a serious fault.

Neck: Long, muscular, clean-cut, without dewlap, slightly arched in the nape, flowing gracefully into the shoulders without creating the impression of a right angle. **Trunk:** The trunk is long and fully muscled. When viewed in profile, the back lies in the straightest possible line between the withers and the short, very slightly arched loin. A body that hangs loosely between the shoulders is a serious fault. Abdomen - Slightly drawn up.

Forequarters: For effective underground work, the front must be strong, deep, long and cleanly muscled. Forequarters in detail: **Chest -** The breast-bone is strongly prominent in front so that on either side a depression or dimple appears. When viewed from the front, the thorax appears oval and extends downward to the mid-point of the forearm. The enclosing structure of the well sprung ribs appears full and oval to allow, by its ample capacity, complete development of heart and lungs. The keel merges gradually into the line of the abdomen and extends well beyond the front legs. Viewed in profile, the lowest point of the breast line is covered by the front leg.

Shoulder blades – long, broad, well-laid back and firmly placed upon the fully developed thorax, closely fitted at the withers, furnished with hard yet pliable muscles.
Upper Arm - Ideally the same length as the shoulder blade and at right angles to the latter, strong of bone and hard of muscle, lying close to the ribs, with elbows close to the body, yet capable of free movement.
Forearm - Short; supplied with hard yet pliable muscles on the front and outside, with tightly stretched tendons on the inside and at the back, slightly curved inwards. The joints between the forearms and the feet (wrists) are closer together than the shoulder joints, so that the front does not appear absolutely straight. The inclined shoulder blades, upper arms and curved forearms form

parentheses that enclose the ribcage, creating the correct "wraparound front." Knuckling over is a disqualifying fault.

Feet - Front paws are full, tight, compact, with well-arched toes and tough, thick pads. They may be equally inclined a trifle outward. There are five toes, four in use, close together with a pronounced arch and strong, short nails. Front dewclaws may be removed.

Hindquarters: Strong and cleanly muscled. The pelvis, thigh, second thigh, and rear pastern are ideally the same length and give the appearance of a series of right angles. From the rear, the thighs are strong and powerful. The legs turn neither in nor out. Rear pasterns - Short and strong, perpendicular to the second thigh bone. When viewed from behind, they are upright and parallel.

Feet - Hind Paws - Smaller than the front paws with four compactly closed and arched toes with tough, thick pads. The entire foot points straight ahead and is balanced equally on the ball and not merely on the toes. Rear dewclaws should be removed. *Croup -* Long, rounded and full, sinking slightly toward the tail.

Tail - Set in continuation of the spine, extending without kinks, twists, or pronounced curvature, and not carried too gaily.

Gait: Fluid and smooth. Forelegs reach well forward, without much lift, in unison with the driving action of hind legs. The correct shoulder assembly and well-fitted elbows allow the long, free stride in front. Viewed from the front, the legs do not move in exact parallel planes, but incline slightly inward. Hind legs drive on a line with the forelegs, with hock joints and rear pasterns (metatarsus) turning neither in nor out. The propulsion of the hind leg depends on the dog's ability to carry the hind leg to complete extension.

Viewed in profile, the forward reach of the hind leg equals the rear extension. The thrust of correct movement is seen when the rear pads are clearly exposed during rear extension. Rear feet do not reach upward toward the abdomen and there is no appearance of walking on the rear pasterns. Feet must travel parallel to the line of motion with no tendency to swing out, cross over, or interfere with each other. Short, choppy movement, rolling or high-stepping gait, close or overly wide coming or going are incorrect. The Dachshund must have agility, freedom of movement, and endurance to do the work for which he was developed.

Temperament: The Dachshund is clever, lively and courageous to the point of rashness, persevering in above- and below-ground work, with all the senses well-developed. Any display of shyness is a serious fault.

Special Characteristics of the Three Coat Varieties: The Dachshund is bred with three varieties of coat: (1) Smooth; (2) Wirehaired; (3) Longhaired and is shown in two sizes, standard and miniature. All three varieties and both sizes must conform to the characteristics already specified. The following features are applicable for each variety:

Smooth Dachshund: *Coat -* Short, smooth and shining. Should be neither too long nor too thick. Ears not leathery. Tail -Gradually tapered to a point, well but not too richly haired. Long sleek bristles on the underside are considered a patch of strong-growing hair, not a fault. A brush tail is a fault, as is also a partly or wholly hairless tail.

Color of Hair – Although base color is immaterial, certain patterns and basic colors predominate. One-colored Dachshunds include red and cream, with or without a shading of interspersed dark hairs. A small amount of white on the chest is acceptable, but not desirable. Nose and nails - black. Two-colored Dachshunds include black, chocolate, wild boar, gray (blue) and fawn (Isabella), each with deep, rich tan or cream markings over the eyes, on the sides of the jaw and underlip, on the inner edge of the ear, front, breast, sometimes on the throat, inside and behind the front legs, on the paws and around the anus, and from there to about one-third to one-half of the length of the tail on the underside. Undue prominence of tan or cream markings is undesirable. A small amount of white on the chest is acceptable but not desirable. Nose and nails – in the case of black dogs, black; for chocolate and all other colors, dark brown, but self-colored is acceptable.

Dappled Dachshunds – The dapple (merle) pattern is expressed as lighter-colored areas contrasting with the darker base color, which may be any acceptable color. Neither the light nor the dark color should predominate. Nose and nails are the same as for one- and two-colored Dachshunds. Partial or wholly blue (wall) eyes are as acceptable as dark eyes. A large area of white on the chest of a dapple is permissible.

Brindle is a pattern (as opposed to a color) in which black or dark stripes occur over the entire body although in some specimens the pattern may be visible only in the tan points.

Piebald (pictured) is a pattern (as opposed to a color) with clearly defined areas and/or patches of white on any allowed one-colored or two-colored dogs. Two-colored piebald patterned dogs may show tan markings on the face and around the anus. There are no patches of lighter shadings within the colored areas as in the dapple pattern. Ticking in the white areas is acceptable *(pictured on the legs).* Eye color, eye rims, nose and lips are well pigmented and in accordance with the base color; eyes are never partially or wholly blue as distinguished from the dapple pattern. Eyes partially or wholly blue is a disqualification.

Head must not be more than 50 percent white and color(s) other than white must cover both ears, back and front, and extend without interruption from the ears over both eyes. A head of more than 50 percent white or white on any portion of either ear, back or front, or around the eyes is a disqualification. Pure white dogs with no body spots except on the head are to be disqualified. Nails may be partially or wholly white.

Sable – the sable pattern consists of a uniform dark overlay on red dogs. The overlay hairs are double-pigmented, with the tip of each hair much darker than the base color. The pattern usually displays a widow's peak on the head. Nose, nails and eye rims are black. Eyes are dark, the darker the better. Colors or patterns other than those specified above are a disqualification.

Wirehaired Dachshund: *Coat* - With the exception of jaw, eyebrows, and ears, the whole body is covered with a uniform tight, short, thick, rough, hard outer coat but with finer, somewhat softer, shorter hairs (undercoat) everywhere distributed between the coarser hairs. The absence of an undercoat is a fault. The distinctive facial furnishings include a beard and eyebrows. On the ears the hair is shorter than on the body, almost smooth.

The general arrangement of the hair is such that the wirehaired Dachshund, when viewed from a distance, resembles the smooth. Any sort of soft hair in the outercoat, wherever found on the body, especially on the top of the head, is a fault. The same is true of long, curly, or wavy hair, or hair that sticks out irregularly in all directions. *Tail -* Robust, thickly haired, gradually tapering to a point. A flag tail is a fault.

Color of Hair - While the most common colors are wild boar **(pictured),** black and tan, and various shades of red, all colors and patterns listed above are admissible. Wild boar (agouti) appears as banding of the individual hairs and imparts an overall grizzled effect which is most often seen on wirehaired Dachshunds, but may also appear on other coats. Tan points may or may not be evident. Variations include red boar and chocolate-and-tan boar. Nose, nails and eye rims are black on wild-boar and red-boar Dachshunds. On chocolate-and tan-boar Dachshunds, nose, nails, eye rims and eyes are self-colored, the darker the better. A small amount of white on the chest, although acceptable, is not desirable. Nose and nails same as for the smooth variety.

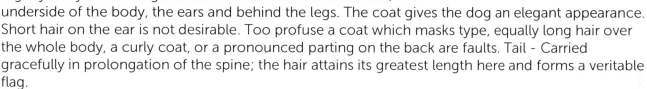

Longhaired Dachshund: *Coat -* The sleek, glistening, often slightly wavy hair is longer under the neck and on forechest, the underside of the body, the ears and behind the legs. The coat gives the dog an elegant appearance. Short hair on the ear is not desirable. Too profuse a coat which masks type, equally long hair over the whole body, a curly coat, or a pronounced parting on the back are faults. Tail - Carried gracefully in prolongation of the spine; the hair attains its greatest length here and forms a veritable flag.

Color of Hair - Same as for the smooth Dachshund. Nose and nails - same as for the smooth. The foregoing description is that of the ideal Dachshund. Any deviation from the above described dog must be penalized to the extent of the deviation keeping in mind the importance of the contribution of the various features toward the basic original purpose of the breed.

Disqualifications: Knuckling over of front legs. In the piebald pattern:

- ❧ Eyes partially or wholly blue
- ❧ A head of more than 50 percent white
- ❧ White covering any portion of the ears, back and front, or around the eyes
- ❧ Pure white with no body spots except on the head
- ❧ Colors or patterns other than those specified above

Approved November 14, 2017 Effective January 1, 2018 Corrected December 29, 2017

Glossary:

Hock - tarsal joint of the hind leg (like the human ankle) but bending in the opposite direction

Occiput - bony bump seen at the top rear of the skull on some breeds

Pastern – the area below the wrist or hock but above the foot

Self color – base colour of hair nearest the body of the dog (not the tip)

Stop - area between a dog's eyes, below the skull

Withers - the ridge between the shoulder blades

3. Finding Your Puppy

Finding a good puppy can be a minefield. If you haven't got yours yet, read this chapter before you commit to anything; it will help you find a healthy, happy puppy with a good temperament

The best way to select a puppy is with your HEAD - not your heart! You'll soon find hundreds of Dachshund puppies advertised, but it requires a bit more time and research to find a first-rate breeder. If you already have your puppy, skip to the next chapter.

....

With their beautiful dark eyes, intelligent expressions and playful personalities, there are few more appealing things on this Earth than a litter of Dachshund puppies. If you go to view a litter, the pups are sure to melt your heart and it is extremely difficult – if not downright impossible - to walk away without choosing one.

 The Dachshund can inherit a number of disorders. A main priority should be to buy a puppy whose parents have been health-screened for the relevant diseases.

If you haven't yet chosen your pup and take only one sentence from this entire book, it is this:

FIND AN ETHICAL BREEDER WHO PRODUCES PUPPIES FROM HEALTH-SCREENED PARENTS WITH GOOD TEMPERAMENTS

– even if that means paying a bit more. It will be worth it.

Find a breeder who knows Dachshunds inside out and who does not breed lots of different types of dogs.

After all, apart from getting married or having a baby, getting a puppy is one of the most important, demanding, expensive and life-enriching decisions you will ever make.

Dachshunds are incredibly loyal and will love you unconditionally - but there is a price to pay. In return for their devotion, you have to fulfil your part of the bargain.

In the beginning, you have to be prepared to devote much of your day to your new puppy. You have to feed her several times a day and housetrain virtually every hour, you have to give her your attention and start to gently introduce the rules of the house. You also have to be prepared to part with hard cash for regular healthcare and pet insurance.

If you are unable to devote the time and money to a new arrival, if you have a very young family, a stressful life or are out at work all day, then now might not be the right time to consider getting a puppy. Dachshunds love their families and thrive on being involved.

If left alone too long, behaviour issues often result. This is a natural reaction and is not the dog's fault; she is simply responding to an environment that is failing to meet her needs. Pick a healthy pup and she should live 10 to 14 years if you're lucky - so this is certainly a long-term commitment. Before taking the plunge, ask yourself some questions:

Do I Have Enough Time for a Puppy?

Even a tenacious Dachshund puppy will feel lonely and possibly even a little afraid after leaving her mother and littermates. Spend time with your new arrival to make her feel safe and sound. Ideally, for the first few days you will be around all the time to help her settle and to start bonding.

If you work, book time off if you can - although this is more difficult for some of our working American readers who get short vacations - but don't just get a puppy and leave her all alone in the house a couple of days later. Leave her a few minutes a day and gradually build up the time so she doesn't over-bond with you and develop separation anxiety.

Housetraining (potty training) starts the moment your pup arrives home. Then, after the first few days and once she's feeling more settled, make time for short sessions of a few minutes of behaviour training. Dachshund puppies are very lively, and this energy can become mischievous if not channelled. You'll also have to find time to slowly start the socialisation process by taking her out of the home to see new places, strangers, other animals, loud noises, busy roads, etc. - but make sure you CARRY her until the vaccinations have taken effect.

FACT The importance of socialising Dachshunds cannot be over-emphasised. Start socialisation as soon as possible, as that critical window up to four months of age is when she is at her most receptive to all things new.

The more positive experiences she is introduced to at this early stage, the better. Good breeders will already have started the process. Once she has had the all-clear after vaccinations, get into the habit of taking her for a short walk every day – more as she gets older. While the garden or yard is fine, new surroundings stimulate interest and help to stop puppies becoming bored.

Also, Dachshunds can become too wary of strangers, so gently introducing her to different people will help her to become more relaxed around people. Initially, get them to sit on the floor at her level. Make time right from the beginning to get your pup used to being handled, gently brushed, ears checked, and later having her teeth touched and cleaned.

 We recommend you have your pup checked out by a vet within a couple of days of arriving home – many good breeders insist on it - but don't put your puppy on the clinic floor where she can pick up germs from other dogs.

Factor in time to visit the vet's surgery for annual check-ups as well as vaccinations, although most now last several years – check with your vet.

How Long Can I Leave My Puppy?

This is a question we get asked a lot and one that causes much debate among new owners. All dogs are pack animals; their natural state is to be with others. So being alone for long periods is not normal for them - although many have to get used to it.

Another issue is the toilet; Dachshund puppies have really tiny bladders. Forget the emotional side of it, how would you like to be left for eight hours without being able to visit the bathroom? So how many hours can you leave a dog alone?

 In the UK, canine rescue organisations will not allow anybody to adopt if they are intending to leave the dog alone for more than four or five hours a day.

The Dachshund was originally bred to perform a task as a working hound, and leaving a Dachshund alone for too long can trigger unwanted behaviour.

A bored or lonely Dachshund may display signs of unhappiness such as nuisance barking, frantic digging, stubbornness, chewing, aggression, disobedience, eliminating or just plain switching off.

 In terms of housetraining, a general rule of thumb is that a puppy can last without urinating for one hour or so for every month of age, sometimes longer.

So, provided your puppy has learned the basics, a three-month-old puppy should be able to last for around three hours without needing to go. Of course, until housetraining kicks in, young puppies just pee at will!

....

Family and Children

Dachshunds really do make excellent family pets - with one or two provisos, and our breeders have some advice on this. With their tiny bodies and bones, Dachshund puppies may not be suitable for some families with very young, boisterous children. Toddlers and young kids are uncoordinated and there can be a risk of injury to a Mini if not well supervised.

Dachshunds can and do form extremely strong and loving bonds with children - once both have learned respect for each other.

 Children (and adults) should be taught how to correctly handle Dachshunds to avoid injuring their backs or necks. Encourage youngsters to interact with the dog on the floor, rather than constantly picking them up to cuddle.

Photo of Erin, courtesy of Lisa Lindfield, Zabannah Dachshunds, Cambridgeshire, UK

Lisa, who breeds all three types of Miniature, added: "It is SO important to pick puppies up properly from Day 1. Don't allow small children to pick them up without supervision, nor wake a sleeping puppy. Puppies mustn't be poked and prodded as they need their sleep.

"It's a case of training the children to be gentle and kind. If you think a Dachshund puppy will help a child with ADHD or a child with anger issues – the answer is no. This is not a toy and it's not fair on the pup. I think very carefully about placing one of my pups with children – it depends on the family."

Kristin Cihos-Williams, of Kinderteckel Standard Smooth Dachshunds, California, agrees: "My Dachshunds grew up with my five children. This breed is excellent with children, as long as the children are well trained to be kind and respectful to animals.

"I did have to separate my youngest child from my dogs during a time in her toddlerhood when she was determined to annoy and tease them. She outgrew this awful stage, but, until that time, it was up to me to make sure my dogs were not subjected to her naughty behavior. I used a baby gate to separate her from the dogs and allowed them space within the house where they had privacy from her.

"Once my children were older, they developed interest in showing the dogs. Three of my daughters did junior showmanship with our Dachshunds. Two of them sustained interest in this wonderful family hobby, and they were ranked #1 Dachshund Juniors in the US, #1 Hound Group Juniors in the US, and #1 Juniors in All Breeds in California!"

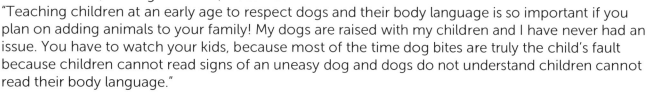

Photo by Bettina Bienefeld of Kristin's daughter Ernalia Pedraza with BISS GCHS Kinderteckel's Paloma CHIC #119615 (2) at the Dachshund Club of America National Specialty. Paloma was top ranked in the US in 2018 with multiple specialty variety wins, group placements, etc.

Brenna Carlisle, Heritage Hounds, Alabama:
"Teaching children at an early age to respect dogs and their body language is so important if you plan on adding animals to your family! My dogs are raised with my children and I have never had an issue. You have to watch your kids, because most of the time dog bites are truly the child's fault because children cannot read signs of an uneasy dog and dogs do not understand children cannot read their body language."

Sandra Robertson, Hartlebury Miniature Dachshunds, Worcester, UK: "Dachshunds are of a fantastic temperament and very much love to be around children. They are very affectionate, loyal and playful. I have and I do prefer to place my puppies with families with small children and other pets; our puppies are raised with children.

"I foster children from all walks of life and couldn't wish for a better breed - they don't get over-excited and can be quite laid-back when they have had their walk and moment of play, Dachshunds and children can be very nurturing and therapeutic for each other; children can be really good at training and teaching their dogs tricks, and the dogs very much enjoy children's company."

Hannah Norton, breeder of Jacksondax Standard and Miniature Smooths, South Devon, UK, said: "My seven-year-old son Jackson, *pictured*, has grown up with dogs and has always been respectful and kind with them. The dogs adore him and make fabulous family pets. He helps me whelp my litters, he rubs the puppies to get them dry and has even helped me tube feed.

"I've had no need to take precautions with Jackson; he is very hands on with the dogs. He teaches the new owners how to hold them correctly and advises them about their backs. My advice for parents would be to teach children boundaries with the puppies and to always hold them correctly, supporting their backs when they are lifted. I try to encourage new owners with young children to handle the puppies on the floor in case they were to drop puppy."

Other breeders added: "Most Dachshunds love people and children, so I would have no worries, but the smooth-haired variety can be snappier, in my opinion, so caution should be used. All children under eight years old should never be left alone with any dog. Every dog is capable of biting a child."

"Respect is hugely important. Dachshunds are lovely with children, but children should be respectful – and not carry puppies about, tempting though it is."

"Dachshunds can be great with children. Children, however, can be not so great with a long-bodied dog, so I don't usually place puppies with families with small children unless those children are VERY well-behaved."

"I have seven grandchildren and yes I would place a puppy with children, if I met the children and they had been taught to show respect for the puppy. For example, by leaving it alone when it's asleep in its bed. If the family had a very small, grabby toddler I would advise them to maybe wait a bit longer!"

"Providing puppies are socialised with children and children learn not to manhandle puppies, Dachshunds make wonderful companions for big and small. All of mine (who do not live with children) just love it when we have children around for visits." Two breeders added that they would definitely place their Dachshund puppies with families.

Puppies regard children as playmates - just like a child regards a puppy as a playmate. Both are playful and excitable, so it's important to teach them both the boundaries of play. A Dachshund puppy would never intentionally harm a child, or vice versa, but either could cause injury if they get over-excited.

Your children will naturally be delighted about your new arrival, but kids and puppy should not be left unsupervised until each has learned to respect the other - no matter how well they get along in the beginning.

 Teach your children to be gentle with your dog and your dog to be gentle with your children.

Photo of Pauline Cheeseman's Colraed Gingerbreadman with granddaughter Eloise, aged eight, by RSA Photography.

Lively behaviour and nipping are not aggression they are normal play for puppies. Put the time in to teach your pup what is acceptable and what is not – and any nipping should be dealt with straight away. See **Chapter 8. Basic Training** for more detailed information.

Your dog's early experiences with children should all be positive. If not, a dog may become nervous or mistrustful - and what you want around children is most definitely a relaxed dog that does not feel threatened by a child's presence. Take things steady in the beginning and your Dachshund will undoubtedly form a deep, lifelong bond that your children will remember throughout their lives.

Single People

Many singles own dogs, but if you live alone, getting a puppy will require a lot of dedication on your part. There is nobody to share the responsibility, so taking on a people-loving, loyal dog like the Dachshund requires a commitment and a lot of your time if the dog is to have a decent life.

If you are out of the house all day, a Dachshund is NOT a good choice. This breed thrives on being involved, and gets bored quite easily. Being alone all day is not much of a life for a dog as intelligent, active and loyal as the Dachshund. However, if you can spend considerable time with the pup, then a Dachshund will definitely become your best friend.

Older People

Dogs can be a great tonic for fit, older people. In his mid-80s my father still walked his dog for an hour to 90 minutes every day – even in the rain or snow. He grumbled occasionally, but it was good for him and it was good for the dog - helping to keep them both fit and socialised! They got fresh air, exercise and the chance to communicate with other dogs and their humans.

You're never alone when you've got a dog. Many older people get a canine companion after losing a loved one - a husband, wife or previous much-loved dog. A pet gives them something to care for and love, as well as a constant companion.

Bear in mind that dog ownership is not cheap, so budget for annual pet insurance, veterinary fees, a quality pet food, etc. The RSPCA in the UK has estimated that owning a dog costs an average of around £1,300 ($1,700) a year!

....

Other Pets

However friendly your puppy is, if you already have other pets in your household, they may not be too happy at the new arrival. Socialised Dachshunds generally get on well with other animals, but it might not be a good idea to leave your hamster or pet rabbit running loose. The Dachshund was bred to hunt badgers and many have strong prey instincts. The pup has first to learn to fit in alongside other pets and if introduced slowly, they may well become best friends.

Dachshund puppies are naturally curious and playful and will sniff and investigate other pets. They may even chase them in the beginning. Depending on how lively your pup is, you may have to separate them initially, or put the pup into a pen or crate for short periods to allow the cat to investigate without being pestered by a hyperactive pup who thinks the cat is a great playmate.

This will also prevent your puppy from being injured. If the two animals are free and the cat lashes out, your pup's eyes could get scratched. A timid Dachshund might need protection from a bold cat - or vice versa. A bold cat and a timid Dachshund will probably settle down together quickest!

If things seem to be going well with no aggression, then let them loose together after one or two supervised sessions. Take the process slowly; if your cat is stressed or frightened, he may decide to leave. Our feline friends are notorious for abandoning home because the board and lodgings are better down the road...

More than One Dog

Most well-socialised Dachshunds have no problem sharing their home with other dogs. Introduce your puppy to other dogs and animals in a positive, non-frightening manner that will give her confidence. Supervised sessions help everyone to get along and for the other dog or dogs to accept your new pup. If you can, introduce them for the first time outdoors on neutral ground, rather than in the house or in an area that one dog regards as her own. You don't want the established dog to feel he has to protect his territory, nor the puppy to feel she is in an enclosed space and can't get away.

If you are thinking about getting more than one pup, consider waiting until your first puppy is a few months old or an adult before getting a second. Waiting means you can give your full attention to one puppy; get housetraining, socialisation and the basics of obedience training out of the way before getting your second. Another benefit is that an older well-trained dog will help teach the new puppy some manners.

 Think very carefully before getting two puppies from the same litter. Apart from the time and expense involved, you want your new Dachshund to learn to focus on YOU, and not her littermate.

In the long term, owning two Dachshunds can be twice as nice — they will be great company for each other - but bear in mind that it's also double the food and vet's bills.

....

Which Type?

With most breeds, you just decide on the breed and that's more or less it. Not so with Dachshunds; I can't think of another dog with so many choices in terms of size, coat type and colour.

If you love Dachshunds but are not sure which size to get, consider how much space you have both indoors and outdoors at home and how much time you can devote to exercising your dog every day. Standard Dachshunds are NOT small dogs, they can weigh 25lb to 30lb, whereas a small Mini may weigh less than 10lb.

Dachshunds have a surprising amount of stamina - an adult Standard that has been regularly exercised can walk all day.

A good rule of thumb is around an hour's daily exercise for adult dogs. Minis may be happy running around the house and garden, but still benefit from getting out on walks to keep them socialised, fit and a healthy weight.

You then have to consider gender - do you want a male or a female Dachshund? Gender should be a consideration if you have other dogs. You can't expect an unneutered male to live in a relaxed manner with an unspayed female in heat. Similarly, two uncastrated males may not always get along; there may simply be too much testosterone and competition.

All females have heat cycles and, unless yours is spayed, you will have to restrict her activities away from the home when she is in heat every six months or so to stop unwanted attention from males.

Temperament often has more to do with the puppy's natural personality and bloodlines, rather than gender - so always ask about the temperament of the father AND mother.

One issue a couple of breeders have pointed out is that some uncastrated males have a tendency to *"mark"* or do a small wee - even inside the house. One said: "The worst thing is the marking by the boys. They tend to do a tiny wee until settled. As they enter the room, or even someone else's house, they can sniff all around the room leaving very small wees. After they have checked out the room they settle and no longer leave little marks.

"They are toilet-trained and go outside to wee and poo, but this need to mark the room is driven from somewhere deeper and is not linked to toilet training, although many owners feel it is. It's more down to saying: **This is my place.** The girls do not need to do this."

Before you all rush out and get females, here are some more comments: "Males seem a little easier, given that females do have PMT (Pre-Menstrual Tension - some of mine want to bite each other's heads off, just before they come into season). Males tend to be a little more chilled - until their hormones kick in and then they may need neutering, depending on their circumstances.

"Boys are more "clingy" and pine or worry more than females. They get upset and won't eat if their favourite person goes away or the routine changes; they are more sensitive to feelings. They also don't always get along in male-only packs if unaltered (uncastrated), but are pretty good in male-only or mixed-sex packs if altered. Females are usually more independent, but still love a cuddle. They usually get along in packs, but it's not a guarantee. Once girls fight, they never forget!"

"No, I don't think there is a difference between the boys and the girls. I have calm boys and calm girls and also have much more active boys and girls. I have boys who love to snuggle in on the sofa but girls who do too! I think it's all down to the individual's personality."

"We have a docile dog (Otto and his son Bruno) and a docile bitch, Clara, who tends to listen better because more she is more focussed on the boss. Django is more tensed and energetic, but he is easily distracted by smell. All males lift their leg when the opportunity is there - even after a long walk outside. Bitches will let you know if they need to pee and be let out."

"I find boys more gentle and cuddly and females a bit more bossy and independent."

"The girls, although they love you and want to be with you, are more independent when relaxing and are happy to snooze on a bed or sofa, whereas the boys would leave with anyone, but are very loving and want to be by your side all of the time."

There are several different colours of Dachshunds - see **Chapter 14. Grooming** for details. If you've set your heart on a particular colour or marking, make sure the health and temperament boxes are ticked as well when you choose your breeder.

 **Your main points of reference in terms of size, physical appearance and temperament are the puppy's parents.**

Plan Ahead

Choosing the right breeder is one of the most important decisions you will make. Like humans, your puppy will be a product of her parents and will inherit many of their characteristics. Natural temperament and how healthy your puppy will be now and throughout her life will depend to some extent on the genes of her parents.

Responsible breeders test their dogs; they check the health records and temperament of the parents and only breed from suitable stock. Sound Dachshund puppies are not cheap – health screening, socialisation and first-rate care come at a cost.

Depending on type, colour markings and which area of the country you live in, expect to pay around £1,000 to £2,500 in the UK and $1,500 to $2,500 or more in the US, for a pedigree pup from **fully health-screened** parents. More for one with show prospects. Anything under £1,000 or $1,000 could be a cause for concern. See **Chapter 12. Dachshund Health** to find out what health certificates to ask to see.

 BE PATIENT. Start looking months or even a year before your planned arrival. There is usually a waiting list for Dachshund pups from health-screened parents and good breeders, so get your name on a list.

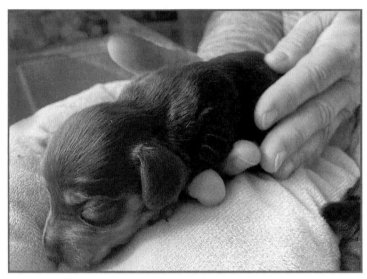

Phone or email your selected breeder or breeders to find out about future litters and potential dates, but don't commit until you've asked lots of questions.

Photo of this beautiful new-born Miniature Long-Haired puppy by AKC Bred With HEART breeder Pame Bates, Doxies Treasures, California.

A healthy Dachshund will be your irreplaceable companion for the next decade or more, so why buy one from a pet shop or general ad? Would you buy an old car or a house with potential structural problems just because it looked pretty in a website photo or was cheap? The answer is probably no, because you know you'd have stress and expense at some point in the future.

Visit the breeder personally at least once. With the distances involved, this is not always possible in the USA, so speak at length on the phone to the breeder, video call, ask lots of questions and ask to see photos and videos of the pups. Reputable breeders will be happy to answer all your questions - and will have lots for you too.

Dachshunds should be eight weeks to 12 weeks old before they leave the breeder. Puppies need this time to physically develop and learn the rules of the pack from their mothers and littermates. In some US states it is illegal to sell a puppy younger than eight weeks.

....

Buyer Beware

Good breeders do not sell their dogs on general purpose websites, Gumtree, eBay, Craig's List or Freeads, in car parks or somebody else's house. In 2020, the Government passed *Lucy's Law* in England (but not as yet Wales or Scotland), saying:

"*'Lucy's Law'* means that anyone wanting to get a new puppy or kitten in England must now buy direct from a breeder, or consider adopting from a rescue centre instead. Licensed dog breeders are required to show puppies interacting with their mothers in their place of birth. If a business sells puppies or kittens without a licence, they could receive an unlimited fine or be sent to prison for up to six months. The law is named after Lucy, a Cavalier King Charles Spaniel who was rescued from a puppy farm."

There is no such law in the US. And if you are looking at dogs on Pets4Homes in the UK, follow their guidelines carefully, check the health screening and see the pup with the mother.

There is a difference between *a hobby breeder* and a *backyard or backstreet breeder*. Both may breed just one or two litters a year and keep the puppies in their homes, but that's where the similarity ends. In the UK, *hobby breeders* often don't have a website and you will probably find out about them via word of mouth.

Good hobby breeders are usually breed enthusiasts or experts; sometimes they show their pedigree dogs. They carry out health tests and lavish care and love on their dogs. They are not professional dog breeders. NOTE: While it is often a good sign in the UK, the term *"hobby breeder"* can have negative implications in the USA.

Backyard breeders are often breeding family pets. They have less knowledge about the breed, pay little attention to the health and welfare of their dogs and are doing it primarily for extra cash. They may be very nice people, but avoid buying a dog from them.

 All GOOD breeders, professional or hobby, have in-depth knowledge of the Dachshund. They take measures to prevent potential health issues being passed on to puppies, and are passionate about the breed.

Here are four reasons for buying from a good breeder:

1. **HEALTH:** Like all breeds, Dachshunds have potentially inheritable health issues. Screening breeding stock and NOT breeding from those that fail the health tests is the best way of preventing genetic disorders from being passed on to puppies.

2. **SOCIALISATION:** Scientists and dog experts now realise that the critical socialisation period for dogs is up to the age of four months. An unstimulated puppy is likely to be less well-adjusted and more likely to have fear or behaviour issues as an adult. Good breeders start this process, they don't just leave the puppies in a shed or barn for eight weeks. Socialisation is important for Dachshunds.

3. **TEMPERAMENT:** Good breeders select their breeding stock based not only on sound structure and health, but also on temperament. They will not breed from an aggressive or overly timid dog.

4. **PEACE OF MIND:** Most good breeders agree to take the dog back at any time in her life or rehome her if things don't work out - although you may find it too hard to part with your beloved Dachshund by then.

Spotting Bad Breeders

Getting a puppy is such an emotional decision - and one that should have a wonderfully positive impact on you and your family's life for over a decade. Unfortunately, the high price of puppies has resulted in unscrupulous people producing litters for the money.

This section helps you avoid the pitfalls of getting a puppy from a puppy mill, a puppy broker (somebody who makes money from buying and selling puppies), a backyard breeder or even an importer. You can't buy a Rolls Royce or a Corvette for a couple of thousand pounds or dollars - you'd immediately suspect that the *"bargain"* on offer wasn't the real thing. No matter how lovely it looked, you'd be right - and the same applies to Dachshunds.

Become Breeder Savvy

- Avoid websites where there are no pictures of the owners' home or kennels

- If the website shows lots of photos of cute puppies with little information about the family, breeding dogs, health tests and environment, click the X button

- Don't buy a website puppy with a shopping cart symbol next to her picture

- See the puppies with their mother face-to-face. If this is not possible due to distances, speak at length on the phone with the breeder and ask lots of questions

- You hear: "You can't see the parent dogs because......" ALWAYS ask to see the parents and, as a minimum, see the mother and how she looks and behaves with the pups, pictured. If the pups are really hers, she will interact with them.

- Good breeders are happy to provide lots of information and at least one reference before you commit

- If the breeder is reluctant to answer your questions, look elsewhere

- Pressure selling: on the phone, the breeder doesn't ask you many questions and then says: "There are only X many puppies left and I have several other buyers interested." Walk away

- You hear "Our Dachshund puppies are cheaper because...." Walk away

- At the breeder's, ask to see where the puppy is living. If the breeding dogs are not housed in the family home, they should be in clean kennels, not too hot or cold, with access to grass and time spent with humans

- Ask to see the other puppies from the litter

- The mother is not with the puppies, but brought in to meet you

- The puppies look small for their stated age

- If the breeder says that the dam and sire are Kennel Club or AKC registered, ask to see the registration papers

- Photographs of so-called "champion ancestors" do not guarantee the health of the puppy

 Look beyond the cute, fluffy exterior. The way to look INSIDE the puppy is to see the parents and, most importantly, check what health screening has been carried out. *"Vet checked"* does NOT mean the pup or parents have passed any genetic health tests

- The person you are buying the puppy from did not breed the dog themselves. Deal with the breeder, not an intermediary

- The only place you meet the puppy seller is a car park, somebody else's house or place other than the puppies' home

- The seller tells you that the puppy comes from top, caring breeders from your or another country. Good breeders don't sell their puppies through brokers

- Ask to see photos of the puppy from birth to present day

- Be wary of "rare colours" or "rare markings" or "double dapple"

- Price – if you are offered a very cheap puppy, there is a reason. The price reflects the time, money and expertise invested in the puppy

- If you get a rescue Dachshund, make sure it is from a recognised rescue group and not a "puppy flipper" who may be posing as a do-gooder, but is in fact getting dogs (including stolen ones) from unscrupulous sources

- NEVER buy a puppy because you feel sorry for it; you are condemning other dogs to a life of misery

- If you have any doubt, go with your gut instinct and WALK AWAY - even if this means losing your deposit. It will be worth it in the long run

 Bad breeders do not have two horns coming out of their heads! Most will be friendly when you phone or visit - after all, they want to make the sale. It's only later that problems develop.

Puppy Mills and Farms

Unscrupulous breeders are everywhere. That's not to say there aren't some excellent Dachshund breeders out there; there certainly are. You just have to do your research.

While new owners might think they have bagged a cheap puppy, it often turns out to be false economy and emotionally disastrous when the puppy develops health problems or behavioural problems due to poor temperament or lack of socialisation. The UK's Kennel Club says as many as one in four puppies bought in the UK may come from puppy farms - and the situation is no better in North America.

The KC Press release states: "As the popularity of online pups continues to soar:

- Almost one in five pups bought (unseen) on websites or social media die within six months

- One in three buys online, in pet stores and via newspaper adverts - outlets often used by puppy farmers – this is an increase from one in five in the previous year

- The problem is likely to grow as the younger generation favour mail order pups, and breeders of fashionable breeds flout responsible steps

"We are sleepwalking into a dog welfare and consumer crisis as new research shows that more and more people are buying their pups online or through pet shops, outlets often used by cruel puppy

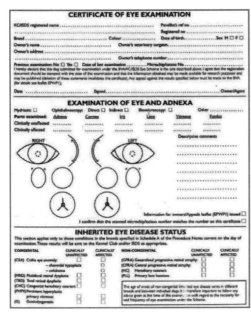

farmers, and are paying the price with their pups requiring long-term veterinary treatment or dying before six months old."

The KC research found that:

❧ One third of people who bought their puppy online, over social media or in pet shops failed to experience "overall good health"

❧ Some 12% of puppies bought online or on social media end up with serious health problems that require expensive on-going veterinary treatment from a young age

The Kennel Club said: "Whilst there is nothing wrong with initially finding a puppy online, it is essential to then see the breeder and ensure that they are doing all of the right things. This research clearly shows that too many people are failing to do this, and the consequences can be seen in the shocking number of puppies that are becoming sick or dying."

Marc Abraham, TV vet and founder of Pup Aid, added: "Sadly, if the *"buy it now"* culture persists, then this horrific situation will only get worse. There is nothing wrong with sourcing a puppy online, but people need to be aware of what they should then expect from the breeder.

"For example, you should not buy a car without getting its service history and seeing it at its registered address, so you certainly shouldn't buy a puppy without the correct paperwork and health certificates and without seeing where it was bred." **Pictured is a UK BVA Eye Certificate.**

"However, too many people are opting to buy directly from third parties, such as the internet, pet shops, or from puppy dealers, where you cannot possibly know how or where the puppy was raised. Not only are people buying sickly puppies, but many people are being scammed into paying money for puppies that don't exist, as the research showed that 7% of those who buy online were scammed in this way."

Visit https://dachshundbreedcouncil.wordpress.com/buying-a-dachshund for The Dachshund Breed Council's tips on buying a puppy and www.thekennelclub.org.uk/paw for the Kennel Club's.

....

Advice From The Experts

Our breeders have lots of advice about what to look for and what to avoid, starting in the UK with **Lisa Cole,** of Foosayo Dachshunds, North Yorkshire: "The first thing is: What does Mum look like? Has she a good coat, are her eyes clear, do her feet face forward or are they pointing out, and does she have a lovely flat back and good teeth?

"The pup should have clear, clean eyes with no weeping at all, clean ears and a clean nose, good pink gums and tongue. Also, the pup should be confident and happy to play with a normal plump tummy. Very fat tummies can indicate worms - walk away.

"Bad breeders are all over the country. Too many try to con buyers by using a bitch that is not the pup's mum if the real mother is unwell or has problems they wish to hide. These breeders can talk you into buying a pup, they are very good at the *"chat"* and often have an answer for all your questions, so do not trust them. Do not take their word, even if they seem very nice. Try to meet all the dogs, see where they have been sleeping, eating and going to the toilet. If the breeder won't show you, ask yourself why.

"Check the paperwork. If you're buying a Miniature, they must have a PRA certificate for the mother's and fathers' eyes (in the UK). At least one of the parents should be "Clear" or the pups could all go blind by the time they are three years old."

Bastiaan Smit, of Daxiesburrow Wire-Haired Dachshunds, Aberdeenshire: "Is the puppy part of the family; bred inside home and in contact with family members, as well as the sire and the dam (mother and father)? Warning signs are puppies left on their own with no social contact, no contact with their dam and sire and kept in outside kennels."

Hannah Norton, of Jacksondax Standard and Miniature Dachshunds, Devon: "Buyers should expect a clean, family environment with happy, healthy, confident puppies. The mother at least should be present and welcoming. The pups should be indoors living as part of the family. I have heard numerous horror stories of badly bred and raised puppies; it's infuriating for breeders like me who put their heart and soul into bringing these amazing dogs into the world."

Judith Carruthers, of Stanegate Wirehaired Dachshunds, Cumbria: "Puppies should look like Dachshunds! So many are actually crossbreeds advertised as Dachshunds - they are often quiet and shy with tear-stained eyes, crooked legs and pot bellies."

Photo of Judith's handsome Wire-Haireds Stanegate Catherine Wheel and her dam Champion Brumberhill Bellina by Will Harris.

Lisa Lindfield, of Zabannah Miniature Dachshunds, Cambridgeshire, has this cautionary tale: "A couple purchased a puppy from me after being caught twice by scammers. They had previously arrived at a house (found the pup via Pets4Homes) and a man with poor English answered the door.

"They asked for "Amy" who they'd been texting and he said she wasn't available, and: "What type of puppy are you here to see?" He then brought out a poorly-looking tiny puppy from the back; it could hardly stand up.

"They argued with him for 30 minutes, refusing to buy the puppy and he eventually admitted that he had imported it the day before. He said he drugged all the puppies so they travelled quietly in the boot of his car so he could get through customs quickly without being noticed, and told them: "The puppy will be fine in a couple of days!"

"The same couple answered another ad on Pets4Homes and arrived very early at a nice big house. There was a guy up a ladder on the house next door who rushed over and told them to get out as it was a set-up. Before they could get away, a big 4x4 arrived and a guy got out with a box which had the puppy in it. He lied and said he'd had a vet check, but couldn't produce papers. When the couple said they'd changed their minds, the guy got REALLY angry and told them they were "time wasters" before he let them leave the property."

Lisa's advice for UK puppy seekers:

- 🐾 See Kennel Club papers/KC change of ownership/KC five- generation pedigree

- Question the health and temperament of the mother and see her interact with the pups, so you know it is the right mother

- Ask for proof of a vet check before sale

- Check the puppy is responsive and active with no weeping eyes or problems with mobility

- Check the puppy responds to light and sound, and looks and smells clean and healthy

- Make sure claws have been trimmed, wormer and vaccinations have been administered and the coat brushed, with no flea dirt in coat

- Good breeders offer five weeks' free Kennel Club insurance

Pictured is Lisa's beloved Pebbles, a six-year-old chocolate and tan Mini Smooth.

Pauline Cheeseman, Colraed Miniature Dachshunds, Surrey: "The puppies should be with mum, they should have a full round tummy (not bloated), coats should be shiny, eyes bright no muck in the corners. They should be confident and outgoing in recognised Kennel Club colours.

"Warning signs to me would be asking for a deposit before viewing puppy, if mum was out on a walk, if puppy was bloated with worms, dull coat and all the opposites of above. Sadly, I've heard of many such stories."

Sandra Robertson, Hartlebury Miniature Dachshunds, Worcester: "The most important things are environment, the condition of dog, also seeing both parents – or at least the mother - and their health records. Warning signs of a bad breeder are caged dogs, dogs confined to a small space and kept out of view of household members, not getting human interaction and dogs in poor condition."

Stefanie Millington, CunAnnun Long-Haired Miniature Dachshunds, Norfolk: "Look for bright eyes, shiny coat, outgoing and friendly puppies happily playing in a clean environment and seen with their mother. Look for a breeder who is a member of a breed club or the KC Assured Breeder scheme, who will show you possibly other family members and is able to tell you a lot about their breed. They will happily provide you with health tests for their dogs, sales contract, vet check, microchip and vaccination cards.

"There are many unscrupulous breeders about. Try to avoid breeders who offer puppies in so-called "rare colours" at inflated prices, as colours which are NOT RECOGNISED by the Kennel Club can come with serious health issues. Also, avoid breeders that do NOT health test, who make excuses if you want to see mum with the puppies or when you can see or feel that the dogs or puppies are uncomfortable around the breeder."

American breeders have this to say, starting with **Kristin Cihos-Williams:** "Unscrupulous breeders can be detected by lack of participation in any Dachshund clubs and by great insistence on obtaining a deposit or money up front; that is a red flag. Responsible breeders take their time to evaluate their litters and screen potential homes based on what is best for each puppy. This is impossible to do before a litter is even born.

"A responsible breeder will care more about the long-term wellbeing of their puppies and find the best home for the puppy in question. Good breeders will always have wait lists and not have puppies constantly available for sale. Puppy mills rely on flashy websites and photos of constantly available cute puppies to lure unsuspecting buyers. It is always best to wait for the right puppy, rather than jump at the first available one. All puppies are cute when they are young - not all grow up to resemble the breed they should be."

Brenna Carlisle, Heritage Hounds, Alabama: "A good breeder will have a detailed contract, and pet puppies will be offered on limited/non-breeding contract. Spay/neuter will be required, but only after sexual maturity. A detailed questionnaire should be offered, with pedigree and genetics as well as health testing provided upon inquiry.

"I do not let people visit my home simply because of the germs they could bring in. When pups are fully vaccinated and ready to go at 12 weeks old, they can come in and see where my pups are raised. I have a Jon art whelping box, and a set-up just for mom and babies.

"I have heard horror stories of dogs being raised in a barn with no heat or air and just free whelping - and other dogs in the same kennel run eating the puppies. It is so important for prospective buyers to ask lots of questions. A GOOD breeder will answer any question, big or little, and will have nothing to hide."

Pame Bates, Doxies Treasures, California: "Shiny eyes, a healthy coat, proportions in accordance with the breed, strong back and legs, good breath, and a curious, engaged puppy are all good signs. Bad breeders do not have a contract to protect themselves and the new owner. Also look for a genetic health guarantee, a physical location (no puppies in a box from a parking lot), and photos of the puppies in their home environment showing development stages."

Melissa Sworab, Rabows Dachshunds, Texas, endorsed much of what has been said and added: "Puppies should have flawless pink bellies, clear eyes and non-smelly ears, and they should not smell of urine. So many breeders clean up a puppy just before delivery, but if they had fleas, etc, that pink belly will show evidence of stains, bumps and debris that don't go away with a quick bath.

"Green flags are breeders who delay puppy going home until 12 weeks and two vaccines before placement. This is SO important as it gives a much smaller chance of contracting Parvo after going home with two shots versus one.

"Also, breeders who ask for a contract first and then offer you copies of health clearances of the breeding stock and Zoom video conference showing where the dogs and puppies are kept, and possibly ask you to do the same."

Photo: Prue (Aust BIS Ch Rabows Charmed One), bred by Melissa and owned by Terry-Anne Keen, who went on to win Best In Show at the 10th National Specialty Show hosted by The Dachshund Club of Victoria, Inc.

Here are some of Melissa's red flags:

- 🐾 Breeders that take your money (deposits included) FIRST without getting a signed contract
- 🐾 Contracts that state you'll only get a replacement puppy if that one dies or gets sick, rather than your money back, as they usually breed a LOT and replacement will always be easier for them

- ❧ No health testing of any breeding stock

- ❧ No questionnaire or interview

- ❧ FULL breeding rights or extra charge for breeding rights on any dog, regardless if pet quality or not

- ❧ Show quality/potential puppy from a NON-show breeder - they really do not know!

- ❧ "Champion lines" – but no Champions in the last two to three generations or more. These breeders are "coat-tail" breeders just trying to charge more for the work of others

- ❧ Breeders that don't have any OLD dogs in their home. It could be they don't live long, or they sell them at auction when they are done breeding, etc. To me, old dogs are the key to seeing your pup's possible longevity

- ❧ Breeders with only outdoor kennels and no dogs in the home. If they have an indoor/outdoor kennel that's clean, that's not terrible, but we prefer dogs being bred under foot and in the home in reasonable numbers so they know how to be house dogs

- ❧ Breeders that will not take you through the house the dogs live in via Zoom or other video chat, but don't expect this until there's a signed contract in place and the breeder knows you are serious first

Where to Find a Good Breeder

1. The Kennel Club in your country. Look for Assured Breeders in the UK, and an AKC Breeder of Merit or a Bred with H.E.A.R.T. breeder in the US.

2. Dachshund Clubs. In the UK https://dachshundbreedcouncil.wordpress.com/breed-clubs has a list of national and regional breed club secretaries. For details of state-by-state breed clubs in the US, visit www.dachshundclubofamerica.org/dca-breeders

3. Visit dog shows or canine events where Dachshunds are participating and talk to competitors and breeders.

4. Get a recommendation from somebody who has a Dachshund that you like - but make sure the breeder health screens her dogs.

5. Ask your vet for details of local, ethical Dachshund breeders.

6. Search the internet - there are hundreds of breeders out there; use the advice in this chapter to find the right one.

7. If you are in the UK, visit the Dachshund stand at Discover Dogs during the annual Crufts dog show in early March.

....

Questions to Ask a Breeder

Here's a list of the questions you should be asking. The Kennel Club also has a three-minute video entitled *The Dos and Don'ts of Buying a Puppy* at: www.youtube.com/watch?v=1EhTu1TQcEc

1. **Have the parents been health screened?** Ask to see certificates and what guarantees the breeder is offering in terms of genetic illnesses.

2. **What veterinary care have the pups had so far?** Ask to see records of flea treatments, wormings and vaccinations, microchipping.

3. **Are you registered with the Kennel Club (UK), AKC (US) or a member of a Dachshund breed club?** Not all good Dachshund breeders are members, but this is a good place to start.

4. **How long have you been breeding Dachshunds?** You are looking for someone who has a track record with the breed.

5. **Can you put me in touch with someone who already has one of your puppies?**

6. **How many litters has the mother had?** Females are better waiting until they are 18 months or two years old, and The UK Kennel Club will not register puppies from a dam that has had more than four litters or is over the age of eight. Check the age of the mother.

7. **What happens to the mother once she has finished breeding?** Are they kept as part of the family, rehomed in loving homes, sent to animal shelters or auctioned off?

8. **Do you breed any other types of dog?** Buy from a specialist, preferably one who does not breed lots of other types of dog - unless you know they have a good reputation.

9. **What is so special about this litter?** You are looking for a breeder who has used good breeding stock and his or her knowledge to produce handsome, healthy dogs with good temperaments.

10. **What is the average lifespan of your dogs?** Generally, pups bred from healthy stock tend to live longer

11. **How socialised and housetrained is the puppy?** Good breeders often start the socialisation and potty training process before they leave.

12. **How would you describe the temperament of the parents?** Temperament is extremely important; try to interact with both parents, or at least the mother.

13. **What do you feed your adults and puppies?** A reputable breeder will feed a top quality dog food and advise that you do the same.

14. **Why aren't you asking me any questions?** A good breeder is committed to making a good match between the new owners and their puppies. If the breeder spends more time discussing money than the welfare of the puppy, draw your own conclusions as to what his or her priorities are – they probably don't include improving the breed. Walk away.

Choosing a Healthy Dachshund

Once you've selected your breeder and a litter is available, you then have to decide WHICH puppy to pick, unless the breeder has already earmarked one for you after asking lots of questions. Here are some pointers on puppy health:

1. Your chosen puppy should have **a well-fed appearance.** She should not, however, have a distended abdomen (pot belly) as this can be a sign of worms or other illnesses. The ideal puppy should not be too thin either - you should be able to feel her ribs, but not see them.

2. **Her nose should be cool, damp and clean** with no discharge.

3. **The pup's eyes should be bright and clear** with no discharge or tear stain. Steer clear of a puppy that blinks a lot. (Bordetella and Kennel Cough vaccines can sometimes cause runny eyes and nose for up to 10 days – ask when she was vaccinated for these).

4. **The pup's ears should be clean** with no sign of discharge, soreness or redness and no unpleasant smell.

5. **Check the puppy's rear end** to make sure it is clean and there are no signs of diarrhoea.

6. **The pup's coat should look clean,** feel soft, not matted - and puppies should smell good! The coat should have no signs of ticks or fleas. Red or irritated skin or bald spots could be a sign of infestation or a skin condition. Also, check between the toes of the paws for signs of redness or swelling.

7. **The puppy should be alert,** *like the pups in this picture,* and curious about you and her surroundings, not timid.

8. **Gums should be clean and pink.**

9. **Choose a puppy that moves freely** without any sign of injury or lameness. It should be a fluid movement, not jerky or stiff, and the pup should have a straight back, not arched.

10. When the puppy is distracted, clap or make a noise behind her - not so loud as to frighten her - to **make sure she is not deaf.**

11. Finally, **ask to see veterinary records** to confirm your puppy has been wormed and had her first vaccinations and a vet check.

If you get the puppy home and things don't work out for whatever reason, good breeders will either take the puppy back or find them a suitable home.

 Take your puppy to a vet to have a thorough check-up within 48 hours of purchase. If your vet is not happy with the pup's condition, return her - no matter how painful it may be. Keeping an unhealthy puppy will only lead to further distress and expense.

Puppy Contracts

Most good breeders provide their puppy parents with an official Puppy Contract. This protects both buyer and seller by providing information on the puppy until he or she leaves the breeder. Puppy Contract will answer such questions as whether the puppy:

🐾 Is covered by breeder's insurance and can be returned if there is a health issue within a certain time period

🐾 Has been micro-chipped (compulsory in the UK) and/or vaccinated and details of worming treatments

🐾 Has been partially or wholly toilet-trained

🐾 Has been socialised and where he or she was kept

- 🐾 What health conditions the pup and parents have been screened for
- 🐾 What the puppy is currently being fed and if any food is being supplied
- 🐾 Was born by Caesarean section
- 🐾 And details of the dam and sire

It's not easy for caring breeders to part with their puppies after they have lovingly bred and raised them, and so many supply extensive care notes for new owners, which may include details such as:

- 🐾 The puppy's daily routine
- 🐾 Feeding schedule
- 🐾 Vet and vaccination schedule
- 🐾 General puppy care
- 🐾 Toilet training
- 🐾 Socialisation

The Royal Society for the Prevention of Cruelty to Animals (RSPCA) has a downloadable puppy contract, *pictured,* endorsed by vets and animal welfare organisations; you should be looking for something similar from a breeder. Type *"RSPCA Puppy Contract"* into a search engine, or *"AKC Preparing a Puppy Contract"* if you're in the US.

 A good course of action would be something like this:

1. **Decide to get a Dachshund.**
2. **Do your research and find a good breeder whose dogs are health screened.**
3. **Decide on a male or female.**
4. **Register your interest - and WAIT until a puppy becomes available.**
5. **Pick one with a suitable temperament to fit in with your family.**
6. **Enjoy 12 or more years with a beautiful, healthy Dachshund.**

Some people pick a puppy based on how the dog looks. If coat type or colour, for example, is very important to you, make sure the other boxes are ticked as well.

4. Bringing Puppy Home

Getting a new puppy is so exciting; you can't wait to bring him home. Before that happens, you probably dream of all the things you are going to do together; going for walks, snuggling down on the couch, playing games, and maybe even taking part in activities or shows.

Your pup has, of course, no idea of your big plans, and the reality when he arrives can be a big shock! Puppies are wilful little critters with minds of their own and sharp teeth. They leak at both ends, chew anything in sight, constantly demand your attention, nip the kids or anything else to hand, cry and don't pay a blind bit of notice to your commands... There is a lot of work ahead before the two of you develop that unique bond!

Your pup has to learn what you require from him before he can start to meet some of your expectations - and you have to learn what your pup needs from you.

Once your new arrival lands in your home, your time won't be your own, but you can get off to a good start by preparing things before the big day. Here's a list of things to think about getting beforehand - your breeder may supply some of these:

Puppy Checklist

- ✓ A dog bed or basket
- ✓ Bedding – a Vetbed or Vetfleece is a good choice
- ✓ A towel or piece of cloth that has been rubbed on the puppy's mother to put in the bed
- ✓ A puppy gate or pen
- ✓ A crate if you decide to use one
- ✓ A collar or puppy harness with ID tag and a lead (leash)
- ✓ Food and water bowls, preferably stainless steel
- ✓ Puppy food – find out what the breeder is feeding and stick with that to start with
- ✓ Puppy treats, healthy ones, carrot and apple pieces are good, no rawhide
- ✓ Newspapers or pellet litter, and a bell if you decide to use one, for potty training
- ✓ Poop bags
- ✓ Toys and chews suitable for puppies
- ✓ A puppy coat if you live in a cool climate or it's winter
- ✓ Old towels for cleaning and drying and partially covering the crate

AND PLENTY OF TIME!

Later on, you'll also need grooming brushes, flea and worming products and maybe a car grille or travel crate. Many good breeders provide Puppy Packs to take home; they contain some or all of the following items:

- ✓ Pedigree certificate
- ✓ Buyer's contract
- ✓ Information pack with details of vet's visits, vaccinations and wormings, parents' health certificates, diet, breed clubs, etc.
- ✓ Puppy food
- ✓ ID tag/microchip info
- ✓ Blanket that smells of the mother and litter
- ✓ Soft toy that your puppy has grown up with, possibly a chew toy as well
- ✓ A month's free insurance

 **By law, all UK puppies have to be microchipped BEFORE they leave the breeder and they must be at least eight weeks old – 10 to 12 weeks is a better age for Dachshunds to leave the litter.**

Puppy Proofing Your Home

Some adjustments will be needed to make your home safe and suitable. Puppies are small bundles of instinct and energy when they are awake, with little common sense and even less self-control. Dachshund puppies have bursts of energy before running out of steam and spending much of the rest of the day sleeping. As one breeder says: "They have two speeds – ON and OFF!"

They also have an incredible sense of smell and love to investigate with their noses and mouths. Check your garden or yard, make sure there are no poisonous or low plants with sharp leaves or thorns that could cause eye injuries.

Photo: A beautiful litter of Mini Smooths bred by Sandra Robertson, Hartlebury Miniature Dachshunds, UK.

There are literally dozens of plants harmful to a puppy if ingested, including azalea, daffodil bulbs, lily, foxglove, hyacinth, hydrangea, lupin, rhododendron, sweet pea, tulip and yew.

The Kennel Club has a list of some of the most common ones, type *"Kennel Club poisonous plants"* into Google or visit: http://bit.ly/1nCv1qJ The ASPCA has an extensive list for the USA at: http://bit.ly/19xkhoG or Google *"ASPCA poisonous plants."*

Fence off any sharp plants, such as roses, that can injure a dog's eyes. Make sure EVERY LITTLE GAP has been plugged in fences. You'd be amazed at the tiny spaces determined puppies can escape through - and your new arrival has no road sense. Don't leave your new puppy unattended in the garden or yard.

FACT **Dognapping is on the increase. Some 2,000 dogs are now being stolen each year in the UK. The figures are much higher for the US, where the AKC reports increasing dog thefts and warns owners against leaving dogs unattended.**

Puppies are little chew machines and puppy-proofing your home involves moving anything sharp, breakable or chewable - including your shoes. Lift electrical cords, mobile phones and chargers, remote controls, etc. out of reach and block off any off-limits areas of the house with a child gate or barrier, especially as he may be shadowing you for the first few days.

Create an area where your puppy is allowed to go, perhaps one or two rooms, preferably with a hard floor that is easy to clean. Keep the rest of the house off-limits, at least until the pair of you have mastered potty training.

This area should be near the door to the garden or yard for toileting. Restricting the puppy's space

also helps him to settle in. He probably had a den and small space at the breeder's home. Suddenly having the freedom of the whole house can be quite daunting - not to mention messy!

You can buy a purpose-made dog barrier or use a sturdy baby gate, which may be cheaper. Choose one with narrow vertical gaps or mesh, and check that your puppy can't get his head stuck between the bars, or put a mesh over the bottom of the gate initially. You can also make your own barrier, but bear in mind that cardboard, fabric and other soft materials will get chewed.

A puppy's bones are soft, and studies have shown that if pups go up and down stairs regularly, or jump on and off furniture, they can develop joint problems later in life.

Don't underestimate your puppy! Young Dachshunds are lively and determined - they can jump and climb, so choose a barrier higher than you think necessary.

The puppy's designated area or room should not be too hot, cold or damp and free from draughts. Little puppies can be sensitive to temperature fluctuations and don't do well in very hot or very cold conditions. If you live in a hot climate, your new pup may need air conditioning in the summertime, especially if he's long-coated.

Just as you need a home, so your puppy needs a den; a haven where your pup feels safe. Young puppies sleep for 18 hours or more a day at the beginning; this is normal. You have a couple of options: you can get a dog bed or basket, or you can use a crate, which can also speed up potty training. **See Chapter 5. Crate and Housetraining** for getting your Dachshund used to - and then to enjoy - being in a crate.

It may surprise American readers to learn that common practice in the UK is to contain the puppy in the kitchen or utility room until he's housetrained, and later to allow the dog to roam around the house at will. Some owners do not allow their dogs upstairs, but many do.

Some owners prefer to create a safe penned area for their pup, rather than a crate, while others use

both a pen and a crate. You can make your own barriers or buy a manufactured metal or fabric playpen, *pictured.*

The time any young children spend with the puppy should be limited to a few short sessions a day. Plenty of sleep is *essential* for the normal development of a young dog. You wouldn't wake a baby every hour or so to play, and the same goes for puppies.

Wait a day or two before inviting friends round to see your handsome new puppy. However excited you are, your new arrival needs a few days to get over the stress of leaving mother and siblings and start bonding with you.

While confident, well-socialised puppies may settle in right away, other puppies may feel sad and a little afraid. Make the transition as gentle and unalarming as possible.

After a few sleep-deprived nights followed by days filled with entertaining your little puppy and dealing with chewed shoes, nipping and a few housetraining "accidents," your nerves might be a tiny bit frayed! Try to remain calm and patient... your Dachshund puppy is doing his best... it just takes a little time for you both to get on the same wavelength.

FACT ▶ This early period is a very important time for your puppy - how you react and interact with each other during these first few days and weeks will help to shape your relationship and your Dachshund's character for the rest of his life.

Bones, Chews and Toys

Like babies, puppies like to explore the world with their mouths, so chew treats and toys are a must. There are some things you can't move out of puppy's way, like kitchen cupboards, doors, sofas, fixtures and fittings, so try not to leave your pup unattended for any length of time where he can chew something that is hard to replace.

Tip Avoid giving old socks, shoes or slippers, or your pup will naturally come to think of your footwear as fair game!

You can give a Dachshund puppy *a raw bone* to gnaw on - NEVER cooked bones as these can splinter. Avoid poultry and pork bones, and ribs - especially pork ribs - are too high in fat. Knuckle bones are a good choice and the bone should be too big for the puppy to swallow. Puppies should be supervised and the bone removed after an hour or so. Don't feed a puppy a bone if there are other dogs around, it could lead to food aggression.

FACT ▶ Raw bones contain bacteria, and families with babies or very young children shouldn't feed them indoors. Keep any bones in a fridge or freezer and always wash your hands after handling them.

Alternatives to real bones or plastic chew bones include natural *reindeer antler* chew toys *(pictured),* which have the added advantage of calcium, although they are hard and have been known to crack teeth. Natural chews preferred by some breeders include ears, dried rabbit pelt and tripe sticks – all excellent for teething puppies - once you have got over the smell!

Tip Rawhide chews are not recommended as they can get stuck in a dog's throat or stomach, but bully sticks (pictured) are a good alternative.

Made from a bull's penis(!) they can be a good distraction from chewing furniture, etc. and help to promote healthy teeth and gums. *Bully sticks* are highly digestible, break down easily in the stomach and are generally considered safe for all dogs. They are made from 100% beef, normally contain no additives or preservatives, come in different sizes and dogs love 'em. NOTE: Puppies should be supervised while eating bully sticks or any other treats.

Dental sticks are good for cleaning your dog's teeth, but many contain preservatives and don't last very long with a determined chewer. One that does last is the *Nylabone Dura Chew Wishbone,* made of a type of plastic infused with flavours appealing to dogs. Get the right size and throw it away if it starts to splinter after a few weeks.

Another long-lasting treat option is the **Lickimat (pictured),** which you smear with a favourite food. This inexpensive mat will keep your puppy occupied for some time – although they can leave a bit of a mess.

Other choices include **Kong toys,** which are pretty indestructible, and you can put treats (frozen or fresh) or smear peanut butter inside to keep your dog occupied while you are out. All of these are widely available online, if not in your local pet store.

As far as toys go, the **Zogoflex Hurley** and the **Goughnut** are both strong and float, so good for swimmers – and you'll get your money back on both if your Dachshund destroys them! For safety, the Goughnut has a green exterior and red interior, so you can tell if your dog has penetrated the surface - as long as the green is showing, you can let your dog "goughnuts."

A **natural hemp** or cotton tug rope is another option, as the cotton rope acts like dental floss and helps with teeth cleaning. It is versatile and can be used for fetch games as well as chewing.

FACT Puppies' stomachs are sensitive, so be careful what goes in. Even non-poisonous garden plants can cause intestinal blockages and/or vomiting. Like babies, pups can quickly dehydrate, so if your puppy is sick or has watery poop for a day or two, seek medical advice.

Collecting Your Puppy

* Let the breeder know what time you will arrive and ask her not to feed the pup for a couple of hours beforehand - unless you have a very long journey, in which case the puppy will need to eat something. He will be less likely to be car sick and should be hungry when he lands in his new home. The same applies to an adult dog moving to a new home

* Ask for an old towel or toy that has been with the pup's mother – you can leave one on an earlier visit to collect with the pup. Or take one with you and rub the mother with it to collect her scent and put this with the puppy for the first few days. It will help him to settle

* Get copies of any health certificates relating to the parents and a Contract of Sale or Puppy Contract – see **Chapter 3. Finding Your Puppy** for details. It should also state that you can return the puppy if there are health issues within a certain time frame. The breeder will also give you details of worming and any vaccinations, as well as an information sheet.

* Find out exactly what the breeder is feeding and how much; dog's digestive systems cannot cope with sudden changes in diet - unless the breeder has deliberately been feeding several different foods to her puppies to get them used to different foods. In the beginning, stick to whatever the pup is used to; good breeders send some food home with the puppy.

The Journey Home

Bringing a new puppy home in a car can be a traumatic experience. Your puppy will be sad at leaving his mother, brothers and sisters and a familiar environment. Everything will be strange and frightening and he may whimper and whine or even bark on the way home.

* If you can, take somebody with you on that first journey – some breeders insist on having someone there to hold and cuddle the pup to make the journey less stressful for the pup

* Under no circumstances have the puppy on your lap while driving. It is simply too dangerous - a Dachshund puppy is extremely cute, wriggly and far too distracting. Have an old towel between your travel companion and the pup as he may quite possibly pee - the puppy, not the passenger!

- If you have to travel any distance, take a crate – a canvas or plastic travel crate with holes in for air flow, or a wire crate he'll use at home. Cover the bottom of the crate with a waterproof material and then put a comfortable blanket on top. You can put newspapers in half of the crate if the pup is partly housetrained

- Don't forget to allow the pup to relieve himself beforehand, and if your journey is more than a couple of hours, take water to give him en route. He may need the toilet, but don't let him outside on to the ground as he is not yet fully vaccinated

- As soon as you arrive home, let your puppy into the garden or yard, and when he "performs," praise him for his efforts

These first few days are critical in getting your puppy to feel safe and confident in his new surroundings. Spend time with the latest addition to your family, talk to him often in a reassuring manner. Introduce him to his den and toys, slowly allow him to explore and show him around the house – once you have puppy-proofed it.

Dachshund puppies are extremely curious - and amusing, you might be surprised at their reactions to everyday objects. Puppies explore by sniffing and mouthing, so don't scold for chewing. Instead, put objects you don't want chewed out of reach and replace them with chew toys. Some puppies can be more "mouthy" than others; if yours is like this, make sure he has safe toys to chew.

If you've got other animals, introduce them to each other slowly and in supervised sessions on neutral territory - or outdoors where there is space so neither feels threatened - preferably once the pup has got used to his new surroundings, not as soon as you walk through the door. Gentleness and patience are the keys to these first few days, so don't over-face your pup.

 Have a special, gentle puppy voice and use his new name frequently - and in a pleasant, encouraging manner. Never use his name to scold or he will associate it with bad things. The sound of his name should always make him want to pay attention to you as something good is going to happen - praise, food, playtime, and so on.

Lifting a Dachshund

Resist the urge to keep picking your puppy up – no matter how irresistible he is! Let him explore on his own little legs, encouraging independence. Make sure everybody, including children and friends, knows the correct way to pick up and handle a Dachshund without causing back injury. It is different from picking up other breeds:

1. Place a hand under the dog's chest and spread your fingers to support as much of the upper body as possible, taking the weight off his spine.

2. Put your other hand, palm up fingers spread, under the dog's bottom to take the weight off his lower body.

3. Lift up the dog, keeping his body and back level.

4. When holding or moving around, keep one hand under his bottom to support his back.

5. Do NOT let his lower body dangle.

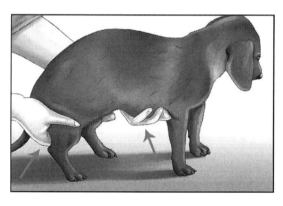

6. If you have to turn him upside down to cradle him (which is a submissive position for a dog), keep using two hands to support both his upper and lower back.

7. With two hands and the dog level, gently lower him all the way back down - do not let go until his paws are touching the ground.

DON'T lift a Dachshund by his armpits, *as shown in the image below.* **Never drop him back on to the ground** - even a drop of a few inches can jar the spine, and never twist or turn him as you lift or place him back on to the ground.

Settling In

One of the most important things at this stage is to ensure that your puppy has enough sleep – **which is nearly all of the time** - no matter how much you want to play with or cuddle him. Our website receives emails from worried new owners. Here are some of the most common concerns:

- My puppy won't stop crying or whining

- My puppy is shivering

- My puppy won't eat

- My puppy is very timid

- My puppy follows me everywhere, he won't let me out of his sight

- My puppy sleeps all the time, is this normal?

These behaviours are quite common at the beginning. They are just a young pup's reaction to leaving his mother and littermates and entering into a strange new world. It is normal for puppies to sleep most of the time, just like babies. It is also normal for some puppies to whine during the first couple of days.

 If you constantly pick up a crying pup, he will learn that your attention is the reward for his crying. Wait until your puppy STOPS crying before giving him your attention.
If your puppy is shivering, check that he's warm enough, as he is used to the warmth of his siblings. If he's on the same food as he was at the breeder's and won't eat, then it is probably just nerves. If he leaves his food, take it away and try it later, don't leave it down all of the time or he may get used to turning his nose up at it.

Make your new pup as comfortable as possible, ensuring he has a warm (but not too hot), quiet den away from draughts, where he is not pestered by children or other pets. Handle him gently, while giving him plenty of time to sleep. Avoid placing him under stress by making too many demands. If your puppy whines or cries, it is usually due one of the following reasons:

- He is lonely

- He is hungry

- He is cold

- He needs to relieve himself

- He wants attention from you

If it is none of these, then physically check him over to make sure he hasn't picked up an injury. Try not to fuss too much! If he whimpers, reassure with a quiet word. If he cries loudly and tries to get out of his allotted area, he may need to go to the toilet. Even if it is the middle of the night, get up and take him outside. Praise him if he performs.

FACT Dachshund puppies from breeders who have already started socialisation and training are often more confident and less fazed by new things. They often settle in quicker than those reared with less human contact.

A puppy will think of you as his new mother, and if you haven't decided what to call him yet, "Shadow" might be apt as he will follow you everywhere! But after a few days start to leave your pup for periods of a few minutes, gradually building up the time. A puppy unused to being left alone can grow up to have separation anxiety - see **Chapter 7. Dachshund Traits** for more information.

Helping a new pup to settle in is virtually a full-time job. If your routine means you are normally out of the house for a few hours during the day, get your puppy on a Friday or Saturday so he has at least a couple of days to adjust to his new surroundings. A far better idea is to book time off work to help your puppy to settle in, if you can. (Easier to do in the UK than the US). If you don't work, leave your diary free for the first couple of weeks.

The strongest bonding period for a puppy is between eight and 12 weeks of age. The most important factors in bonding with your puppy are TIME and PATIENCE, even if he makes a mess in the house or chews something. Spend time with your Dachshund pup and you will have the most loyal lifelong friend.

 FACT ⟩ Dachshunds are very focused on their human and hugely affectionate. That emotional attachment may grow to become one of the most important aspects of your life – and certainly his.

Where Should the Puppy Sleep?

Where do you want your new puppy to sleep? In the beginning, you cannot simply allow a pup to wander freely around the house. Ideally, he will be in a contained area, such as a pen or crate, at night. While it is not acceptable to shut a dog in a cage all day, you can keep your puppy in a crate at night until housetrained. Some adult dogs still prefer to sleep in a crate.

You also have to consider whether you want the pup to permanently sleep in your bedroom or elsewhere. If it's the bedroom, don't let him jump on and off beds or couches, or race up and down stairs, as this can cause joint damage.

Tip Many breeders recommend putting the puppy in a crate (or similar) next to your bed for the first two or three nights before moving him to the permanent sleeping place. Knowing you are close and being able to smell you will help overcome initial fears.

He may still cry when you move him further away or out of your bedroom, but that should soon stop - you just have to block your ears for a couple of nights! He will have had those few days to get used to his new surroundings and feeling safe with you.

Young puppies can't go through the night without needing to pee (and sometimes poo); their bodies simply aren't up to it. To speed up housetraining, consider getting up in the night from Day One for the first week or so to let your pup outside for a pee. Just pick him up, take him outside with the minimum of fuss, praise the pee and put him back into the crate. After that, set your alarm for an early morning wake-up call.

NOTE: While I and many breeders recommend getting up in the night in the beginning, a few breeders are against it, as they don't believe it speeds up housetraining. Ask your own breeder's advice on this one.

We don't recommend letting a new pup sleep on the bed. He will not be housetrained and also a puppy needs to learn his place in the household and have his own special place. It's up to you whether to let him on the bed or not once he's housetrained.

If your Dachshund is to be allowed on the bed and sofa, consider investing or making a ramp so he can get up there under his own steam – and don't let him race up and down stairs at any age. As a new Dachshund owner, get into the habit of considering the effect any activity might have on your dog's delicately-structured back.

If you do allow your dog to sleep in the bedroom but not on the bed, be aware that dogs snuffle, snore, fart and - if not in a crate - pad around the bedroom in the middle of the night and come up to the bed to check you are still there - or see if you want to play! None of this is conducive to a good night's sleep.

While it is not good to leave a dog alone all day, it is also not healthy to spend 24 hours a day together, as a dog can become too dependent. While this is very flattering for you, it actually means that the dog is nervous and less sure of himself when you are not there. The last thing you want on your hands is an anxious Dachshund.

A Dachshund puppy used to being on his own every night is less likely to develop attachment issues, so consider this when deciding where he should sleep.

Breeders' Advice for New Owners

Bastiaan Smit, Daxiesburrow, Aberdeenshire: "Let the puppy rest throughout the day for at least the first six months, and allow rest before any training. Home training should start from the very beginning, but let your puppy be a puppy; show patience and allow sufficient time. Training sessions should only be 5-10 minutes at a time.

"Digging is part of the Dachshund's survival tool package and natural behaviour. He will find the place where he can dig: between stones, wood piles, badger burrows and even rocks, so create an area where he can be a Dachshund and dig!"

Hannah Norton, Jacksondax, South Devon: "Replace everything that puppy attempts to chew or bite that he or she shouldn't with a toy or something that they are allowed. Always turn away and ignore a puppy that jumps up."

Pictured is Hannah's Gracie with her new-born litter.

Judith Carruthers, Stanegate Wirehaired Dachshunds, Cumbria: "Allow your puppy to explore safely to get his bearings. Don't allow puppies to jump up or down stairs or furniture. Introduce him to his crate and ensure he's secure when left on his own. Be careful he's not able to chew cables, electrics or toys."

"Ignore barking - no eye contact or verbal communication and remove the dog from the situation. If a puppy is jumping up, again, don't make eye contact or verbal communication. Fold your arms and turn away; do not squeal or wave your arms!"

Lisa Cole, Foosayo Dachshunds, North Yorkshire: "Dangers for any Dachshund pup are: jumping on a sofa, running upstairs, being trodden on, onions or any bulbs like daffodils, chocolate, macadamia nuts, corn on the cob, avocado, artificial sweetener (xylitol), alcohol, cooked bones, grapes and raisins.

"Don't allow the pup to have the whole house to play in; you cannot keep all your things and the pup safe - keep the pup in manageable spaces that can be increased as the pup grows. Your pup cannot toilet under your dining table every day if he cannot go under the dining table every day.

"My advice for dealing with a puppy biting is easy: scream as if the pup has just bitten your arm off! Grab hold of the "wounded" arm and rush out of the room. A pup will be shocked at what has happened and you will find the pup stops the mouthing. Unfortunately, I have not been so successful with stopping my dogs digging. They won't do it in front of me, they wait until I am not looking and sneak off! They love to chew the roots of grass, not to be sick but because they love the sweet taste, so I have lots of little bare patches in my lawn.

"As far as sleeping goes, start as you mean to go on. If you use a crate or just a dog bed in the kitchen, do that from Day 1. Never let them sleep with you unless you want a dog in bed with you for the next 14 to 16 years!"

Lisa Lindfield, Zabannah Dachshunds, Cambridgeshire: "It is SO important to pick Dachshunds up properly from Day 1. Don't allow small children to pick them up without supervision nor to wake a sleeping puppy; they need their sleep and mustn't be poked and prodded. Dachshunds shouldn't be allowed to jump from the furniture either.

Photo: Nevaeh Fiske (8) carefully handling nine-week-old Gordan, bred by Lisa.

"Other tips are:

* Your garden needs to be secure from means of escape

* Your house needs to have wires tidied and not in the way

* No collars on in the house, so they don't get trapped

* All members of the household not to wear shoes as pups are so small and fast when they're 8-10 weeks old, you literally have to feel them under your feet

* When you start exercising after vaccinations, build it up slowly and gradually to ensure you're building good strong ligaments and muscles. Don't over-walk a puppy: five minutes of daily exercise per month of life

* Nipping is an absolute no-no. Puppy must be told "NO!" in a loud voice and if they're biting fingers, put the palm of your hand up and say "STOP!"

"My puppies leave crate trained and "bomb proof" so they go to bed at 9pm and sleep through. I advise not to bring the crate up to the bedroom if owners can avoid it, otherwise it takes weeks or months of gradually moving the crate out of the bedroom, across the hall, near the kitchen etc."

Sandra and Karl Robertson, Hartlebury Miniature Dachshunds, Worcester: "Make the garden secure, and make sure there is nothing too high that they can jump off, as they are prone to back problems.

"Be sure there are puppy gates where needed, lock away cleaning supplies, take chews away when they get small to avoid possible choking. Put your puppy in a designated safe, clean, warm area. Treat your puppy with plenty of love and stimulation and look for dangers at all time.

Photo of mother and pups courtesy of Sandra.

With biting, we let out a high-pitched yelp, shake our hands and say "NO!" like we mean it. If our dogs get excited and jump up a lot, we say "Down" or leave the room. We will do this until the dog learns he will only get attention when four paws are kept on the floor.

"Our dogs stop barking to command, but in young puppies if we are going out for a short while, we put a cover over the crate and leave them with a toy. We leave a little background noise, such as radio or TV, on very low. We also teach our puppies from a young age to spend a little bit of time away from litter to get them being used to being on their own. This helps very much with transitioning and our puppies settle really well."

Stefanie Millington, CunAnnun Long-Haired Miniature Dachshunds, Norfolk: "To avoid future back problems, avoid the puppy running up and down stairs, jumping on and off sofas, beds etc. Recent statistics have shown that Dachshunds have a much higher probability of IVDD problems if spayed/neutered at an early age so I advise not to spay or neuter until 24 months old.

"With nipping or mouthing, I say "No!" and with two fingers gently move the mouth away from where they are nipping. If puppy is persistent, I say "No!" and hold the mouth gently shut for 10 seconds or so. I don't discourage my dogs from digging - that's what they were bred to do, go to ground. Hence my garden looks like a minefield! But most dogs dig, in the summer they dig up dry soil to lie on the cool damp soil underneath and they dig holes to hide food for bad times."

Pauline Cheeseman, Colraed Miniature Dachshunds, Surrey: "New owners shouldn't let the puppy have the run of the whole house; make them a cosy den to feel safe in and don't be constantly picking them up. I advise they sleep with you on the first few nights, then in a crate by the bed and then move the crate slowly further away until it's where you want them to sleep permanently.

"Give the puppy time to settle, teach them early that you leave the room for a while, always without acknowledging them when you return. When you start to leave them alone for short periods, put them in their den with a stuffed Kong or Lickimat so they are occupied when you leave unnoticed – that's good for stopping Separation Anxiety. Also, Dachshund puppies are very small and will get under your feet - so shuffle!

"Barking can be an issue, as they are bred to tell you what they have found down the hole when hunting. I teach mine with treats or toys to bark on command and to stop on command, so if they start barking, they will stop on command, but you can also distract them and then reward Quiet. Try to divert any nipping with a toy. If it continues, remove yourself from the game. You can try the loud screech like puppies do, but some have a high prey drive and that can make them worse! As for jumping up, I ignore it, stand tall with arms folded. I look at their head, wait for them to stop and then praise feet on the floor."

Photo of Marianne McCullough and nine-month-old Kenmar's A Million Dreams, "Dreamy," going Best In Sweepstakes at the Dachshund Club of America Specialty in Hoosier, Indiana.

Marianne says: "Crate training is vital and a crate should be utilized throughout life in some capacity. For the first few nights the puppy should sleep in a crate. After that, depending on families' personal wishes, in a crate at night always or in your bed. Though I believe a puppy should be crated overnight for at least the first six months before they are introduced to the bed.

"It is normal for puppies to bite their siblings when they play. It is not, however, acceptable behaviour for them to bite people. Utilize the pen as a time-out for unacceptable behaviour. The worst punishment a Dachshund can receive is being ignored. If you don't want your Dachshund to dig up your yard or garden, don't leave them out unattended. They are a digging breed - they will dig."

Brenna Carlisle, Heritage Hounds, Ragland, Alabama: "My advice is crate, crate, crate! It is their safe place and never a punishment. My dogs eat in their crates and sleep in them. This is their safe place."

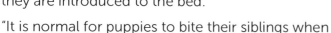

Still looking good! Ten-year-old GCH Twelfth Night Be My Sugar, "Domino," competing in the Veterans class with Brenna at the Dachshund National Show.

"The biggest concern for pups of any kind is chewing on cords or eating random objects. I had an eight-month-old female eat a sock and get an obstruction and she had to have emergency surgery to remove it. It was scary and she is fine now, but she was a little chewer as a pup."

Kristin Cihos-Williams, Kinderteckel Standard Smooth Dachshunds, California: "Dachshunds were developed as hunting hounds, bred to go to ground after badger and other fierce prey. Because of this heritage, this breed digs - and chews if they are not properly exercised and mentally stimulated.

"If you do not want a Dachshund to dig in your yard or garden, either fence off that area and allow the dog to dig in a different area that is authorized, or reconsider your desire to own this breed. I always allow my dogs to dig as much as they want. They get healthy exercise, stay busy, and wear down their nails naturally this way.

"It is up to the owner to not allow any negative behaviour, such as nipping or jumping, to continue. It is not "cute" for a Dachshund to misbehave. There are many different ideas when it comes to training methods. Whether you use positive reinforcement training, aversion training, etc., make sure to use the training method consistently, to address negative behaviors.

Melissa Sworab, Rabows Dachshunds, Texas: "The most important thing in bringing a puppy home is preventing that first accident as long as possible. We recommend when someone buys a puppy from us to purchase two www.peekeeper.com puppy outfits to teach them not to void in the home, as well as a crate for those times you cannot watch them 100%. We prefer these to 'belly bands.'"

Photo: WiFi (Rabows 4G Wireless) and Thumbelina (Rabows 4G Thumbdrive), two inquisitive littermate sisters, aged nine-months, bred by Melissa.

"Dachshunds are prone to chewing when their adult teeth come in and you have to keep your shoes put up and cords managed because when they start chewing, they sometimes never stop as adults. Appropriate chews are absolutely essential to avoid the chewing of personal items.

"Not all barky puppies will grow up to be barky adults, but sometimes they do just get worse, so curbing the barking early is important. I've yet to find a cure that works, but I now raise puppies away from barking adults and they tend to not learn to bark at all until they do, and then it's usually a more appropriate bark, not just "because the others do."

"You have to correct biting the SECOND it happens the first time. We also do not encourage playing tug-o-war with puppies, as that can establish more aggressive behaviors as an adult. With digging, give them a space they are allowed to dig and fill it with sand to help make it easy and fun - then pray they leave your manicured lawn and garden alone! They are diggers, so it's going to happen and hard to avoid, but keeping nails very short can help to reduce it."

"New owners must protect their new puppies from themselves and prevent them from chewing and ingesting foreign bodies that may lead to expensive and dangerous obstruction surgery. Dachshunds will chew drywall, baseboards, wooden door jambs, and even vinyl flooring and carpet, as well as shoes, undergarments, etc."

"Mini Longs seem especially prone to eating rocks! This habit is very dangerous and leads to multiple surgeries, since the habit is not easily prevented and dogs tend to be repeat offenders."

"I am a firm advocate of early crate training. This is a process that takes months, rather than days or weeks, to establish reliable housetraining. After early housetraining is accomplished, I have no problem with my dogs sleeping in bed with us. We use a six-foot-long carpeted ramp up to our bed, so there is no jumping."

Vaccinations and Worming

We recommend having your Dachshund checked out by a vet soon after picking him up. In fact, some Puppy Contracts stipulate that the dog should be examined by a vet once he has settled in and within a few days. This is to everyone's benefit and, all being well, you are safe in the knowledge that your puppy is healthy, at least at the time of purchase.

NOTE: Keep your pup on your lap away from other dogs in the waiting room as he will not yet be fully protected against canine diseases.

Vaccinations

All puppies need immunisation and currently the most common way of doing this is by vaccination. An unimmunised puppy is at risk every time he meets other dogs as he has no protection against potentially fatal diseases – and it is unlikely a pet insurer will cover an unvaccinated dog.

It should be stressed that vaccinations are generally safe and side effects are uncommon. If your Dachshund is unlucky enough to be one of the *very few* that suffer an adverse reaction, here are some signs to look out for; a pup may exhibit one or more of these:

MILD REACTION - Sleepiness, irritability and not wanting to be touched. Sore or a small lump at the place where he was injected. Nasal discharge or sneezing. Puffy face and ears.

SEVERE REACTION - Anaphylactic shock. A sudden and quick reaction, usually before leaving the vet's, which causes breathing difficulties. Vomiting, diarrhoea, staggering and seizures.

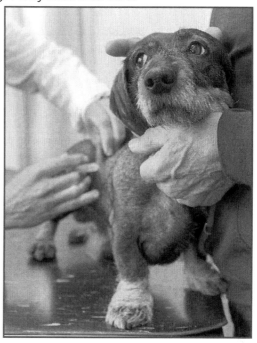

A severe reaction is rare. There is a far greater risk of your Dachshund either being ill or spreading disease if he does not have the injections. The usual schedule is for the pup to have the first vaccination at eight or nine weeks of age, usually before leaving the breeder. This gives protection from a number of diseases in one shot.

In the UK these are Distemper, Canine Parvovirus (Parvo), Infectious Canine Hepatitis (Adenovirus) and Leptospirosis. In the US, the core vaccines are known as DHPPv (no Lepto) and DHPPv-L (with Lepto). Many vets also recommend vaccinating against Kennel Cough (Bordetella). In the US this is known as DHPP.

Puppies in the US also need vaccinating separately against Rabies after 16 weeks, but this varies by state. There are optional vaccinations for Coronavirus (C) and - depending on where you live and if your dog is regularly around woods or forests - Lyme Disease.

A puppy requires a second vaccination two to four weeks later (but the timing and number of courses of vaccination do vary). He is clear to mix with other animals two weeks after the second vaccinations.

- Boosters for Distemper, Parvo and Canine Hepatitis are recommended no more often than every three years (yearly in the US)
- Boosters for Leptospirosis are every year

Leptospirosis is a bacterial infection that attacks the body's nervous system and organs. It is spread through infected rat urine and contaminated water, so dogs are at risk if they swim in or drink from stagnant water or canals. Outbreaks can often happen after flooding.

In the US, breeders are aware of reactions to the Lepto vaccine. Melissa Sworab suggests staying at the vet for at least 30 to 45 minutes after the injection in case of anaphylaxis. Although rare, it may occur after the second vaccination, rather than the first.

Diseases such as Parvo and Kennel Cough are highly contagious and you should not let your new arrival mix with other dogs - unless they are your own and have already been vaccinated - until two weeks after his last vaccination, otherwise he will not be fully immunised. Parvovirus can also be transmitted by the faeces of many animals, including foxes.

The vaccination schedule for the USA is different, depending on which area you live in and what diseases are present. Full details can be found by typing *"AKC puppy shots"* into Google, which will take you to this page: www.akc.org/content/health/articles/puppy-shots-complete-guide

 Avoid taking your new puppy to places where unvaccinated dogs might have been, like the local park. This does not mean that your puppy should be isolated - far from it.

This is an important time for socialisation. It is OK for the puppy to mix with other dogs that you absolutely know are up-to-date with their vaccinations and annual boosters. Perhaps invite a friend's dog round to play in your garden or yard to begin the socialisation process.

The vet should give you a record card or send you a reminder when a booster is due, but it's also a good idea to keep a note of the date in your diary. Tests have shown that the Parvovirus vaccination gives most animals at least seven years of immunity, while the Distemper jab provides immunity for five to seven years. In the US, many vets now recommend that you take your dog for a titer test once he has had his initial puppy vaccinations and one-year booster.

Titres (Titers in the USA)

Some breeders and owners feel strongly that constantly vaccinating our dogs is having a detrimental effect on our pets' health. Many vaccinations are now effective for several years, yet some vets still recommend annual "boosters."

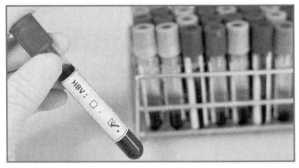

One alternative is titres. The thinking behind them is to avoid a dog having to have unnecessary repeat vaccinations for certain diseases as he already has enough antibodies present. Known as a *VacciCheck* in the UK, they are still relatively new here; they are more widespread in the USA.

To *"titre"* is to take a blood sample from a dog (or cat) to determine whether he has enough antibodies to guarantee immunity against a particular disease, usually Parvovirus, Distemper and Adenovirus (Canine Hepatitis).

If so, then an annual injection is not needed. Titering is NOT recommended for Leptospirosis, Bordetella or Lyme Disease, as these vaccines provide only short-term protection. Many US states also require proof of a Rabies vaccination.

The vet can test the blood at the clinic without sending off the sample, thereby keeping costs down for the owner. A titre for Parvovirus and Distemper currently costs around $100 in the US, sometimes more for Rabies, and a titre test in the UK costs as little as £40.

Titre levels are given as ratios and show how many times blood can be diluted before no antibodies are detected. So, if blood can be diluted 1,000 times and still show antibodies, the ratio would be 1:1000, which is a strong titre, while a titre of 1:2 would be "weak."

A *strong (high) titre* means that your dog has enough antibodies to fight off that specific disease and is immune from infection. A *weak titre* means that you and your vet should discuss revaccination - even then your dog might have some reserve forces known as *"memory cells"* that will provide antibodies when needed. If you are going on holiday and taking your dog to kennels, check whether the kennel accepts titre records; many don't as yet.

One UK breeder said: "When my puppies go to their new homes, I tell all my owners to follow their vet's advice about worming and vaccinating, as the last thing new owners require is to be at odds with their vets. All dogs must have their puppy vaccinations; it is now thought that the minimum duration of immunity is between seven and 15 years.

"However, a few owners do express concern about all the chemicals we are introducing into our puppies' lives and if they do, I explain how I try to give my dogs a chemical-free life, if possible, as adult dogs.

"Instead of giving my adult dogs their core vaccinations for Canine Distemper, Parvovirus and Adenovirus (Hepatitis) every three years, I just take my dogs down to the local vet and ask them to do something called a titre test, also known as a VacciCheck. They take a small amount of blood and send it to a lab and the lab checks for antibodies to the diseases. If they have antibodies to the diseases, there is no reason to give dogs a vaccination.

"However, you should note that there is a separate vaccination for Leptospirosis and Canine Parainfluenza, which is given annually. Leptospirosis is recommended by the BSAVA (British Small Animal Veterinary Association). Leptospirosis is more common in tropical areas of the world and not that common in England.

"In order to make a decision about whether to give this to your dog annually, you need to talk to your vet and do some research yourself so you can make an informed decision. It may be that Leptospirosis is a problem in your area.

"We vaccinate our children up to about the age of 16. However, we don't vaccinate adults every one to three years, as it is deemed that the vaccinations they receive in childhood will cover them for a lifetime. This is what is being steadily proved for dogs and we are so lucky that we can titre test our dogs so we don't have to leave it to chance. "

Another breeder added: "I do not vaccinate my dogs beyond the age of four to five years, I now have them titre-tested. Every dog I have titre tested aged five to 10 years has been immune to the diseases vaccinated against when younger. I believe many vets over-vaccinate."

The (UK) Kennel Club now includes titre testing information into its Assured Breeder Pack, but has yet to include it under its general information on vaccines on its website. In the US, type *"titer test Embrace Pet Insurance"* into Google for more info.

Worming

All puppies need worming (technically, deworming). A good breeder will give the puppies their first dose of worming medication at around two weeks old, then probably again at five and eight weeks before they leave the litter – or even more often. Get the details and inform your vet exactly what treatment, if any, your pup has already had.

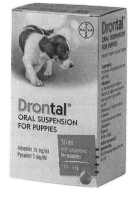

The main worms affecting puppies are roundworm and tapeworm. In certain areas of the US, the dreaded heartworm can also pose a risk. If you live in an affected area, discuss the right time to start heartworm medication when you visit your vet for puppy vaccinations – it's usually from a few months old.

The pill should be given every month when there is no heavy frost (frost kills mosquitos that carry the disease); giving it all year round gives the best protection. The heartworm pill is by prescription only and deworms the dog monthly for heartworm, round, hook, and whip worm.

Roundworm can be transmitted from a puppy to humans – often children - and can in severe cases cause blindness, or miscarriage in women, so it's important to keep up to date with worming.

 Worms in puppies are quite common, usually picked up through their mother's milk. If you have children, get them into the habit of washing their hands after they have been in contact with the puppy – lack of hygiene is the reason why children are susceptible.

Most vets recommend worming a puppy once a month until he is six months old, and then around every two to three months.

If your Dachshund is regularly out and about running through woods and fields, it is important to stick to a regular worming schedule, as he is more likely to pick up worms than one that spends more time indoors.

Fleas can pass on tapeworms to dogs, but a puppy would not normally be treated unless it is known for certain he has fleas - and then only with caution. You need to know the weight of your puppy and then speak to your vet about the safest treatment to get rid of the parasites.

NOTE: Buy age-appropriate worming treatments.

Several people living in the US have contacted our website claiming the canine parasite treatment **Trifexis** has caused health issues and even death. http://www.max-the-schnauzer.com/trifexis-side-effects-in-schnauzers.html

Breeders worm their puppies. However, there are ways to reduce worming treatments for adult dogs.

Following anecdotal reports of some dogs experiencing side effects with chemical wormers, more owners are looking to use natural wormers on their dogs. If you go down this route, check exactly which worms your chosen herbal preparation deals with – it may not be all of them.

A method of reducing worming medication by testing your dog's stools is becoming more popular. You send a small sample of your dog's poo(p) off in an envelope every two to three months. If the result is positive, your dog needs worming, but if negative, no treatment is necessary.

In the UK this is done by veterinary labs like Wormcount www.wormcount.com and similar options are available in the USA – there is even a *"fecal worm test"* available at just over $20 from Amazon.com.

5. Crate and Housetraining

Crates are becoming more popular year on year. Used correctly, they speed up housetraining (potty training), give you and your puppy short breaks from each other and keep him safe at night or when you are out. Many adult dogs grow to love their crates. Breeders, trainers, behaviourists, and people who show, compete or train working dogs all use them.

Using A Crate

A crate should always be used in a humane manner. If you decide to use one, spend time getting your puppy or adult dog used to it, so he comes to regard the crate as his own safe haven and not a punishment cell or prison.

Crates may not be suitable for every dog – or owner. Dogs are social animals; they thrive on interaction. Being caged for long periods is a miserable existence for any dog, but particularly an alert, affectionate breed like the Dachshund.

We prefer a wire crate that allows air to pass through, although some breeders like the plastic ones. A crate should never be used as a means of confinement while you are out of the house for six, or eight or more hours every day.

 Dogs can suffer from joint problems if confined in a small space for too long.

1. Always remove your dog's collar before leaving him inside when you are not there. Sadly, dogs have been known to die after panicking when their collars or tags got caught.

2. If the door is closed, your dog must have access to water while inside during the day. Non-spill water bowls are available from pet shops and online, as are bowls to attach to the bars.

Crates are ideal for giving you or the puppy some down time. You cannot watch a puppy 24/7 and a crate is a safe place for him while you get on with doing other things. Young puppies need lots and lots of sleep – but they are easily distracted, so a crate is a quiet, safe place where they can get some of that sleep during the day. He has to first get used to the crate so he looks forward to going in there - some breeders may have already started the process.

NOTE: An eight-week-old puppy should not be in a crate for longer than two hours at a time.

Not every owner wishes to use a crate, but used correctly they:

- ❧ Are a useful housetraining tool
- ❧ Create a canine den
- ❧ Give you a break

❧ Limit access to the rest of the house until potty trained

❧ Are a safe place for the dog to nap or sleep at night

❧ Provide a safe way to transport your dog in a car

Another very good reason to crate-train a Dachshund is that if he has to be confined for several weeks as conservative treatment for IVDD, he will already be used to a crate. Confining a Dachshund NOT used to a crate is very stressful for both dog and owner.

Which Crate and Where?

The crate should be large enough to allow your dog to stretch out flat on his side without being cramped, and he should be able to turn around easily and sit up without hitting his head on the top.

A Miniature Dachshund will require a 24" (61cm) crate, while a 30" (76cm) crate is a good size for most Standards.

But if the crate is too big for your pup, it will slow down housetraining as he can mess in one area and sleep in another. Many owners use a crate divider *(pictured, above)* or block off a part of the crate while the pup is growing. A smaller area also helps him to feel more secure.

Tip Partially covering the crate with an old blanket creates a den for your new puppy at night. Only cover on three sides - leave the front uncovered - and leave a gap of a few inches at the bottom of all three sides to allow air flow. During the day, many owners cover half of the crate to make it cosier for the pup.

Place the crate in the kitchen or another room where there are people during the day, preferably one with a hard, easy-to-clean floor. Puppies are curious pack animals and like to see what is going on. If you have children, strike the balance between putting the crate in a place where the pup won't feel isolated, yet allowing him some peace and quiet from the kids.

Avoid putting the crate in a closed utility room or garage away from everybody, or he will feel lonely and sad. If you are using a room off the kitchen, allow the pup free run of the room and use a pet gate or baby gate *(pictured)*, so he can see what's going on. I suggest buying one higher than this one - Dachshunds can jump and scramble!

The chosen location should be draught-free, not too hot and not in bright sunshine.

You can also buy or create a puppy playpen to use as well as (or instead of) a crate.

Some breeders recommend putting the crate right next to the bed for the first night or two – even raised up next to the bed - to help the puppy settle in quicker. A few owners have even been known to sleep downstairs on the sofa or an air mattress next to the crate for the first one or two nights! After that, you might put the crate in a place where the dog can hear or smell you during the night, e.g. the landing, or leave it in the same place downstairs all the time. Put the following items inside the crate:

❧ Bedding – Vet Bed or other bedding your puppy won't chew in a few days

❧ A towel or similar item that has been rubbed with the mother's scent

❧ A non-spill water bowl

🐾 A healthy chew to stop him gnawing the crate and bedding

🐾 A toy to keep him occupied

At night, remove the water from the crate. Add an extra blanket if you think he might get cold overnight; he has been used to the warmth of his littermates and mother.

Puppies are little chew machines so, at this stage, don't spend a lot of money on a fluffy floor covering for the crate, as it is likely to get destroyed. The widely available and washable "Vet Bed" is a good choice for bedding.

Made from double-strength polyester, they retain extra heat, allow air to flow through and are widely used in vets' clinics to make dogs feel warm and secure. They also have drainage properties, so your pup will stay dry if he has an accident.

Vet Beds are also a good option for older dogs, as the added heat is soothing for aging muscles and joints. You can buy "Vet Bedding" by the roll, which keeps costs down. One breeder added: "Don't use beds with stuffing at this age, as once they learn to de-stuff a bed, it may become a lifelong habit and possibly graduate into de-stuffing furniture or pillows later!"

 Consider putting a Snuggle Puppy in the crate with the new puppy. The Snuggle Puppy *(pictured)* is a safe soft toy with a heartbeat. (Remove it if your dog chews it and exposes the internal mechanism).

Whining

If your puppy is whining or whimpering in the crate, make sure:

A. He doesn't need the toilet.

B. He is warm.

C. He is physically unharmed.

Then the reason he is whimpering is because he doesn't want to be alone. He has come from the warmth and security of his mother and litter, and the Brave New World can be a very daunting place for a few-weeks-old puppy all alone in a new home. He is not crying because he is in a cage. He would cry if he had the freedom of the room - he is crying because he is separated. Dogs are pack animals and being alone is not a natural state for them.

However, with patience and the right training, he will get used to being alone and being in the crate. Some adult Dachshunds choose the crate as their favourite resting place. Some owners make the crate their dog's only bed, so he feels comfortable and safe in there. Here are some other tips to help your puppy settle in his crate:

🐾 Leave a ticking clock next to the crate

🐾 Leave a radio on softly nearby

🐾 Lightly spray DAP on a cloth or small towel and place in the crate

 DAP, or Dog Appeasing Pheromone, is a synthetic form of the pheromone that nursing Dachshunds (and other breeds) give off after giving birth and then again after weaning to reassure their puppies that everything is fine.

DAP has been found to help reduce fear in young puppies, as well as separation anxiety, phobias and aggression caused by anxiety in adult dogs. According to one French study: "DAP has no toxicities or side effects and is particularly beneficial for sick and geriatric dogs." Google **"Canadian Veterinary Journal Dog Appeasing Pheromone"** for more details of the study.

NOTE: There is also an ADAPTIL collar with slow-release DAP, which is designed to reduce fear in anxious adult dogs. It gets good reports from many, not all, owners.

Whether or not you decide to use a crate, it's important to know that those first few days and weeks are a critical time for your puppy. Make him feel as safe and comfortable as you can.

Travel Crates

Special travel crates are useful for the car, or for taking your dog to the vet's or a show or competition. Choose one with holes or mesh in the side to allow free movement of air, rather than a solid one in which a dog can soon overheat. You can also use your regular crate in the car.

Put the crate on the shady side of the interior and make sure it can't move around and put the seatbelt around it. If it's very sunny and the top of the crate is wire mesh, cover part of it so your dog has some shade and put the windows up and the air conditioning on.

Don't leave your Dachshund unattended in a vehicle. They can overheat, be targeted by thieves or get into mischief.

Here are two breeders' comments: "I've had them stand on the window controls and roll the

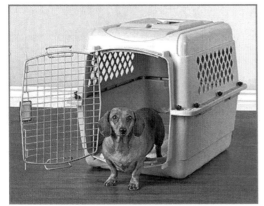

window down in the back seat while driving down the highway! So, it's not safe to leave them in the car even for a minute, because they can lock YOU out or roll down a window while you aren't looking." "They should not ever be left unattended in running cars or trusted to ride with windows down."

We recommend using a crate fastened with a seatbelt, rather than a metal grille in the back of the car. And allowing your dog to roam freely inside the car is simply too dangerous as he is likely to get thrown around and injured.

Avoid letting your Dachshund ride with his head out of the window - even if his Easy Rider look does make you smile! Wind pressure can cause ear infections or bits of dust, insects, etc. to fly into unprotected eyes. Your dog will fly forward if you suddenly hit the brakes.

··

Getting your Puppy Used to a Crate

Once you've got your crate, you'll need to learn how to use it properly so that it becomes a safe, comfortable den for your dog. Many breeders will have already started the process but, if not, here's a tried-and-tested method of getting your dog firstly to accept a crate, and then to actually want to spend time in there. These are the first steps:

1. **Drop a few puppy treats around and then inside the crate.**

2. **Put your puppy's favourite toy in there.**

3. **Keep the door open.**

4. Feed your puppy's meals inside the crate. Again, keep the door open.

Place a chew or treat INSIDE the crate and close the door while your puppy is OUTSIDE the crate. He will be desperate to get in there! Open the door, let him in and praise him for going in. Fasten a long-lasting chew inside the crate and leave the door open. Let your puppy wander inside to spend some time eating the chew.

5. **After a while, close the crate door and feed him some treats through the mesh.** At first just do it for a few seconds at a time, then gradually increase the time. If you do it too fast, he may become distressed.

6. **Slowly build up the amount of time he's in the crate.** For the first few days, stay in the room, then gradually leave first one minute, then three, then 10, 30 and so on.

Next Steps

7. Put your dog in his crate at regular intervals during the day - maximum two hours.

8. **If your pup is not yet housetrained, make sure he has relieved himself BEFORE you put him in the crate.** Putting him in when he needs to eliminate will slow down training.

9. **Don't crate only when you are leaving the house.** Put him in the crate while you are home as well. Use it as a *"safe zone"* or *"quiet zone."* By using the crate both when you are home and while you are gone, your dog becomes comfortable there and not worried that you won't come back, or that you are leaving him alone. This helps to prevent separation anxiety.

10. If you are leaving your dog unattended, give him a chew and remove his collar, tags and anything else that could become caught in an opening or between the bars.

11. Make it very clear to any children that the crate is NOT a den for them, but a *"special room"* for the dog.

    Photo: Well-behaved Ella (2) with five-week-old Daniel by Vera Peltier Brock.

12. Although the crate is your dog's haven and safe place, it must not be off-limits to humans. You should be able to reach inside at any time.

13. **Try and wait until your dog is calm before putting him in the crate.** If he is behaving badly and you grab him and shove him in the crate, he will associate the crate with punishment. If you can't calm him down, try NOT to use the crate. A better option is to remove the privilege of your attention by either leaving the room or putting the dog in another room until he calms down.

14. The crate should ALWAYS be associated with a positive experience in your dog's mind.

15. **Don't let your dog out of the crate when he is barking or whining, or he'll think that this is the key to opening the door.** Wait until he has stopped whining for at least 10 or 20 seconds before letting him out.

Reminder:

- 🐾 During the day the crate door should not be closed until your pup is happy with being inside

- 🐾 At night-time it is OK to close the door

- 🐾 Consider keeping the pup right next to you for the first one or two nights

- 🐾 If you don't want to use a crate, use a pet gate, section off an area inside one room, or use a puppy pen to confine your pup at night

Housetraining

While the Dachshund has many endearing qualities, being quick to housetrain is not one of them! A Dachshund is a hound, and all hounds have an independent streak running through them. Some, particularly males, can be a bit slow about learning to pee and poop in the right place.

Although they are intelligent, Dachshunds can also be stubborn and sensitive, so the right approach is essential. Lots of repetition with praise and rewards along the way are key, but scolding and making a fuss about accidents are counter-productive.

The good news is that a puppy's instinct is not to soil his own den. From about the age of three weeks, a pup will leave his sleeping area to go to the toilet. The bad news is that when you bring your little pup home, he doesn't realise that your whole home is not his den – and off-limits for making a mess!

He may think that a corner of the crate, the kitchen, behind the sofa or anywhere else in the house is an acceptable place for him to relieve himself. The aim of housetraining (potty training) is to teach him exactly WHERE this space starts and finishes.

It could take a few weeks - or anything up to six months if neither of you is vigilant.

FACT ❯ The speed and success of housetraining depends to some degree on the individual dog and how much effort the breeder has already put in. However, the single most important factor in success is undoubtedly the owner.

Like all dogs, Dachshunds are creatures of routine - not only do they like the same things happening at the same times every day, but establishing a regular routine with your dog also helps to speed up housetraining.

Dogs are tactile creatures, so they pick a place to eliminate which feels good under their paws. Many dogs like to go on grass - but this will do nothing to improve your lawn, so think carefully about what area to encourage your Dachshund to use as a toilet. Consider a small patch of gravel, or a dog litter tray if you live in an apartment.

Clear your schedule and make housetraining your No.1 priority - it will be worth it. I get complaints from some American readers for advising: "Book a week or two off work to housetrain your dog." I know Americans get much shorter vacation time than almost anybody else, but honestly, if you can take time off to monitor housetraining at the beginning, it will undoubtedly speed up the results.

If you've rescued a Dachshund, he may have picked up some unwanted habits before arriving at your home. In such cases, extra time, patience and vigilance are essential to gently teach your dog the new ways.

A general rule of thumb is that puppies can last for one hour per month of age without urinating, sometimes a bit longer. So:

- 🐾 *An eight-week pup can last for two hours*
- 🐾 *A 12-week-old pup can last for three hours*
- 🐾 *A 16-week pup can last for four hours*
- 🐾 *A six-month-old can last for six hours*

NOTE: This only applies when the puppy is calm and relaxed.

 **FACT** ❯ If a puppy is active or excited, he will urinate more often, and if he is excited to see you, he may urinate at will.

To speed up the process even more, set your alarm clock to get up in the night to let the pup out to relieve himself for the first week or two. You might hate it, but it will shorten the overall time spent housetraining.

··

Housetraining Tips

Follow these tips to speed up housetraining:

1. Constant supervision is essential for the first week or two if you are to housetrain your puppy quickly. If nobody is there, he will learn to pee or poop inside the house.

2. Take your pup outside at the following times:

- 🐾 As soon as he wakes – every time
- 🐾 Shortly after each feed
- 🐾 After a drink
- 🐾 When he gets excited
- 🐾 After exercise or play
- 🐾 Last thing at night
- 🐾 Initially every hour or two - whether or not he looks like he wants to go

Photo of Mini Long, Marlene, courtesy of Stefanie Millington, CunAnnun, Norfolk. Photo by Marcio Garcia.

You may think that the above list is an exaggeration, but it isn't! Housetraining a pup is almost a full-time job in the beginning. If you are serious about toilet training your puppy quickly, then clear your diary for a week or two and keep your eyes firmly glued on your pup...learn to spot that expression or circling motion just before he makes a mess on your floor.

1. Take your pup to **the same place** every time, you may need to use a lead (leash) in the beginning - or tempt him there with a treat. Some say it is better to only pick him up and dump him there in an emergency, as it is better if he learns to take himself to the chosen toilet spot. Dogs naturally develop a preference for going in the same place or on the same surface. Take or lead him to the same patch every time so he learns this is his toilet area.

2. **No pressure – be patient. Dachshunds do not perform well under pressure.** You must allow your distracted little darling time to wander around and have a good sniff before performing his duties – but do not leave him, stay around a short distance away. Unfortunately, puppies are not known for their powers of concentration, so it may take a while for him to select the perfect bathroom spot!

3. **Housetraining a Dachshund should ALWAYS be reward-based, never negative or aggressive.** Give praise and/or a treat IMMEDIATELY after he has performed his duties in the chosen spot. Persistence, praise and rewards are best for quick results with a Dachshund.

4. **Share the responsibility.** It doesn't have to be the same person who takes the dog outside all the time. In fact, it's easier if there are a couple of you, as this is a very time-demanding business. Just make sure you stick to the same principles, command and patch of ground.

5. **Stick to the same routine.** Sticking to the same times for meals, exercise, playtime, sleeping and toilet breaks will help settle him into his new home and housetrain him quicker.

   This determined little gal is eight-week-old silver dapple Mini Smooth Kaziah's Bonnie Little Legs at Colraed, owned by Pauline Cheeseman. Photo by RSA Photography.

6. **Use the same word** or command when telling your puppy to go to the toilet – or while he is in the act. He will gradually associate this phrase or word with toileting.

7. **Use your voice ONLY if you catch him in the act indoors.** A short sharp sound is best - ACK! EH! It doesn't matter, as long as it is loud enough to make him stop. Then either pick him up or run enthusiastically towards your door, calling him to the chosen place and wait until he has finished what he started indoors. Only use the ACK! sound if you actually catch him MID-ACT.

8. **No punishment, no scolding, no smacking or rubbing his nose in it.** Dachshunds are surprisingly sensitive and hate it. **He** will become either more stubborn or afraid to do the business in your presence, so may start going secretly behind the couch or under the bed. Accidents will happen. He is a baby with a tiny bladder and bowels and little self-control.

Housetraining a Dachshund takes time - remain calm, ignore him (unless you catch him in the act) and clean up the mess.

FACT ❯ Dachshunds are scent hounds. If there's an "accident" indoors, use a special spray from your vet or a hot washing powder solution to completely eliminate the smell, which will discourage him from going there again.

9. **Look for the signs.** These may be:

   a. Whining

   b. Sniffing the floor in a determined manner

   c. Circling and looking for a place to go

   d. Walking uncomfortably - particularly at the rear end!

Take him outside straight away, and try not to pick him up all the time. He has to learn to walk to the door himself when he needs to go outside.

10. **Use a crate at night-time** and, for the first few nights, consider getting up four hours after you go to bed to take the pup outside, gradually increasing the time. By the age of four or five months a Dachshund pup should be able to last through a short night – provided you let him out last thing at night and first thing in the morning. Before then, you will have a lot of early mornings!

Troubleshooting

Don't let one or two little accidents derail your potty training - accidents WILL happen! Here is a list of some possible scenarios and action to take:

🐾 **Puppy peed when your back was turned** – Don't let him out of his crate or living space unless you are prepared to watch his every move

🐾 **Puppy peed or pooped in the crate** - Make sure the crate isn't too big; it should be just enough for him to stand up and turn around. Also, make sure he is not left in the crate for too long

🐾 **Puppy pooped without warning** - Observe what he does immediately beforehand. That way, you'll be able to scoop him up and take him outside next time before an accident happens

🐾 **Puppy pees on the same indoor spot daily** - Make sure you get rid of the smell completely and don't give your puppy too much indoor freedom too soon. Some breeders use *"tethering"* where the puppy is fastened to them on a lead indoors. That way they can watch the puppy like a hawk and monitor his behaviour. They only do this for a short time - a week or so – but it can speed up housetraining no end

🐾 **Puppy not responding well** - Increase the value of your treats for housetraining and nothing else. Give a tiny piece of meat, chicken etc. ONLY when your Dachshund eliminates outdoors in the chosen spot.

Even after all your hard work, some Dachshunds continue to eliminate indoors, often males, even though they understand housetraining perfectly well.

This is called "marking" and they do it to leave a scent and establish your home as their territory. This is very hard to cure - although neutering generally reduces the urge to mark indoors.

Other reasons for peeing indoors when housetrained include a urinary tract infection, or an older dog losing continence or forgetting housetraining,

 Many Dachshunds grow to dislike bad weather. Get yours used to going out in the rain right from the beginning - invest in a little puppy coat and an umbrella!

Breeder Melissa Sworab added: "If YOU go out with an umbrella and stay out of the rain, so will your puppy, who looks to you for guidance. Be sure to go out and play in a light mist of rain without an umbrella and show them there is nothing to fear and they will not dislike rain after that."

Apartment Living

If you live in a high-rise apartment, housetraining can be a little trickier, as you don't have easy access to the outdoors. One method is to indoor housetrain your puppy.

Most dogs can be indoor housetrained fairly easily, especially if you start early. Stick to the same principles already outlined, the only difference is that you will be placing your Dachshund on puppy pads or newspaper instead of taking him outdoors.

Start by blocking off a section of the apartment for your pup. Use a baby gate or make your own barrier, but make sure you choose a chew-proof material! You will be able to keep a better eye on him than if he has free run of the whole place, and it will be easier to monitor his "accidents."

Select a corner away from his eating and sleeping area that will become his permanent bathroom area – a carpeted area is to be avoided if at all possible.

At first, cover a larger area than is actually needed - about 3x3 or 4x4 feet - with puppy pads or newspapers and gradually reduce the area as training progresses. Take your puppy there as indicated in the **Housetraining Tips** section.

Praise him enthusiastically when he eliminates on the puppy pad or newspaper. If you catch him doing his business out of the toilet area, pick him up and take him back there. Correct with a firm voice - never a hand. With positive reinforcement and close monitoring, he will learn to walk to the toilet area on his own.

Owners attempting indoor housetraining should be aware that it does generally take longer than outdoor training. Some dogs will resist. Also, once a dog learns to go indoors, it can be difficult to train them to go outdoors on their walks. If you don't monitor your puppy carefully enough in the beginning, indoor housetraining will be difficult. The first week or two is crucial to your puppy learning what is expected of him.

Melissa added: "We also do litterbox training with pine pellet with every litter by three weeks of age, and they are trained so that you can sprinkle the pellets wherever you'd like them to go after that, including starting them going outdoors to wee."

NOTE: Some breeders advise against using newspapers or puppy pads in homes with gardens or yards, as they can slow down potty training. Newspapers can encourage a pup to soil inside the house. Because dogs are tactile, and puppy pads are soft and comfy - dogs like going on them! When you remove the pads, the puppy may be tempted to find a similar surface - like a carpet or rug. The decision is yours.

Bell Training

Bell Training is a method that works well with some dogs. There are different types of bells, the simplest are inexpensive and widely available. They consist of a series of adjustable bells that hang on a nylon strap from the door handle.

Another option is a small metal bell attached to a metal hanger that fixes low down on the wall next to the door with two screws. As with all puppy training, do bell training in short bursts of five to 10 minutes or your easily-distracted little student will switch off!

1. Show your dog the bell, either on the floor, before it is fixed anywhere or by holding it up. Point to it and give the command *"Touch," "Ring,"* or whatever word you decide.

2. Every time he touches it with his nose, reward with praise.

3. When he rings the bell with his nose, give him a treat. You can rub on something tasty, like peanut butter, to make it more interesting.

4. Take the bell away between practice sessions.

5. Once he rings the bell every time you show it to him, move on to the next step.

6. Take the bell to the door you use for housetraining. Place a treat just outside the door while he is watching. Then close the door, point to the bell and give the command.

7. When he rings the bell, open the door and let him get the treat outside.

8. When he rings the bell as soon as you place a treat outside, fix the bell to the door or wall.

9. The next time you think he needs to relieve himself, walk to the door, point to the bell and give the command. Give him a treat or praise if he rings it, let him out immediately and reward him again with enthusiastic praise when he performs his duty.

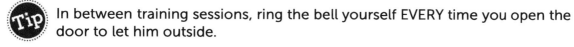 **In between training sessions, ring the bell yourself EVERY time you open the door to let him outside.**

Some dogs can get carried away by their own success and ring the bell any time they want your attention, fancy a wander outdoors or see a squirrel!

Make sure that you ring the bell every time your puppy goes out through the door to relieve himself, but DON'T ring the bell if he is going out to play. And if he starts playing or dawdling around the garden or yard, bring him in!

Breeders on Crates and Housetraining

Breeders shares their experiences, starting in the USA with Brenna Carlisle, Heritage Hounds, Alabama: "Crate, crate, crate! It is their safe place and never a punishment! My dogs eat in their crates and sleep in them. This is their safe place.

"I say the biggest concern for pups of any kind is chewing on cords or eating random objects. I had an eight-month-old female eat a sock and get an obstruction and she had to have emergency surgery to remove it. It was scary and she is fine now, but she was a little chewer as a pup. My pups all leave knowing what a crate is."

On potty training: "Repetition and consistency. Make sure you are not disciplining and scaring them, and always praise for right and re-correct for wrong."

Photo of GCHB Heritage Mustang Sally, bred by Brenna and her Mom, Laura Potash.

Kristin Cihos-Williams, Kinderteckel Standard Smooth Dachshunds, California: "I am a firm advocate of early crate training. This is a process that takes months, rather than days or weeks, to establish reliable housetraining. After early housetraining is accomplished, I have no problem with my dogs sleeping in bed with us. We use a six-foot long carpeted ramp up to our bed, so there is no jumping!

"Housetraining begins at age three to four weeks, when the puppy first emerges from the confines of the whelping box with high sides and is given a pan with litter pellets within the larger whelping enclosure. Eventually, the puppy learns that there is a place for toileting, a place for sleeping, and a place for eating and playing.

"Once my pups are old enough, they go outside to potty and sleep all night in an appropriately-sized crate. Crate training immensely speeds up the house training process for new owners, and it also keeps a curious puppy safe from electrical cords and other dangers when the new owner cannot directly supervise. I always advise new owners that housetraining is a long slow process. It is not accomplished in a few weeks but rather over a period of many months."

Marianne McCullough, Kenmar Hounds, Florida: "Absolutely, I use crates! Crating is vital for Dachshunds. Not only is it an excellent housebreaking tool, but it allows them their "quiet space." Dachshunds are a mischievous breed, if you allow them too much freedom when you are not home, they will get into things. Crate them and you know they are safe.

"A crate should be utilized throughout life in some capacity - a reputable breeder will send puppies home crate-trained. Make sure you never let them out when they are crying or making noise."

Pame Bates, Doxies Treasures, California: "We put our dogs to bed in crates and let them out when we get up. We do not like to keep them crated any other time, unless it is a travel or safety issue. Housetraining takes about six months. Take them out regularly and establish a routine."

Melissa Sworab, Rabows Dachshunds, Texas: "The most important thing in bringing a puppy home is preventing that first accident as long as possible. When someone buys a puppy from us, we recommend that they purchase two puppy outfits from www.peekeeper.com outfits to teach them not to void in the home. We prefer these to "belly bands." The longer you can prevent that first accident, the better the housebreaking will be for the rest of their lives.

"If you start off thinking the puppy will sleep while you sleep for eight hours and not have an accident, you are setting that puppy up to fail. So, we recommend not sleeping more than four hours at a time to take the puppy outside often, and lengthen that gradually."

"Crates are great for food/water time and for training in the early months, as well as a place they can be safe if you have to be away for a couple of hours and want to protect from getting into dangerous plants, garbage, pillows, etc. Overnight would be the longest they should ever be in a crate at one time and no more than a couple of hours during the day.

"They love to be out and will usually sleep on the couch or in their crates with the door left open when they want to. We NEVER suggest crating more than one per crate, EVER. One dog per crate, so they have their own food, water, toys and treats and, while enclosed in their own space, no squabbling will happen when you aren't there to stop it. You can monitor their food intake and water intake in a crate and see who vomited, etc., which is critical in catching illnesses quickly."

UK breeder Stef Millington, of CunAnnun, Norfolk: "I use crates; my puppies leave crate-trained and sleep in the crate or a puppy pen at night. If a puppy is not crate-trained when arriving at his new home, use the crate as part of a reward. Feed in the crate, give stuffed Kongs, filled hooves or other long-lasting treats to take to bed."

Pictured is Stef's Oliver (CunAnnun Veni Vedi Vici). Photo by Marcio Garcia.

"Make sure the crate is at least double the size the puppy needs, put a toy and a comfortable bed inside. Cover half of the crate with a blanket to turn it into a den and NEVER use the crate as punishment. With housetraining, I advise consistency with praise and rewards for doing "the job" outside. Don't acknowledge accidents you find later and have lots of patience."

Pauline Cheeseman, Colraed Miniature Dachshunds, Surrey: "I do use crates, but for no more than two hours. I tell the owners to put a blanket over to make them dark with a cosy bed, blanket or duvet in there.

"Start by feeding them in there with the doors open, give them stuffed Kongs with their dinner and shut the door for a few seconds. As they are busy, walk away.

"Come back, open the door while they are still busy and go away again, slowly building up the time. Once your puppy has been out playing and shows signs of sleeping, pop them into the crate with a toy and they will soon learn to sleep in there.

"I don't think housetraining takes too long if the owners are vigilant, but they can't go all night when they are tiny. I also tell the owner to take them to the same place in the garden and leave a stool (poop) there so they can scent the area."

Sandra Robertson, Hartlebury Miniature Dachshunds, Worcester: "We crate our dogs overnight; depending on age they are put in the crate late evening and let out early morning to do their business and a little run before breakfast. Through the day we leave the crate doors open for our older dogs to go in and out as they please and we have never had barking and whining to come out if their door is closed."

"We encourage our new owners to carry on where we left off with housetraining. From seven weeks when our puppies wake up, we put them straight on a puppy pad. As they get used to it, we eventually start moving pads to the back door, then eventually out the door and by 12 weeks they are adjusting. Depending on the commitment and perseverance of the owner, puppies can be fully potty trained by four to six months."

Lisa Cole, Foosayo Dachshunds, North Yorkshire: "Crates, if used, should be a happy safe place. My dogs love crates; my old girl, who is 13, will go into a crate to have a snooze if she wants to get away from the younger dogs. Crates should not be used to lock a dog up all day or because the dog has been "naughty."

"I am not doing it unless sausages are involved!" Photo of shaded red Standard Long, Schnitzel, courtesy of Lisa.

"Start on Day 1 with soft toys, soft blankets. You can place a warm (not hot) water bottle under the blankets for the first few nights. Some people even place a ticking clock under the blankets to calm the pup the first few nights, as it makes a sound like the mother's heartbeat.

"My crates are only ever closed at night - the doors are open all day and evening. The length of time depends on the size of the dog and size of the crate, but for me, a full day while owners are at work is far too long."

"Housetraining is not hard you just need to: Repeat, Repeat, Repeat. A lot of people do it for a day or two and after that it's a bit slapdash.

"Pups need the toilet when they wake, after eating and when at play, so when any of the above happen take the pup outside. When the pup goes to the toilet in the garden, reward him in some way. You can use a food treat, a favourite toy or just lots of fuss and a happy owner.

"However, if he goes to the toilet indoors don't react - to the point where you don't look at him or talk to him. When you walk across the room, you almost walk through him as if he was not there. Then he has a pee outside and: Yes, Good Boy! He will understand that toileting outside gets him something nice, but when he toilets inside, he is almost invisible, which he will not like as all pups just want attention."

Lisa Lindfield, Zabannah Dachshunds, Cambridgeshire "Mine leave crate-trained and "bomb proof," so they go to bed at 9am and sleep through. I advise owners not to bring the crate up to the bedroom if they can avoid it, otherwise it takes weeks/months gradually moving the crate out of the bedroom, across the hall, near the kitchen etc."

Hannah Norton, Jacksondax, South Devon: "All dogs are different and learn at their own rate. I would say, however, that a puppy should be fully housetrained by around six months of age.

"I suggest taking puppy outside to his or her toilet area every 20 minutes when they are awake and always straight after they have had a drink or have eaten. I give mine a lot of praise when they toilet in the right place, but would never scold a puppy for an accident indoors. He or she will then associate having a wee with being told off and it can have an adverse effect on the training."

"I believe all dogs should be crate-trained, regardless of whether you want to use a crate at home. In an emergency situation or a stay at the vet's, they should feel comfortable being confined to a smaller area."

Judith Carruthers, of Stanegate Wirehaired Dachshunds, Cumbria, has bred Long-Haired and Wire-Haireds for almost 50 years and is also a firm believer in crates.

Pictured is Judith's 18-month-old Stanegate Catherine Wheel, "Sparkle." Photo by Will Harris.

She says: "The crate is happy place for bed, food and quiet time, not a punishment cell.

"Don't make an issue of the pup going into the crate, just pop him in and turn away. They can be left for an hour at a time as babies, and up to three or four hours when older."

6. Feeding a Dachshund

Providing the right nutritional fuel helps keep your dog's biological machine in excellent working order. And while it is important for all breeds to have a healthy diet, it is especially important for Dachshunds, because:

1. They are prone to obesity.

2. Good nutrition can delay or lessen the effects of back or joint problems and arthritis.

3. Some Dachshunds have skin issues or sensitive stomachs. The right food can help reduce or eliminate potential problems.

....

The topic of feeding can be a minefield; owners are bombarded with advertisements and numerous choices. There is not one food that gives every single Dachshund the strongest bones, the most energy, the best coat, the easiest digestion, the least gas and the longest life.

You could feed a high-quality food to a group of Dachshunds and find that most of them thrive on it, some do not so well, while a few might put weight on, get an upset stomach or itchy skin. The question is: *"Which food is best for MY Dachshund?"*

We don't recommend one brand of dog food over another, but we do have lots of tips to help you decide, and several Dachshund breeders share their thoughts on nutrition.

Life Stages

Dachshund puppies should stay with the litter until at least eight to 12 weeks old, to give the mother enough time to teach her offspring important rules about life. Initially, pups get all their nutrients from their mother's milk and then are gradually weaned (put on to a different food by the breeder) from three or four weeks of age.

Unless the puppy has had an extremely varied diet at the breeder's, continue feeding the same puppy food and at the same times as the breeder when you bring your puppy home. It is always a good idea to find out what the breeder feeds, as she knows what her bloodlines do well on. If you decide to switch foods, do so gradually, as dogs' digestive systems cannot handle sudden changes of diet. (By the way, if you stick to the identical brand, you can change flavours in one go). These ratios are recommended by Doctors Foster & Smith Inc:

- ❧ Days 1-3 add 25% of the new food
- ❧ Days 4-6 add 50%
- ❧ Days 7-9 add 75%
- ❧ Day 10 feed 100% of the new food

Feed your puppy three or four times a day up to the age of 12-16 weeks. If at any time your puppy starts being sick, has loose stools or is constipated, slow the rate at which you are switching the food. Puppies soon dehydrate, so seek veterinary advice if vomiting or diarrhoea continues for more than a day. Some breeders purposely feed their pups lots of different foods over the first few weeks of life to reduce the risk of them developing sensitive stomachs or becoming fussy eaters.

 If you live far away from the breeder, fill a large container with water from the breeder's house and mix it with your own water back home. Different types of water, e.g. moving from a soft to a hard water area or vice versa, can upset a sensitive pup's stomach.

During the first six months, puppies grow quickly and it is important that they grow at **a controlled rate.** Giving your puppy more or less food will not affect his adult size, it will only affect his weight and rate of growth.

FACT > Dachshund puppies should look well-covered, not fat. Overfeeding leads to excess weight, which makes them vulnerable to lots of health issues in later life.

There are three **Life Stages** to consider when feeding: **Puppy, Adult. Senior**, also called **Veteran.**

Some manufacturers also produce a Junior feed for adolescent dogs. If you decide on a commercially-prepared food, choose one approved either for **Puppies** or for **All Life Stages**. An **Adult** feed won't have enough protein, and the balance of calcium and other nutrients will not be right for a pup. Puppy food is very high in calories and nutritional supplements.

Also choose a **Small Breed** formula as Dachshund puppies are tiny - especially Miniatures - and they cannot cope with large pieces of kibble. Manufacturers such as Royal Canin make a food specially prepared for Dachshunds.

Look at switching to an adult food when your pup is around 10 to 14 months old and consider reducing feeds from three to two a day at this time.

 Because Dachshunds are small or medium-sized energetic dogs with fast metabolisms, feed your adult at least twice a day - not once. Some owners feed three times a day.

NOTE: Feeding elderly dogs is covered in **Chapter 17. Caring for Older Dachshunds.**

Reading Dog Food Labels

A NASA scientist would have a hard job understanding some manufacturers' labels, so it's no easy task for us lowly dog owners. Here are some things to look out for on the manufacturers' labels:

- ❧ **The ingredients are listed by weight and the top one should always be the main content,** such as chicken or lamb. Don't pick one where grain is the first ingredient; it is a poor-quality feed. If your Dachshund has a food allergy or intolerance to wheat, check whether a food is gluten free; all wheat contains gluten

- ❧ **Chicken meal (dehydrated chicken) has more protein than fresh chicken, which is 80% water.** The same goes for beef, fish and lamb. So, if any of these "meals" are No. 1 on the ingredient list, the food should contain enough protein

Ingredients:
Deboned Chicken, Chicken Meal, Turkey Meal, Potatoes, Peas, Tomato Pomace, Dried Ground Potatoes, Ground Flaxseed, Chicken Fat (preserved with Mixed Tocopherols), Natural Chicken Flavor, Pea Fiber, Potassium Chloride, Spinach, Broccoli, Vitamin E Supplement, Carrots, Parsley, Apples, Blueberries, Kale, Sweet Potatoes, Taurine, L-Carnitine, Mixed Tocopherols added to preserve freshness, Zinc Proteinate, Glucosamine Hydrochloride, Chondroitin Sulfate, Zinc Sulfate, Calcium Carbonate, Niacin, Ferrous Sulfate,

Ingredients:
Ground Yellow Corn, Chicken By-Product Meal, Corn Gluten Meal, Whole Wheat Flour, Animal Fat Preserved with Mixed-Tocopherols (form of Vitamin E), Rice Flour, Chicken, Soy Flour, Water, Propylene Glycol, Salt, Tricalcium Phosphate, Salt, Phosphoric Acid, Animal Digest, Calcium Phosphate, Potassium Chloride, Sorbic Acid (a Preservative), Dried Carrots, Dried Tomatoes, Avocado, Calcium Propionate (a Preservative), Choline Chloride, L-Lysine Monohydrochloride, Added Color (Yellow 5, Red, 40, Blue 2, Yellow 6), Vitamin E

- Anything labelled *"human-grade"* is higher quality than normal dog food ingredients. E.g. Human-grade chicken includes the breast, thighs and other parts of the chicken suitable for human consumption. Human-grade chicken complies with United States Department of Agriculture (USDA) welfare standards

- A certain amount of flavourings can make a food more appetising for your dog. **Choose a food with a specific flavouring,** like *"beef flavouring"* rather than a general *"meat flavouring,"* where the origins are not so clear

- **Find a food suitable for the Dachshund breed and your dog's age and activity level.** Talk to your breeder or vet, or visit an online Dachshund forum to ask other owners' advice.

- **Natural is best.** Food labelled *'natural'* means that the ingredients have not been chemically altered, according to the FDA in the USA. However, there are no such guidelines governing foods labelled *"holistic"* – so check ingredients and how they have been prepared

- In the USA, dog food that meets American Feed Control Officials' (AAFCO) minimum nutrition requirements has a label that states: *"[food name] is formulated to meet the nutritional levels established by the AAFCO Dog Food Nutrient Profiles for [life stage(s)]"*

 If you live in the USA, we recommend looking for a food "as fed" to real pets in an AAFCO-defined feeding trial. The AAFCO label is the gold standard, and brands that do costly feeding trials indicate so on the package.

Dog food labelled *'supplemental'* isn't complete and balanced. Unless you have a specific, vet-approved need for it, it's not something you want to feed your dog long term. The *Guaranteed Analysis* listed on a sack or tin legally guarantees:

- Minimum percentages of crude protein and crude fat, and

- Maximum percentages of crude fibre and moisture

While it is a start, don't rely on it too much. One pet food manufacturer made a mock product with a guaranteed analysis of 10% protein, 6.5% fat, 2.4% fibre, and 68% moisture (similar to what's on some canned pet food labels) – the ingredients were old leather boots, used motor oil, crushed coal and water!

- **Protein** – found in meat and poultry, protein should be the first ingredient and is very important. It helps build muscle, repair tissue and contributes to healthy hair and skin. According to AAFCO, a growing puppy requires a diet with minimum 22% **protein,** while an adult requires 18% minimum

- **Fats** – these are a concentrated form of energy that give your dog more than twice the amount of

GUARANTEED ANALYSIS	
Crude protein (min.)	28.00 %
Crude fat (min.)	12.00 %
Crude fiber (max.)	4.50 %
Moisture (max.)	11.00 %
Docosahexaenoic acid (DHA) (min.)	0.05 %
Calcium (min.)	1.20 %
Phosphorus (min.)	1.00 %
Omega-6 fatty acids* (min.)	2.20 %
Omega-3 fatty acids* (min.)	0.30 %
Glucosamine* (min.)	500 mg/kg
Chondroitin sulfate* (min.)	500 mg/kg

* Not recognized as an essential nutrient by the AAFCO Dog Food Nutrient Profiles.

energy that carbohydrates and proteins do. Common fats include chicken or pork fat, cottonseed oil, vegetable oil, soybean oil, fish oil, safflower oil, and many more. They are highly digestible and are the first nutrients to be used by the body as energy. AAFCO recommends minimum 8% fat for puppies and 5% for adults

- **Fibre** – found in vegetables and grains. It aids digestion and helps prevent anal glands from becoming impacted. The average dry dog food has 2.5%-4.5% crude fibre, but reduced-calorie feeds may be as high as 9%-10%

- **Carbohydrates** typically make up anywhere from 30%-70% of a dry dog food. They come mainly from plants and grains, and provide energy in the form of sugars

- **Vitamins and Minerals** – have a similar effect on dogs as humans. Glucosamine and chondroitin are good for joints

- **Omegas 3 and 6** – fatty acids that help keep Dachshunds' skin and coat healthy. Also good for inflammation control, arthritic pain, heart and kidneys

Well-formulated dog foods have the right balance of protein, fat, carbohydrates, vitamins, minerals and fatty acids. If you're still not sure what to choose for your Dachshund, check out these websites: www.dogfoodadvisor.com/best-dog-foods/german-Dachshunds run by Mike Sagman in the USA and www.allaboutdogfood.co.uk run by UK canine nutritionist David Jackson.

How Much Food?

Maintaining a healthy body weight is all about balancing calories taken in with calories burned. If a dog is exercised two or three times a day or taking part in a physical competition, he will need more calories than a relatively inactive or older Dachshund.

- Breed
- Gender
- Age
- Natural energy levels
- Metabolism
- Amount of daily exercise
- Health
- Environment
- Number of dogs in the house or kennel
- Quality of the food
- Whether your Dachshund is competing or simply a pet

Dachshunds are lively dogs, but energy levels vary from one dog to the next. Dogs that have been spayed may be more likely to put on weight. Certain health conditions, e.g. underactive thyroid, diabetes, arthritis or heart disease, can lead to dogs putting on weight. And just like us, a dog kept in a very cold environment will need more calories to keep warm than a dog in a warm climate, as he burns extra calories in keeping warm.

 **FACT** A Dachshund kept on his own is more likely to be overweight than one kept with other dogs, as he receives all of the food-based attention.

Manufacturers of cheap foods may recommend feeding more than necessary, as a major ingredient is cereal, which is not doing much except bulking up the weight of the food – and possibly triggering allergies. The daily recommended amount listed on dog food sacks or tins can be too high – after all, the more your dog eats, the more they sell!

 There is an excellent leaflet that clearly explains each component of a dog's diet and how much to feed your dog based on weight and activity level. It can be found by searching for *"Your Dog's Nutritional Needs National Academies"* online.

Feeding Options

We are what we eat. The right food is a very important part of a healthy lifestyle for dogs as well as humans. Here are the main options explained:

Dry dog food – or kibble, is a popular and relatively inexpensive way of providing a balanced diet. Millions of dogs thrive on kibble. It comes in a variety of flavours and with differing ingredients to suit the different stages of a dog's life. Cheap kibble is often false economy with Dachshunds.

Canned food – dogs love the taste and it generally comes in a variety of flavours. Some owners feed kibble mixed with some canned food. These days there are hundreds of options, some are high quality made from natural, organic ingredients with herbs and other beneficial ingredients. Read the label closely, the origins of cheap canned food are often somewhat dubious. Some dogs can suffer from stomach upsets with too much soft food. Avoid fillers and preservatives and brands with lots of grain or recalls.

Semi-Moist – this food typically has a water content of around 60%-65%, compared to 10% in dry food, making it easier to digest. It also has more sugar and salt, so is not suitable for some dogs. Semi-moist treats are shaped like pork chops, bacon *(pictured)*, salamis, burgers, etc. They are the least nutritional of all dog foods, full of sugars, artificial flavourings and colourings, so avoid giving them regularly.

Home-Cooked - some owners want the ability to be in complete control of their dog's diet and to know exactly what their dog is eating. Feeding a home-cooked diet can be time-consuming and expensive. The difficult thing (as with the raw diet) is sticking to it once you have started out with the best of intentions, but your dog will love it and he won't be eating preservatives or fillers. Some high-end dog food companies now provide boxes of freshly-prepared meals with natural ingredients.

Dehydrated - this dried food *(pictured)* is becoming increasingly popular. It looks similar to kibble, but is only minimally processed. It offers many of the benefits of raw feeding, including lots of nutrients, but with none of the mess or bacteria. Gentle heating slowly cooks proteins and helps start the digestive process, making it easier on the digestive tract of older Dachshunds, or those with sensitive stomachs. Owners just add water and let it stand for a minute or two to reconstitute the meal.

Freeze-Dried – this is usually raw, fresh food that has been freeze-dried by frozen food manufacturers. It's a more convenient, hygienic and less messy option than raw, and handy if you're going on a trip. It contains healthy enzymes but no preservatives, is highly palatable and keeps for six months to a year. It says *"freeze-dried"* on the packet, but the process bumps up the cost. A good option for owners who can afford it.

The Raw Diet

Opinions are divided on a raw diet. There is anecdotal evidence that some dogs thrive on it, particularly those with food intolerances or allergies, although scientific proof is lagging behind. Claims made by fans of the raw diet include:

- Reduced symptoms of - or less likelihood of - allergies, and less scratching
- Better skin and coats
- Easier weight management
- Improved digestion
- Less doggie odour and flatulence
- Higher energy levels
- Reduced risk of bloat
- Helps fussy eaters
- Fresher breath and improved dental health
- Drier and less smelly stools, more like pellets
- Overall improvement in general health and less disease
- Most dogs love a raw diet

If your Dachshund is not doing well on a dry dog food or has skin issues, you might consider a raw diet. Some commercial dog foods contain artificial preservatives, grains and excessive protein and fillers – causing a reaction in some dogs. Dry, canned and other styles of processed food were mainly created as a means of convenience – for humans, not dogs!

Some nutritionists believe there are inherent beneficial enzymes, vitamins, minerals and other qualities in meats, fruits, vegetables and grains in their natural, uncooked state. However, critics of a raw diet say that the risks of nutritional imbalance, intestinal problems and food-borne illnesses caused by handling and feeding raw meat outweigh any benefits.

It is true that owners must pay strict attention to hygiene when preparing a raw diet and it may not be a suitable option if you have children. The dog may also be more likely to ingest bacteria or parasites such as Salmonella, E. Coli and Ecchinococcus - although freeze-dried meals reduce the risk.

If you do switch your dog over to raw feeding, do so over a period of at least a week.

 **Raw is not for every dog; it can cause loose stools, upset stomach and even vomiting in some, and there are other dogs who simply don't like the taste.**

There are two main types of raw diet, one involves feeding raw, meaty bones and the other is known as the BARF diet *(Biologically Appropriate Raw Food or Bones And Raw Food)*, created by Dr Ian Billinghurst.

Raw Meaty Bones

- Raw meaty bones or carcasses form the bulk of the diet. **Cooked bones should NOT be fed, as they can splinter**
- Table scraps both cooked and raw, such as vegetables

Australian veterinarian Dr Tom Lonsdale is a leading proponent of the raw meaty bones diet. He believes the following foods are suitable:

- Chicken and turkey carcasses, after the meat has been removed for human consumption
- Poultry by-products, e.g. heads, feet, necks and wings
- Whole fish and fish heads
- Sheep, calf, goat, and deer carcasses sawn into big pieces of meat and bone
- Pigs' trotters and heads, sheep heads, brisket, tail and rib bones
- A certain amount of offal can be included in the diet, e.g. liver, lungs, trachea, hearts, tripe
- Table scraps and some fruit and vegetable peelings, but should not make up more than one-third of the diet

Low-fat game animals, fish and poultry are the best source of food. If you feed meat from farm animals (cattle, sheep and pigs), avoid excessive fat and bones too large to be eaten. It depends on price and what's available locally - start with your local butcher or farm shop.

 **Dogs are more likely to break their teeth eating large knuckle bones and bones sawn lengthwise than when eating meat and bone together**.

You'll also need to think about WHERE and WHEN you are going to feed. A dog takes some time to eat a raw bone and will push it around the floor, so the kitchen may not be the most hygienic place. Outside is one option, but what do you do when it's raining? If you live in a hot climate, evening feeding may be best to avoid flies. Establishing the right quantity to feed is based on your dog's activity levels, appetite and body condition. A very approximate guide of raw meaty bones for the average dog is:

15%-20% of body weight per week, or 2%-3% a day.

Dr Lonsdale says: "Wherever possible, feed the meat and bone ration in one large piece requiring much ripping, tearing and gnawing. This makes for contented pets with clean teeth." More information is available from www.rawmeatybones.com

NOTES: Pregnant or lactating females and growing puppies need more food. This diet may not be suitable for old dogs used to a processed diet or those with dental issues, or in households with children due to the risk of bacterial infection from raw meat.

Monitor your dog while he eats, especially in the beginning. Don't feed bones with sharp points, and remove any bone before it becomes small enough to swallow. Raw meaty bones should be kept separate from human food and any surface the uncooked meat or bones have touched should be thoroughly cleaned afterwards

Puppies can and do eat diets of raw meaty bones, but consult your breeder or vet before embarking on raw with a young dog.

The BARF diet - A variation of the raw meaty bones diet is the BARF created by Dr Ian Billinghurst, who owns the registered trademark "Barf Diet." A typical BARF diet is made up of 60%-75% of raw meaty bones - with about 50% meat, such as chicken neck, back and wings - and 25%-40% of fruit and vegetables, offal, meat, eggs or dairy foods. There is lots of information on the BARF diet online.

Dachshund Feeding Tips

1. If you choose a manufactured food, pick one where meat or poultry (or meat or poultry meal) is the first item listed. Most Dachshunds do not do well on cheap cereals or sugar. Choose a high quality one specially formulated for small breed dogs or Dachshunds.

2. If a Dachshund has sensitive skin, "hot spots" or allergies, a cheap food bulked up with grain will only make this worse. A dry food described as *"hypoallergenic"* on the sack means *"less likely to cause allergies."*

3. Consider feeding a probiotic, such as a spoonful of natural, live yoghurt, to each meal to help maintain healthy gut bacteria.

4. Feed your adults twice a day, rather than once. Smaller feeds are easier to digest, and reduce the risk of Bloat as well as gas.

5. Establish a feeding regime and stick to it. Dogs like routine. Stick to the same times, morning and tea-time. Feeding too late won't give your dog's body time to process the food before bed. Feeding at the same times also helps your dog establish a toilet regime.

6. Take away uneaten food between meals. Most Dachshunds love their food, but any dog can become fussy if food is constantly available. Remove the bowl after 15-20 minutes – even if there is some left. A healthy, hungry dog will look forward to the next meal and should soon stop leaving food. If he's off his food for a couple of days or more, it could be a sign of illness.

7. Feeding time is a great training opportunity - particularly for the commands **SIT** and **STAY** and the release.

8. Use stainless steel or ceramic bowls. Plastic bowls don't last as long and can trigger an allergic reaction around the muzzle in some sensitive dogs.

9. Use apple or carrot slices, or other healthy alternatives, as training treats for puppies.

10. Don't feed too many tidbits or treats between meals. As they throw a balanced diet out of the window and cause obesity. Feed leftovers in the bowl as part of a meal, rather than from the table, as this encourages attention-seeking behaviour, begging and drooling.

11. Don't feed cooked bones, as these can splinter and cause choking or intestinal problems. And avoid rawhide, as a dog can gulp it without chewing, causing an internal blockage.

12. Obesity leads to all sorts of health issues, such as joint problems, diabetes, high blood pressure and organ disease. Your Dachshund's tummy should be higher than his rib cage - if his belly is level or hangs down below it, reduce his food.

13. These are poisonous to dogs: grapes, raisins, chocolate, onions, Macadamia nuts, any fruits with seeds or stones, tomatoes, avocados, rhubarb, tea, coffee and alcohol.

14. Check your dog's faeces (aka stools, poo or poop)! If the diet is suitable, the food should be easily digested and produce dark brown, firm stools. If your dog is producing light or sloppy poo or lots of gas, his diet may well need changing. Consult your vet or breeder for advice.

15. And finally, always make sure that your dog has access to clean, fresh water. Change the water and clean the bowl every day or so – it gets slimy!

 If your dog is not responding well to a particular family member, get him or her to give the feeds - the way to a Dachshund's heart is through his stomach!

Food Allergies

Dog food allergies are a reaction to food that involves the body's immune system and affect about one in 10 dogs. They are the third most common canine allergy after atopy (inhaled or contact allergies) and flea bite allergies.

Food allergies affect males and females in equal measure as well as neutered and intact pets. They can start when your dog is five months or 12 years old - although the vast majority start when the dog is between two and six years old. It is not uncommon for dogs with food allergies to also have other types of allergies. Here are some common symptoms of food causing problems:

- Itchy skin (this is the most common). Your dog may lick or chew his paws or legs and rub his face with his paws or on the furniture, carpet, etc.

- Excessive scratching

- Hair loss

- Hot patches of skin – *"hot spots"*

- Redness and inflammation on the chin and face

- Increased bowel movements (maybe twice as often as usual)

- Recurring ear or skin infections that clear up with antibiotics but recur when the antibiotics run out

The problem with food allergies is that the symptoms are similar to symptoms of other issues, such as environmental or flea bite allergies, intestinal problems, mange and yeast or bacterial infections. There's also a difference between dog food *allergies* and dog food *intolerance*:

ALLERGIES = SKIN PROBLEMS AND/OR ITCHING

INTOLERANCE = DIARRHOEA AND/OR VOMITING

Dog food intolerance can be compared to people who get an upset stomach from eating spicy curries. Symptoms can be cured by changing to a milder diet. With dogs, certain ingredients are more likely to cause a reaction than others. Unfortunately, these are also the most common ingredients in dog foods! In order of the most common triggers in dogs in general, they are:

Beef - Dairy Products – Chicken – Wheat – Eggs – Corn - Soya (Soy in the US)

 A dog is allergic or sensitive to an <u>ingredient</u>, not to a particular brand, so it's important to read the label. If your Dachshund reacts to beef, for example, he'll react to any food containing beef, regardless of how expensive it is or how well it has been prepared.

AVOID corn, corn meal, corn gluten meal, artificial preservatives (BHA, BHT, Propyl Gallate, Ethoxyquin, Sodium Nitrite/Nitrate and TBHQBHA), artificial colours, sugars and sweeteners, e.g. corn syrup, sucrose and ammoniated glycyrrhizin, powdered cellulose, propylene glycol.

Food Trials

The only way to completely cure a food allergy or intolerance is complete avoidance, which is not as easy as it sounds. First you have to determine your dog DOES have an allergy to food - and not pollen, grass, etc. - and then you have to discover WHICH food is causing the reaction.

A **food trial or exclusion diet** involves feeding one specific food for 12 weeks, something the dog has never eaten before. Before you embark on one, know that they are a real pain-in-the-you-know-what! You have to be incredibly vigilant and determined, so only start one if you are prepared to see it through to the end or you are wasting your time.

The chosen food must be the **only thing** eaten during the trial. During the trial, your dog shouldn't roam freely, as you can't control what he is eating or drinking when out of sight. Don't give:

- ❧ Treats
- ❧ Rawhide (not recommended anyway)
- ❧ Pigs' ears
- ❧ Cows' hooves
- ❧ Flavoured medications (including heartworm treatments) or supplements
- ❧ Flavoured toothpastes
- ❧ Flavoured plastic toys

A more practical, less scientific approach is to eliminate ingredients one at a time by switching diets over a period of a week or so. If you switch to home-cooked or raw, you know exactly what your dog is eating; if you choose a commercial food, a hypoallergenic one is a good place to start. They all have the word *"hypoallergenic"* in the name and do not include wheat protein or soya. They are often based around less common ingredients.

Grain Intolerance

Although beef is the food most likely to cause allergies in the general dog population, there is plenty of anecdotal evidence to suggest that GRAIN can also be a problem. *"Grain"* is wheat or any other cultivated cereal crop. Some dogs also react to starch, which is found in grains and potatoes, as well as bread, pasta rice, etc.

Dogs, especially Miniatures, have short digestive tracts and don't process grains as well as humans. Foods high in grains and sugar can cause increases in unhealthy bacteria and yeast in the stomach, which crowds out the good bacteria and allows toxins to affect the immune system.

The itchiness related to food allergies can then cause secondary bacterial and yeast infections, which may show as hot spots, ear or bladder infections, excessive shedding, reddish or dark brown tear stains. You may also notice a musty smell.

 Drugs like antihistamines and steroids will help temporarily, but they do not address the root cause.

Before you automatically switch to a grain-free diet, a recent study by University of California, Davis, vets found a link between a form of heart disease called *taurine-deficient dilated cardiomyopathy* and some popular grain-free dog foods where legumes (e.g. beans, lentil, peas, soy) or potatoes were the main ingredients. Lead author Joshua Stern said that while many owners may not want to see *"by products"* listed in their dog's food, they often contain organ meat like heart and kidney, which are good sources of taurine.

Some food allergy symptoms - particularly the scratching, licking, chewing and redness - can also be a sign of environmental allergies or flea bites. See **Chapter 13. Skin Conditions** for more details.

 If you've switched diet to little effect, it's time to see a vet. Many vets promote specific dog food brands, which may or may not be the best option for your Dachshund. Do your research.

Bloat

Bloat occurs when there is too much gas in the stomach. It is known by several different names: **_twisted stomach, gastric torsion_** or **_Gastric Dilatation-Volvulus (GDV)_** and occurs mainly in larger breeds. The Dachshund isn't large, but he does have the other major risk factor - a deep chest. Bloat is statistically more common in males than in females and in dogs over seven years old.

 As the stomach swells with gas, it can rotate 90° to 360°. The twisting stomach traps air, food and water inside and the bloated organ stops blood flowing properly to veins in the abdomen, leading to low blood pressure, shock and even damage to internal organs.

The causes are not fully understood, but there are some well-known risk factors. One is the dog taking in a lot of air while eating - either because he is greedy and gulping the food too fast, or stressed, e.g. in kennels where there might be food competition.

A dog that is fed once a day and gorges himself could be at higher risk; another reason why Dachshund owners feed twice a day. Exercising straight after eating or after a big drink also increases the risk - like colic in horses.

Another potential cause is diet. Fermentable foodstuffs that produce a lot of gas can cause problems for the stomach if the gas is not burped or passed into the intestines. Symptoms are:

- Swollen belly
- Standing uncomfortably or hunched
- Restlessness, pacing or looking for a place to hide
- Rapid panting or difficulty breathing
- Dry retching, or excessive saliva or foam
- White or colourless gums
- Excessive drinking
- Licking the air
- General weakness or collapse

Tips to Avoid Canine Bloat

- Some owners buy a frame for food bowls so they are at chest height for the dog, other experts believe dogs should be fed from the floor – do whichever slows your Dachshund down

- Avoid dog food with high fats or those using citric acid as a preservative, also avoid tiny pieces of kibble

- Buy a bowl with nobbles *(pictured)* and moisten your dog's dry food – both of these will slow down a gulper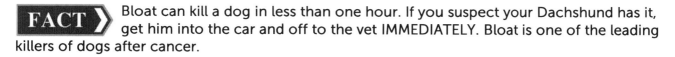

- Feed twice a day rather than once

- Don't let your dog drink too much water just before, during or after eating

- Stress can possibly be a trigger, with nervous and aggressive dogs being more susceptible. Maintain a peaceful environment, particularly around his mealtimes

- Avoid vigorous exercise before or after eating, allow one hour either side of mealtimes before strenuous exercise

FACT ⟩ Bloat can kill a dog in less than one hour. If you suspect your Dachshund has it, get him into the car and off to the vet IMMEDIATELY. Bloat is one of the leading killers of dogs after cancer.

Overweight Dachshunds

Dachshunds are notorious for piling on the pounds - one US study put Dachshunds in the top three breeds for obesity. You may think you are being kind to your beloved Dachshund by giving him extra treats and scraps, but the reality is that you are shortening his life.

The extra weight puts huge strain on his short legs, back and organs, often resulting in a reducing lifespan. It is far easier to regulate your dog's weight and keep it at a healthy level than to slim down a pleading Dachshund once he becomes overweight. Overweight dogs are susceptible to:

IVDD – a study by the Royal Veterinary College found that dogs that were fat or obese were more likely to suffer from IVDD than fitter, slimmer ones.

Joint disease – excessive body weight increases joint stress, which then tends to lead to a vicious circle of less exercise and weight gain, further reducing exercise.

Heart and lung problems – fatty deposits within the chest cavity and too much circulating fat contribute to cardio-respiratory and cardiovascular disease.

Diabetes – is a major risk factor for overweight Dachshunds.

Tumours – obesity increases the risk of mammary tumours in female dogs.

Liver disease – fat degeneration can result in liver insufficiency.

Reduced Lifespan - one of the most serious proven findings in obesity studies is that obesity in both humans and dogs reduces lifespan.

Most Dachshunds are extremely loyal companions and very attached to their humans. They are a part of our family. However, beware of going too far.

FACT ⟩ Studies show that dogs regarded as "family members" by the owner (anthropomorphosis) are at greater risk of becoming overweight. This is because attention given to the dog often results in food being given as well.

To see diagrams and descriptions of overweight, underweight and correct weight Dachshunds, type *"Dachshund health UK body condition and weight"* into an online search engine.

If you have to put your dog on a diet, be aware that a reduced amount of food will also mean reduced nutrients, so he may need a supplement during this time.

Don't despair if your Dachshund is overweight. Many problems associated with being overweight are reversible with weight loss.

What the Breeders Feed

We asked a number of breeders what they give their dogs. This is what they said, starting with the UK breeders, who are all Kennel Club Assured Breeders: Hannah Norton, Jacksondax, South Devon: "I feed Royal Canin to all of my dogs. They look fabulous and I highly recommend it."

Judith Carruthers, Stanegate Wirehaired Dachshunds, Cumbria: "I feed a complete kibble, either Royal Canin Dachshund or Arden Grange Sensitive, to ensure each dog gets a balanced diet. Dachshunds should not be overfed."

Long-Haired breeder Lisa Cole, Foosayo Dachshunds, North Yorkshire: "I feed my dogs kibble and raw fresh eggs from my hens, every day. The BARF diet is fine, but you need to make sure you have the right vitamins and herbs added to the diet to get it right. I don't change my dog's food, just slightly soaked kibble with a raw egg and nothing else - no treats unless training and then the treat is the size of a pea."

Lisa Lindfield, Zabannah Dachshunds, Cambridgeshire, who breeds all three types of Miniature: "I feed Royal Canin food and raw. I start my pups on raw, it's so easy to mulch it up, then they move on to Royal Canin. So, they have the Puppy formula, then the Adult one, and then the Lightweight or Senior as they get older."

Bastiaan Smit, Daxiesburrow, Aberdeenshire: "We feed tripe or meat and Josera dry food. Some pellets are very salty or have a high quantity of ash, which is a filler."

Pictured thriving on his diet is Bastiaan's 11-year-old Otto.

Bastiaan adds: "Otto von Konigstannen is now 11 years young and he does not show signs of fatigue. In particular, when his girl is in heat he is as proud as a young stag!"

Sandra and Karl Robertson, Hartlebury Miniature Dachshunds, Worcestershire: "We feed our dogs on James Wellbeloved. It's a well-balanced diet with natural ingredients, no synthetic colours or preservatives and it has natural antioxidants. Our dogs have beautiful coats and no bowel or gut problems whatsoever."

Mini Smooth breeder Pauline Cheeseman, Colraed Miniature Dachshunds, Surrey: "I feed raw as it's my view that's what dogs should be fed. It's mainly a BARF diet but I do use completes as well."

Stefanie Millington: "I feed my dogs very naturally: BARF. None of mine have had any allergies, which I put down to a natural diet. I've fed BARF for years. I tried various different foods in the past, but never for long and have always gone back to BARF – and I worked for almost 10 years for one of the largest pet food companies in the world. My dogs always looked their best on BARF, be it the German Shepherds or the Mini Longs."

Now the US breeders, all AKC Breeders of Merit or members of the Bred With HEART programme, starting with Melissa Sworab, Rabows Dachshunds, Texas: "We rotate. In today's world, you cannot guarantee ingredients or quality, so we feed A LOT of fresh fruits and vegetables every day and feed a kibble base that does NOT include peas, pea protein, pea fiber, legumes, and chickpeas.

"Taurine deficiencies are causing DCM (Dilated Cardiomyopathy) and it's reversible if caught early, but the studies so far only suspect peas, and legumes, etc. We rotate kibble but do NOT mix the kibble, ever. Freeze dried Duck and Duck Liver once a week will help with taurine levels as well as raw or cooked beef hearts or beef liver, or a commercial raw that includes heart."

Marianne McCullough, Kenmar Hounds, Florida: "We feed Purina Pro Plan Sport 30/20. It is an excellent food and my dogs have been healthy and happy on it for well over a decade. I'm not a fan of a raw or BARF diet." Mini Long breeder Pame Bates, Doxies Treasures, California: "There are so many different opinions on this subject. We feed our dogs a high-quality dry food."

Kristin Cihos-Williams Kinderteckel Standard Smooth Dachshunds, California: "I have fed basically every brand of quality kibble that is available in the US market.

"I look for a meat-based food that gets at least 90% of its protein from actual meat sources, not cheaper plant-based protein sources like chickpeas, peas, or other legumes. I do not feed kibble with flaxseed meal, peas, or other phytoestrogens, as there is some evidence that phytoestrogens can impair fertility."

Looking the picture of health is Kristin's Lily (CH Kinderteckel's Fourstar Lily ROMO), aged 10, in the Veteran Class at the Dachshund Club of Santa Ana's Specialty Show.

"At this point in time, I am happy with Farmina Ancestral Grains Chicken and Pomegranate, a meat-based kibble that meets the above criteria.

"I fed raw meaty bones 20 years ago, after reading the Ian Billinghurst books, but I had a young dog that had to have emergency obstruction surgery because of a raw meaty bone. I have had much better success using raw food that has ground bone. I purchase raw green tripe for my dogs, as well as various raw ground organ meat blends, entire raw ground chicken blends, etc. I start my puppies on raw ground meat blends."

If your Dachshund is happy and healthy, interested in life, has lots of energy, is not too fat and not too thin, doesn't scratch a lot and has dark brown, firm stools, then...CONGRATULATIONS, you've got it right!

7. Dachshund Traits

With a Dachshund, you are getting a big dog in a small body. And if you've decided to share your life with one, it helps to have an insight into what is going on in that maverick mind of his!

To get the best out of your dog, you first have to learn what makes him tick and what motivates him to learn. This chapter helps you to do that.

....

Just as with humans, a dog's personality is made up of a combination of temperament and character – or **Nature and Nurture.**

Temperament is the nature – or inherited characteristics - a dog is born with; a predisposition to act or react to the world around her. Natural temperament is where good breeders come into their own. Not only do they produce puppies from physically healthy dams and sires, but they also look at temperament and only breed from Dachshunds with good traits.

Character is what develops through the dog's life and is formed by a combination of temperament and environment. How you treat your dog will have a huge effect on his personality and behaviour.

Start off on the right foot with your puppy by establishing the rules of the house and good routines. Treat him well and make lots of time for socialisation, training and, as his body matures, exercise.

FACT ❯ Socialisation means "learning to be part of society." With dogs, it means helping them learn to be comfortable living within a human society that includes many different types of people, environments, buildings, sights, noises, smells and other animals.

All dogs need different environments and experiences to keep them stimulated and well-balanced. As hounds, Dachshunds enjoy running free off the lead and activities that challenge their minds as well as their bodies. The Dachshund was originally bred as a working dog whose job was to hunt badgers. Some of those natural instincts are evident in the modern Dachshund.

....

Typical Dachshund Traits

1. They are scent hounds with a keen sense of smell. They love to follow a scent with their nose to the ground, so teaching The Recall while young is very important

2. Dachshunds often worked alone or in pairs when hunting and acted on their own initiative when underground inside a badger's sett, or burrow, which is why they are regarded as independent thinkers. This can sometimes develop into stubbornness without sufficient training

3. Because they were bred to hunt, they have a keen prey drive and most love to chase small animals and birds

4. Nobody has told the Dachshund that he's small (Miniature) or medium-sized (Standard), and he is bold and fearless – sometimes to the point of rashness. On a hunt he'd burrow into a sett and face down a badger. He will take on a big dog if he feels threatened, so socialisation with other dogs is important

5. They are champion diggers, especially if bored; it's what they were bred for. They enjoy burrowing outside and inside.... under bedcovers blankets or cushions, behind the couch....

6. They were bred to work alongside Man and are fiercely loyal. Their natural tendency is often to strongly bond with one person, rather than the whole family

7. They have territorial instincts and, if not well socialised, can become over-protective of their owner, property, toys or food

8. They are very affectionate and LOVE snuggling up with their beloved owners

9. They are very smart and tenacious. They don't give up easily and enjoy problem-solving, so bolt down or move out of reach (which is higher than you think) anything you don't want yours to get into

10. They are lively dogs that love to be busy – physically and mentally. They thrive on an hour or more exercise a day and, once they've built up to it, can walk all day. They also enjoy the challenge of canine competitions

11. They have no road sense, so keep yours on a lead at all times near traffic

12. They are playful and love noisy, squeaky toys and playing Fetch - although they don't always fetch the ball right back to you. They also enjoy learning new tricks and showing off

13. They are surprisingly fast for their size and can run at speeds of up to 20mph. This is about eight meters faster than Usain Bolt over 400 meters, so make sure you've instilled The Recall before you let yours loose in the park!

14. Most Dachshunds are controlled by two things – their noses and their stomachs! Keeping them at a healthy weight can be a challenge, but on the plus side, food treats are often highly effective motivation when training

15. Dachshund are not quiet dogs; they bark at everything. They make excellent watchdogs and have a very deep, loud bark for their size. They also have a surprising array of other sounds, including howling, whining, barking, yapping, squeaking, squealing - some owners even say they "talk"

16. Due to their independent-mindedness, which is common in hounds, they are not the quickest breed to housetrain. The trick is to persuade them that what YOU want them to do is really what THEY want to do – this often involves bribery!

17. Many are not too keen on going out in the rain. Their short legs mean their bellies get wet, but a waterproof jacket can help keep them dry

18. They have a reputation for being extraordinarily good with children - provided they and the kids are well-trained and socialised

19. They are quirky freethinkers with amusing antics and make for entertaining companions

Canine Emotions

As pet lovers, we are all too keen to ascribe human characteristics to our dogs; this is called **anthropomorphism** – "the attribution of human characteristics to anything other than a human being."

Most of us dog lovers are guilty of that, as we come to regard our pets as members of the family - and Dachshunds certainly regard themselves as members and guardians of the family.

An example of anthropomorphism might be that the owner of a male dog might not want to have him neutered because he will "miss sex," as a human might if he or she were no longer able to have sex. This is simply not true.

A male dog's impulse to mate is entirely governed by his hormones, not emotions. If he gets the scent of a bitch in heat, his hormones (which are just chemicals) tell him he has to mate with her. He does not stop to consider how attractive she is or whether she is *"the one"* to produce his puppies.

No, his reaction is entirely physical, he just wants to dive in there and get on with it!

It's the same with females. When they are in heat, a chemical impulse is triggered in their brain making them want to mate – with any male, they aren't at all fussy. So, don't expect your little princess to be all coy when she is in heat, she is not waiting for Prince Charming to come along - the tramp down the road or any other scruffy pooch will do! It is entirely physical, not emotional.

Food is another issue. A dog will not stop to count the calories of a delicious treat – you have to do that. No, he is driven by food and just thinks about getting the treat. Most Dachshunds will eat far too much, given the opportunity.

Dachshunds are incredibly loyal and loving. They are amusing characters and if yours doesn't make you smile from time to time, you must have had a humour by-pass. All of this adds up to one thing: a beloved family member that is all too easy to spoil.

 Dachshunds form deep bonds with their humans and respond well to the right motivation - usually treats. Teach yours to respect the authority figure, which is you - not him! In the beginning, think of yourself as a kindly but firm teacher with a slightly stubborn young student.

Learn to understand his mind, patiently train him to be comfortable with his place in the household, teach him some manners and household rules – like not jumping up or constantly barking - and you will be rewarded with a companion who is second to none and fits in beautifully with your family and lifestyle.

Dr Stanley Coren is well known for his work on canine psychology and behaviour. He and other researchers believe that in many ways a dog's emotional development is equivalent to that of a young child. Dr Coren says: "Researchers have now come to believe that the mind of a dog is roughly equivalent to that of a human who is two to two-and-a-half years old. This conclusion holds for most mental abilities as well as emotions.

"Thus, we can look to human research to see what we might expect of our dogs. Just like a two-year-old child, our dogs clearly have emotions, but many fewer kinds of emotions than found in adult humans.

"At birth, a human infant only has an emotion that we might call excitement. This indicates how excited he is, ranging from very calm up to a state of frenzy. Within the first weeks of life the excitement state comes to take on a varying positive or a negative flavour, so we can now detect the general emotions of contentment and distress.

"In the next couple of months, disgust, fear, and anger become detectable in the infant. Joy often does not appear until the infant is nearly six months of age and it is followed by the emergence of shyness or suspicion. True affection, the sort that it makes sense to use the label "love" for, does not fully emerge until nine or ten months of age."

So, our Dachshunds can truly love us – but we knew that already!

According to Dr Coren, dogs can't feel shame. So, if you are housetraining your puppy, don't expect him to feel ashamed if he makes a mess in the house, he can't; he simply isn't capable of feeling shame. But he will not like it when you ignore him when he's behaving badly, and will love it when you praise or reward him for relieving himself outdoors.

FACT ❯ He is simply responding to you with his simplified range of emotions.

Although Dachshunds can sometimes be stubborn, they are surprisingly sensitive and certainly show empathy - *"the ability to understand and share the feelings of another."* They can pick up on the mood and emotions of the owner.

One emotion that all dogs can experience is jealousy. It may display itself by being overly-protective of humans, food or toys.

An interesting article was published in the PLOS (Public Library of Science) Journal in 2014 following an experiment into whether dogs get jealous.

Building on research that shows that six-month old infants display jealousy, the scientists studied 36 dogs in their homes and videoed their actions when their owners showed affection to a realistic-looking stuffed canine *(pictured).*

Over three-quarters of the dogs pushed or touched the owner when they interacted with the decoy. The envious mutts were more than three times as likely to do this for interactions with the stuffed dog, compared to when their owners gave their attention to other objects, including a book.

Around a third tried to get between the owner and the plush toy, while a quarter of the put-upon pooches snapped at the dummy dog!

Professor Christine Harris from University of California in San Diego said: "Our study suggests not only that dogs do engage in what appear to be jealous behaviours, but also that they were seeking to break up the connection between the owner and a seeming rival."

The researchers believe that the dogs thought that the stuffed dog was real. The authors cite the fact that 86% of the dogs sniffed the toy's rear end during and after the experiment!

Professor Harris said: "We can't really speak of the dogs' subjective experiences, of course, but it looks as though they were motivated to protect an important social relationship. Many people have assumed that jealousy is a social construction of human beings - or that it's an emotion specifically tied to sexual and romantic relationships.

"Our results challenge these ideas, showing that animals besides ourselves display strong distress whenever a rival usurps a loved one's affection."

Cause and Effect

When treated well, socialised and trained, Dachshunds make wonderful canine companions. Once you've had one, no other dog seems quite the same. But sometimes they, just like other breeds, can develop behaviour problems. Poor behaviour may result from a number of factors, including:

- Lack of socialisation
- Lack of training
- Poor breeding
- Boredom, due to lack of exercise or mental challenges
- Being left alone too long
- Being badly treated
- A change in living conditions
- Anxiety, insecurity or fear
- Being spoiled

Bad behaviour may show itself in different ways:

- Becoming overly protective of a person, toys or food
- Excessive barking or whining
- Growling
- Nipping, biting
- Aggression towards people or other dogs
- Chewing or destructive behaviour
- Excessive digging
- Snarling and lunging on the leash
- Jumping up
- Soiling or urinating inside the house
- Constantly demanding your attention

 **FACT** Avoid poor behaviour by devoting lots of time early on to socialise and train your Dachshund, and to nip any potential problems in the bud.

If you are rehoming a Dachshund, you'll need extra time and patience to help your new arrival unlearn some bad habits.

10 Ways to Avoid Bad Behaviour

Here are some tips to help you start out on the right foot:

1. **Buy from a good breeder**. They use their expertise to match suitable breeding pairs, taking into account factors such as good temperament, health and being *"fit for function."*

2. **Start socialisation right away**. Dachshunds are naturally protective. Give a new puppy a couple of days to get used to his new surroundings and then start socialising him – even if this means carrying him places until the vaccination schedule is complete.

Some Dachshunds naturally tend to fixate on one person. They can become needy and too attached to that person if they are not well socialised.

Socialisation does not end at puppyhood. Dogs are social creatures that thrive on sniffing, hearing, seeing, and even licking. While the foundation for good behaviour is laid down during the first few months, good owners reinforce social skills and training throughout a dog's life.

Dachshunds love to be at the centre of the action and it is important that they learn when young that they are not also the centre of the universe. Socialisation helps them to learn their place in that universe and to become comfortable with it.

3. **Start training early** - you can't start too soon. Start teaching your puppy to learn his own name as well as some simple commands a day or two after you bring him home.

4. **Basic training should cover several areas:** housetraining, chew prevention, puppy biting, simple commands like SIT, COME, STAY and familiarising him with collar and lead or puppy harness. Adopt a gentle approach and keep training sessions short. Dachshunds are sensitive to you and your mood and do not respond well to harsh treatment. Start with five minutes a day and build up.

   Puppy classes or adult dog obedience classes are a great way to start; be sure to do your homework together afterwards. Spend a few minutes each day reinforcing what you have both learned in class - owners need training as well as dogs!

5. **Reward your dog for good behaviour.** All behaviour training should be based on positive reinforcement. Dachshunds love rewards and praise, and this trait speeds up the training process. The main aim of training is to build a good understanding between you and your dog.

6. **Ignore bad behaviour**, no matter how hard this may be. If, for example, your dog is chewing his way through your kitchen, shoes, or couch, jumping up or chasing the kids, remove him from the situation and then ignore him. For most dogs even negative attention is some attention. Or if he is constantly demanding your attention, ignore him. Remove him or yourself from the room so he learns that you give attention when you want to give it, **not** when he demands it. If your pup is a chewer – and most are - make sure he has plenty of durable toys to keep him occupied.

7. **Take the time to learn what sort of temperament your dog has.** Is he by nature confident or anxious? What was he like as a tiny puppy, did he rush forward or hang back? Does he fight to get upright when on his back or is he happy to lie there? Is he a couch potato or a ball of fire? Your puppy's temperament will affect his behaviour and how he reacts to the world. A nervous Dachshund will certainly not respond well to a loud approach on your part,

whereas an energetic, strong-willed one will require more patience and exercise, and a firm hand.

Photo: The handsome, characterful Cadbury and Crunchie, courtesy of Sue and Ian Seath, Sunsong Dachshunds.

8. **Exercise and stimulation.** A lack of either is another reason for dogs behaving badly. Regular daily exercise, games and toys and organised activities are all ways of stopping your dog from becoming bored or frustrated.

9. **Learn to leave your dog.** Just as leaving your dog alone for too long can lead to problems, so can being with him 100% of the time. The dog becomes over-reliant on you and then gets stressed when you leave; this is called *separation anxiety*. When your dog first arrives at your house, start by leaving him for a few minutes every day and gradually build it up so that after a while you can leave him for up to four hours.

10. **Love your Dachshund – but don't spoil him,** however difficult that might be. You don't do your dog any favours by giving too many treats, constantly responding to his demands for attention or allowing him to behave as he wants inside the house.

Separation Anxiety

It's not just dogs that experience separation anxiety - people do too. About 7% of adults and 4% of children suffer from this disorder. Typical symptoms for humans are:

❧ Distress at being separated from a loved one

❧ Fear of being left alone

Our canine companions aren't much different. When a puppy leaves the litter, his owner becomes his new pack. It's estimated that as many as 10% to 15% of dogs suffer from separation anxiety, which is an exaggerated fear response caused by being apart from their owner. Separation anxiety affects millions of dogs and is on the increase. According to behaviourists, it is the most common form of stress for dogs.

FACT ❯ Dachshunds CAN suffer from it, especially if they have not spent enough time away from their owners when young. Even if yours does not have separation anxiety, being over-reliant on you can lead to other insecurity issues, such as becoming:

❧ Anxious

❧ Over-protective

❧ Too territorial

❧ Too suspicious or aggressive with other people

Separation anxiety can be equally distressing for the owner - I know because one of our dogs suffered from it. He howled whenever we left home without him. He'd also bark if one of us got out of the car - even if other people were still inside.

Fortunately, his problem was relatively mild. If we returned after only a short while, he was usually quiet. Although if we silently sneaked back and peeked in through the letterbox, he was never asleep. Instead he'd be waiting by the door looking and listening for our return.

It could be embarrassing. Whenever I'd go to the Post Office, I'd tie him up outside, where I could still see him and, even though he could see me through the glass door, he'd still bark his head off - so loud that the people inside couldn't make themselves heard. Luckily, the postmistress was a dog lover and, despite the large **'GUIDE DOGS ONLY'** sign outside, she'd let him in. He'd promptly dash through the door and sit down beside me...quiet as a mouse!

Tell-Tale Signs

Does your Dachshund do any of the following?

- Follow you from room to room — even the bathroom - whenever you're home?

- Get anxious or stressed when you're getting ready to leave the house?

- Howl, whine or bark when you leave?

- Tear up paper or chew things he's not supposed to?

- Dig or scratch at the carpet, doors or windows trying to join you?

- Soil or urinate inside the house, even though he is housetrained? (This **only** occurs when left alone)

- Exhibit restlessness - such as licking his coat excessively, pacing or circling?

- Greet you ecstatically every time you come home — even if you've only been out to empty the bins?

- Wait by the window or door until you return?

- Dislike spending time alone in the garden or yard?

- Refuse to eat or drink if you leave him?

- Howl or whine when one family member leaves - even when others are still in the room or car?

If so, he may suffer from separation anxiety. Fortunately, in many cases this can be cured.

Causes

Dogs are pack animals and being alone is not a natural state for them. Puppies have to be taught to get used to periods of isolation slowly and in a structured way before they can become comfortable with being alone.

A Dachshund puppy will emotionally latch on to his new owner, who has taken the place of his mother and siblings. He will want to follow you everywhere initially and, although you want to shower him with love and attention, it's best to start leaving him, starting with a minute or two, right from the beginning. In our case, I was working from home when we got Max. With hindsight, I should have left him alone more often in those critical first few days, weeks then months.

Adopted dogs may be particularly susceptible to separation anxiety. They may have been abandoned once already and fear it happening again.

One or more of these causes can trigger separation anxiety:

20. Not being left alone for short periods when young

21. Being left for too long by owners who are out of the house for most of the day

22. Anxiety or lack of confidence due to insufficient socialisation, training or both

23. Boredom

24. Being given TOO MUCH attention

25. All of the dog's attention being focussed on one person – usually because that person spends time with him, plays, feeds, trains and exercises him

26. Making too much of a fuss when you leave and return to the house

27. Mistreatment in the past, a rescue dog may well feel anxious when left alone

FACT ❯ It may be very flattering that your Dachshund wants to be with you all the time, but separation anxiety is a form of panic that is distressing for your dog. Socialisation helps a dog to become more confident and self-reliant.

A different scenario is separation anxiety in elderly dogs. Pets age and their senses, such as scent, hearing and sight, diminish. They often become "clingier" and more anxious when they are separated from their owners - or even out of view.

You may even find that your elderly Dachshund reverts to puppyhood and starts to follow you around the house again. In these cases, it is fine to spend more time with your old friend and gently help him through his final years.

So, what can you do if your dog is showing signs of canine separation anxiety? Every dog is different, but here are tried and tested techniques that have worked for some dogs.

Tips to Combat Separation Anxiety

28. After the first couple of days at home, leave your new puppy or adult dog for short periods, starting with a minute, then two, then gradually increasing the minutes you are out of sight.

29. Use a crate. Crate training helps a dog to become self-reliant.

30. Introduce your Dachshund to other people, places and animals while young.

31. Get other members of your family to feed, walk and train the dog, so he doesn't become fixated on just one person.

32. Tire your Dachshund out before you leave him alone. Take him for a walk, do an activity or play a game before leaving and, if you can, leave him with a view of the outside world, e.g. in a room with a patio door or low window.

33. Keep arrivals and departures low key and don't make a big fuss.

34. Leave him a *"security blanket,"* such as an old piece of clothing that still has your scent on it, a favourite toy, or leave a radio on softly in the room with the dog. Avoid a heavy rock station! If it will be dark when you return, leave a lamp on a timer.

35. Associate your departure with something good. Give him a rubber toy, like a Kong, filled with a tasty treat, or a frozen treat. This may take his mind off your departure. (Some dogs may refuse to touch the treat until you return home).

36. Structure and routine can help to reduce anxiety. Carry out regular activities, such as feeding and exercising, at the same time every day.

37. Dogs read body language very well; many Dachshunds are sensitive and may start to fret when they think you are going to leave them. One technique is to mimic your departure routine when you have no intention of leaving. Put your coat on, grab your car keys, go out of the door and return a few seconds later. Do this randomly and regularly and it may help to reduce your dog's stress levels when you do it for real.

38. However lovable your Dachshund is, if he is showing early signs of anxiety when separating from you, do not shower him with attention all the time when you are there. He will become too reliant on you.

39. If you have to regularly leave the house for a few hours at a time, try to make an arrangement so the dog is not on his own all day every day during the week. Consider dropping him off with a neighbour or doggie day care if you can afford it.

40. Getting another dog to keep the first one company can help, but ask yourself if you can afford double the food and veterinary bills?

41. There are many natural calming remedies available for dogs in spray, tablet or liquid form, such as CBD oil. Another option is to leave him with a Snuggle Puppy, which is warm and has a heartbeat.

Sit-Stay-Down

Another technique for helping to reduce separation anxiety is the *"sit-stay"* or *"down-stay"* exercises using positive reinforcement. The goal is to be able to move briefly out of your dog's sight while he is in the *"stay"* position. Through this, he learns that he can remain calmly and happily in one place while you go about your normal daily life.

You have to progress slowly. Get your dog to sit and stay and then walk away from him for five seconds, then 10, 20, a minute and so on. Reward your dog every time he stays calm. Then move out of sight or out of the room for a few seconds, return and give him a treat if he is calm, gradually lengthen the time you are out of sight.

If you're watching TV snuggled up with your dog and you get up for a snack, say *"Stay"* and leave the room. When you return, praise him quietly. It is a good idea to practise these techniques after exercise or when your dog is a little sleepy (but not exhausted), as he is likely to be more relaxed.

FACT > Canine separation anxiety is not the result of disobedience or lack of training. It's a psychological condition; your dog feels anxious and insecure.

NEVER punish your dog for showing signs of separation anxiety – even if he has chewed your best shoes or dug a hole in your expensive rug. This will only make him more anxious.

NEVER leave your dog unattended in a crate for long periods or if he is frantic to get out, as it can cause physical or mental trauma. If you're thinking of leaving an animal in a crate all day while you are out of the house, get a rabbit or a hamster - not a Dachshund.

....

Breeders on Temperament

We asked our contributing breeders about their Dachshunds' typical temperaments and traits. This is what they said:

Judith Carruthers (Standard Wires): "In the 50-plus years that I've been associated with Dachshunds, they've never been as popular as they are now, although they've always had a very loyal following: once a Dachshund owner, always a Dachshund owner. All six varieties are different but, although they're small in stature, they're big dogs in their behaviour.

"They are intelligent, and trainable - but not as easily as some other breeds due to their hound instincts. They can be independent and noisy, but are loyal to their family and adore those they live with and know. Dachshunds are lovely with children, but the latter should be respectful. Children should not carry puppies about, tempting though it is. Respect is hugely important."

Pictured is Judith's Alex (Aikton Alexander at Stanegate) at 12 weeks, bred by her granddaughter Eliza Carruthers. Photo: Will Harris.

"From our experience, the Standard Longs are the most gentle and laid-back of the varieties, and the Standards generally have the character of a much larger breed. Miniatures tended to be treated more as lapdogs, though their temperament doesn't reflect this."

Lisa Lindfield (all three types of Mini): "Mini Wires are definitely the clowns of the breed. They are very happy, funny and bouncy. One of mine waves her paw, and a friend of mine has one that "smiles," which is hilarious!

"Mini Smooths are the most highly strung. They can sit for hours barking at the odd leaf dropping to the ground or the wind blowing. They are funny little things who definitely need company - either from humans or other pets. Mini Longs are very loving and quite laid back with sweet temperaments."

Hannah Norton (Standard and Mini Smooths): "I have 24 Dachshunds and all my dogs live in my home - no kennels, no crates, just free range! We have a big detached house, but don't have a huge garden, so I rent three acres of land - which they have all to themselves.

"I'd say they all vary so much in temperament. I have calm and collected dogs and some who act like toddlers! Some would rather spend their days snoozing on the sofa, whereas others want to be in the field for most of the day. My Standards have more of a "look at me" nature - almost as if they know how stunning they are, and are full of airs and graces.

"Mine bark if the doorbell goes. They make good watchdogs and have impeccable hearing. However, I am yet to see them protect their territory. They tend to welcome people and dogs into their home, rather than protect it!"

Watchdogs par excellence! Photo of one-year-old Hudson keeping an eye out at home, courtesy of Hannah.

Florida breeder Marianne McCullough (Mini Longs): "As a teenager I worked in a pet store and there was a Longhair Dachshund puppy for sale. Back then the Longhairs were not common; people thought he was "mixed" with something else, so he was there a long time. I felt bad for him because he was getting older and older.

"As I spent more time with him, I discovered how amazing he was. Even though I said I would never have a wiener dog, I discovered the reality of the amazing treasure they are as a breed. I took that little puppy home - and that was the start of it all, 38 years ago! They are the best dog breed ever."

Amazingly, Lisa Cole (Standard Longs) had an almost identical experience to Marianne's in the UK: "I was working at a kennels and one of the dogs that used to come to stay was a Long-Haired cream called Fudge who I fell in love with, even though he was totally blind.

"When I lost my fantastic Cocker Spaniel Belle, aged 13, my husband bought me a Standard shaded red Dachshund named Ruby, who is now 13 years old. I fell in love with her and have been hooked on the breed ever since.

"Mini Dachshunds are very popular. The Standard is not as desired; however, I feel they are a much better dog! They are incredibly loyal and keen to learn - with food! They love long walks through the woods or along the river bank. With super intelligence and a very loving nature, while often sleeping in the most uncomfortable positions, they are amazing dogs and a delight."

Big Personality

Melissa Sworab (Mini Longs): "Over the years, the biggest theme amongst Dachshund owners is how they didn't want a "little dog," but Dachshunds don't know they are little! They are a big dog with a big bark, just wrapped in a little package.

"They are mighty and stubborn and can occasionally raise your blood pressure, but lowering it is more their style. They can be cuddly yet still independent. A very versatile breed who can do almost anything: tracking/scent, field hunting, earth dog, dance, obedience (with some work), some agility, etc. They come in the most colors, patterns, coat types and sizes, so there's really a perfect one for nearly any household. They can be litterbox-trained and live in an apartment or run on an acre of fenced property. There's no other breed like them and they really do steal your heart!

"They love to chew, love to lick, and sleep in bed with you. A few think that if you eat it, they must eat it too and will take it right off your plate or cup. More than half will chase a wild animal and not look both ways before crossing a street. Occasionally, however, some are not interested in giving chase and would rather stay by your side, but they are few and far between.

"They love belly rubs. They think they are part cat and will climb up on arm rests and backs of couches and occasionally your shoulders if they can get there. They don't know they are small and will give chase to a dog several times their size. Some give chase to cars, and will need secure fencing.

"Miniature Longhairs are my first love. They are cuddly and sleep generally on top of the covers - and on top of their owners if they let them! Miniature Smooths can be a little more edgy and have a stronger prey drive. Miniature Wires are totally Terrier-like and love to be the clowns, and super rough-and-tumble and playful. The Standards are nearly a different breed.

"Dachshunds in any size and coat do great alone or with the opposite sex, but two neutered boys are great together as well. Having multiple girls can be problematic because, if they start to squabble like no other combination, they never forget."

Pauline Cheeseman (Mini Smooths): "I was attracted to the breed's unique look and the fact that they have a big personality. All mine have super loving temperaments. I only have bitches, and some can become ball-and-chase orientated. They are courageous, loyal companions."

Photo of Pauline's pups.

"I have seven grandchildren and I would place a puppy with a young family if I met the children and if they'd been taught to show respect for the puppy, for example leaving it alone when sleeping. If the family had a small, grabby toddler, I would advise them to maybe wait a bit longer."

Intelligent Hunters

Bastiaan Smit (Standard Wires): "Dachshunds have been in our family for over 20 years. They have a character all of their own, they are intelligent, curious hunters.

"Their attention span is limited, so when training you have to first get their attention and then get them interested. The dog should be relaxed, not excited, and you should be calm, structured and "pack leader" in your approach. Repeat, repeat, repeat and never lose your temper. Your Dachshund should obey you because he WANTS to, not because he has been forced to."

Stefanie Millington (Mini Longs): "I was fascinated by them from childhood; with their tenacity to flush and track small and even large game and their fearlessness. This, combined with their even temperament inside a family home, has always made them a favourite in a lot of German dog lovers' hearts." (Stef is German).

"Dachshunds are highly intelligent, but can be rather stubborn. They are not naturally obedient, but they know what they want and when they want it. Therefore, consistent and firm training from a very young age is important. And with positive re enforcement and rewards, obedience can be achieved. They make excellent guards; they are fiercely protective of their territory and family."

Brenna Carlisle, Heritage Hounds, (Standard Longs), Alabama: "My Doxies are so smart! But they can be extremely stubborn, they require a lot more patience than some breeds and owners need to be able to give them a job. Many owners forget that they are a working breed and not just lapdogs. They need something to get them focused.

"The typical temperament of my dogs is loving and goofy, and they have some big personalities. Wilbur is my six-year-old and he can open the baby gates in my house. But he also pretends he doesn't know what "kennel" means, until I get a cookie and actually show him the cookie to make him go in his crate while other dogs are out!

"I think Longhair Standards have the most loving, goofy temperament, then the Standard Smooths, then the Mini Longs. I find some of the Miniatures to be a little timid, but recently I have seen some Standards with that similar trait. Wires are harsher and much like a Terrier."

"Socialization is extremely important as dogs are social animals and they need to figure things out for themselves. It also helps animals gain confidence."

Children

Sandra Robertson (Mini Smooths): "Before deciding on the Miniature Dachshund, we spoke with many vets who told us they don't see Dachshunds visit them as often as many other breeds; they are quite resilient.

"We investigated breeds for over two years and discovered that the Miniature Dachshund met our expectations, not only for their nature and temperament, but also for being a nice size for children. We really needed to do our research, as we are foster carers for very vulnerable children. All our Minis pass health checks and temperament tests, which is a one-off visit lasting two or three hours by a local vet.

"He or she likes to see where the dog sleeps and eats and spends time playing with the dog - this will involve play fighting, playing tug of war, throwing toys and taking favourite toys or food away to

see how our dog reacts, as in many cases a small child will snatch a toy away from their pet. The vet also tests the dog's responses to commands, especially Stop! Down! and No!

"If we are looking for another dog, we do everything the vet does, spending a couple of hours with them to judge the puppy's and mother's nature and temperament. We check the health certificates, then most of all we look for a puppy that's had lots of love and attention, so they learn to give it back - and they are easier to train."

Photo: Best of friends. Sandra's grandson Charlie and Dark Princess Pryah.

Kristin Cihos William (Standard Smooths): "My Standard Smooths tend to be aloof with strangers who invade their space suddenly, yet can be very kind and outgoing with young children who approach with respect. I find it uncanny that my dogs can sense when someone is "off" in personality or intent.

"I love when families come to the dog shows and want to meet a Standard Smooth Dachshund in person, as I have several dogs who love to do meet and greet with the public - if there are treats involved! I have had both sizes of Dachshunds and all three coat varieties stay at my home or travel with me to shows. I find the Mini Smooths to be a bit more timid, which can lead to fear biting.

This portrait by Bettina Bienefeld beautifully illustrates the nobility of the Dachshund. This red Standard Smooth is CH Kinderteckel N Crazy Q Coppertone, aged 11 months, bred by Kristin.

"I am not sure if this is because their owners tend to pick them up and not let them down on the ground as much in new environments and situations, and even during exhibition. It may be a combination of both genetics and socialization. Early socialization and training are imperative with this breed."

Best Dogs Ever!

Pame Bates (Mini Longs): "Dachshunds are the best dogs ever! They are loveable and will take over your life - but in the best way. They adore their people.

"Whatever you do the first nights is forever with a Dachshund; if you let them sleep in your bed, you have made a lifetime commitment - but they also need their own dog bed or kennel. It is critical to socialize them, and training should be consistent - they respond to treats and praise."

"They love other dogs and do well with cats if around them from an early age. I have seen photos where Dachshunds are companions to lions, giraffes and other larger animals. No one told them they are short. As loud and ambitious as they can appear, they are cuddlers and very loving. They will also pick the softest, coziest spot and make a human squeeze in."

"Mine have to greet and greet again people in my home. Unless it is a well-known individual, they run over and bark to say "Hello." It sometimes startles those not used to it, we, on the other hand, love the cacophony of noise.

"They are hunters and a particular animal scent can send them off towards unknown areas chasing prey; leashes are important for safety. They will climb on tables and counters in search of food crumbs or your dinner - they are not discriminating, they are pirates!

"The older ones are less excitable, but give them some birds floating on a lake and they decide they will swim out to get them. We have all ours wear life vests at the lake because they are overly ambitious in the estimation of their swimming abilities! They will dive into the water after a ball or birds or each other. They love the competition of who is going to get the ball or bird first, barking all the way.

"'Unfettered' is the best way to describe these loveable and insane dogs. They will easily chase off larger predators without any sense and, if there are a couple of them, they do it with panache!"

8. Training a Dachshund

Training a young dog is not unlike bringing up a child. Put lots of time in early on to work towards a good mutual understanding and you'll be rewarded with a well-adjusted, sociable member of the family who you can take anywhere.

Some Dachshunds are more strong-willed and independent than others and energy levels vary, so training should be tailored to meet the needs of the individual dog. Dog trainer Lisa Cole has some tips on this in the next chapter.

A well-trained Dachshund doesn't magically appear overnight - it requires time and patience on your part. Dachshunds are super family dogs and companions, but let yours behave exactly how he or she wants and you could finish up with a stubborn, attention-seeking adult who rules YOU!

....

Dachshunds are highly motivated by rewards, particularly food. But you shouldn't discount the power of praise, as they are incredibly loyal to their owners and love your attention. This motivation is a big bonus when it comes to training.

Dachshunds are also hounds, and hounds are known for having an independent streak. This is because they have been selectively bred to use their initiative and work independently while hunting.

They are not like Border Collies, who are desperate to please their owners and need a job to do. With training, you have to persuade your Dachshund that what YOU want him to do is actually what HE wants to do, because good things will happen.

If you can get him interested, the Dachshund enjoys challenge, so keep training sessions fun, stimulating - and short. In **Chapter 11. Dachshund Activities,** three breeders talk about how much their Dachshunds enjoy the challenge of various competitions - and how this has improved their interest and receptiveness to training.

 Bear in mind that most Dachshunds are greedy little love machines and show-offs! So, give yours a chance to shine, praise and reward him often until the particular training task becomes ingrained.

Shouting, scolding or physical punishment will have the opposite effect. Dachshunds are sensitive and respond badly to rough or negative training methods. The secret of good training can be summed up in four words:

1. Consistency
2. Praise
3. Patience
4. Reward

 Police and service dogs are trained to a very high level with only a ball for reward. Don't always use treats with your Dachshund; praise or play time is often enough. Also, try getting your pup used to a small piece of carrot or apple as a healthy treat.

The Intelligence of Dogs

Psychologist and canine expert Dr Stanley Coren has written a book called *The Intelligence of Dogs* in which he ranks the breeds. He surveyed dog trainers to compile the list and used *Understanding of New Commands* and *Obeying First Command* as his standards of intelligence. He says there are three types of dog intelligence:

5. Adaptive Intelligence (learning and problem-solving ability). Specific to the individual dog and is measured by canine IQ tests

6. Instinctive Intelligence. Specific to the individual dog and is measured by canine IQ tests

7. Working/Obedience Intelligence. This is breed-dependent

He divides dogs into six groups and the brainboxes of the canine world are the 10 breeds ranked in the 'Brightest Dogs' section of his list. It will come as no surprise to anyone who has ever been into the countryside and seen sheep being worked by a farmer and his right-hand man (his dog) to learn that the Border Collie is the most intelligent of all dogs.

Number Two is the Poodle, followed by the German Shepherd, Golden Retriever, Doberman Pinscher, Shetland Sheepdog, Papillon, Rottweiler and Australian Cattle Dog. All dogs in this class:

8. Understand New Commands with Fewer than Five Repetitions

9. Obey a First Command 95% of the Time or Better

You will be disappointed to read that the Dachshund (no distinction between types) is ranked 92 out of 138 breeds. They are in the fourth group our of six: 'Average Working/Obedience Intelligence.' Understanding of new commands: 25 to 40 repetitions. Obey first command: 50% of the time or better. The full list can be seen here: https://en.wikipedia.org/wiki/The_Intelligence_of_Dogs

By the author's own admission, the drawback of this rating scale is that it is heavily weighted towards obedience-related behavioural traits, which are often found in working dogs, rather than understanding or creativity found in hunting dogs. As a result, some hounds and Terriers are ranked quite low on the list, due to their independent or stubborn nature.

Photo: Top of the class is Melissa Sworab's Rabows 4G Wireless "WiFi"

The ranking does not mean that Dachshunds are not intelligent — far from it. It does mean, however, that you you've got your work cut out when it comes to training!

....

Five Golden Rules

1. Training must be reward-based, not punishment based.

2. Keep sessions short or your dog will get bored.

3. Never train when you are in a rush or a bad mood.

4. Training after exercise is fine, but never train when your dog is exhausted.

5. Keep sessions fun

Energetic, stubborn or independent Dachshunds may try to push the boundaries when they reach adolescence – any time between six months and two years old. They may start behaving badly, and some males may start "marking" or urinating in the house, even when they are housetrained. In all cases, go back to basics and put the time in – sadly, there is no quick fix.

You need to be firm with a strong-willed or stubborn dog, but all training should still be carried out using positive techniques.

 Establishing the natural order of things is not something forced on a dog through shouting or violence; it is brought about by mutual consent and good training.

Dogs are happiest and behave best when they are familiar and comfortable with their place in the household. If you have adopted an older dog, you can still train him, but it will take a little longer to get rid of bad habits and instil good manners. Patience and persistence are the keys here.

Socialisation is a very important aspect of training. A good breeder will have already begun this process with the litter and then it's up to you to keep it going when puppy arrives home. Young pups can absorb a great deal of information, but they are also vulnerable to bad experiences.

They need exposing – in a positive manner - to different people, other animals and situations. If not, they can find them very frightening when they do finally encounter them later. They may react by cowering, urinating, barking, growling or even snapping.

If they have a lot of good experiences with other people, places, noises, situations and animals before four or five months old, they are less likely to either be timid or nervous or try to establish dominance later. Don't just leave your dog at home in the early days, take him out and about with you, get him used to new people, places and noises. Dogs that miss out on being socialised can pay the price later.

All pups are chewers. If you are not careful, some young pups and adolescents will chew through anything – wires, phone chargers, remote controls, bedding, rugs, etc. Young dogs are not infrequent visitors to veterinary clinics to have *"foreign objects"* removed from their stomachs. Train your young pup only to chew the things you give – so don't give him your old slippers, an old piece of carpet or anything that resembles something you don't want him to chew, he won't know the difference between the old and the new. Buy purpose-made long-lasting chew toys.

A puppy class is one of the best ways of getting a pup used to being socialised and trained. This should be backed up by short sessions of a few minutes of training a day back home.

 Some Dachshund puppies, especially those with a lot of working instinct, can be "mouthy." Do not give your young pup too much attention, and choose training times when he is relaxed, perhaps slightly tired, but not exhausted.

Dachshunds are a good choice for first-time dog owners, and anybody prepared to put in a fair bit of time can train one. If you do need some professional one-on-one help (for you and the dog), choose a trainer registered with the Association of Professional Dog Trainers (APDT) or other positive method organisation, as the old Alpha-dominance theories have gone out the window.

17 Training Tips

10. **Start training and socialising straight away.** Like babies, puppies learn quickly and it's this learned behaviour that stays with them through adult life. Start with just a few minutes a day a couple of days after arriving home.

11. **Your voice is a very important training tool.** Your dog has to learn to understand your language and you have to understand him. Commands should be issued in a calm, authoritative voice - not shouted. Praise should be given in a happy, encouraging voice, accompanied by stroking or patting. If your dog has done something wrong, use a stern voice, not a harsh shriek. This applies even if your Dachshund is unresponsive at the beginning.

12. **Avoid giving your dog commands you know you can't enforce.** Every time you give a command you don't enforce, he learns that commands are optional. One command equals one response. Give your dog only one command - twice maximum - then gently enforce it. Repeating commands will make him tune out, and teach him that the first few commands are a bluff. Telling your dog to *"SIT, SIT, SIT, SIT!!!"* is neither efficient nor effective. Say a single *"SIT,"* gently place him in the Sit position and praise him.

13. **Train your dog gently and humanely.** Dachshunds are sensitive by nature and do not respond well to being shouted at or hit.

14. Keep training sessions short and upbeat. If obedience training is a bit of a bore, pep things up a bit by *"play training"* by using constructive, non-adversarial games.

15. **Do not try to dominate your dog.** Training should be mutual, i.e. your dog should do something because he WANTS to do it and he knows that you want him to do it. Dachshunds are not interested in dominating you – although they might try and push the boundaries.

16. **Begin training at home around the house and garden/yard.** How well your dog responds at home affects his behaviour away from the home. If he doesn't respond well at home, he certainly won't respond any better out and about where there are 101 distractions, e.g. interesting scents, people, food scraps, other dogs and small animals or birds.

17. **Mealtimes are a great time to start training.** Teach Sit and Stay at breakfast and dinner, rather than just putting the dish down and letting him dash over immediately.

18. **Use his name often and in a positive manner** so he gets used to the sound of it. He won't know what it means at first, but it won't take long before he realises you're talking to him.

19. **DON'T use his name when reprimanding, warning or punishing.** He should trust that when he hears his name, good things happen. He should always respond to his name with enthusiasm, never hesitancy or fear. Use words such as *"No," "Ack!"* or *"Bad Boy/Girl"* in a stern (not shouted) voice instead. Some parents prefer not to use "No" with their dog, as they use it so often around the kids that it can confuse the pup! When a puppy is corrected

by his mother, e.g. – if he bites her – she growls to warn him not to do it again. Using a short sharp sound like **"Ack!"** can work surprisingly well; it does for us.

20. **Don't give your dog lots of attention (even negative attention) when he misbehaves.** Dachshunds love attention and if yours gets lots when he's naughty, you are inadvertently reinforcing bad behaviour.

21. **Timing is critical.** When your puppy does something right, praise him immediately. If you wait a while, he will have no idea what he has done right. Similarly, when he does something wrong, correct him straight away.

22. **If he has an "accident" in the house, don't shout or rub his nose in it; it will have the opposite effect with a Dachshund.** He may start hiding and peeing or pooping behind the couch or other inappropriate places. **If you catch him in the act**, use your **"No!"** or **"Ack!"** sound and immediately carry him out of the house. Then back to basics with housetraining. If you find something but don't catch him in the act, ignore it. If your pup is constantly eliminating indoors, you are not keeping a close enough eye on him.

23. **In the beginning, give your dog attention when YOU want to – not when he wants it.** When you are training, give your puppy lots of positive attention when he is good. But if he starts jumping up, nudging you constantly or barking to demand your attention, ignore him. Wait a while and pat him when you are ready and AFTER he has stopped demanding your attention.

24. **You can give Dachshunds TOO MUCH attention in the beginning.** This may create a rod for your own back when they grow into needy adults that are over-reliant on you. They may even develop Separation Anxiety, which is stressful for both dog AND owner.

25. **Start as you mean to go on.** In terms of training, treat your cute little pup as though he were fully-grown. Introduce the rules you want him to live by as an adult.

26. **Make sure that everybody in the household sticks to the same set of rules.** If the kids lift him on to the couch or bed and you forbid it, your dog won't know what is allowed and what isn't.

Teaching Basic Commands

The Three Ds

The three Ds – **Distance, Duration** and **Distraction** – are the cornerstone of a good training technique.

Duration is the length of time your dog remains in the command.

Distance is how far you can walk away without your dog breaking the command.

Distraction is the number of external stimuli - such as noise, scents, people, other animals, etc. - your dog can tolerate before breaking the command.

Only increase one of the Three Ds at a time. For example, if your new pup has just learned to sit on command, gradually increase the time by a second or two as you go along. Moving away from the dog or letting the kids or the cat into the room would increase the Distance or Distraction level and make the command too difficult for your pup to hold.

If you are teaching the Stay, gradually increase EITHER the distance OR the time he is in the Stay position; don't increase both at once. Start off by training your dog in your home before moving into the garden or yard where there are more distractions - even if it is quiet and you are alone, outdoor scents and sights will be a big distraction for a young dog. Once you have mastered the commands in a home environment, progress to the park.

 Implement the Three Ds progressively and slowly, and don't expect too much too soon. Work within your dog's capabilities, move forward one tiny step at a time and thereby set your dog up to consistently SUCCEED, not fail.

The Sit

Teaching the Sit command to your Dachshund is relatively easy. Teaching a young pup to sit still for any length of time is a bit more difficult! If your little protégé is very distracted or high energy, it may be easier to put him on a lead (leash) to hold his attention. Stand facing each other and hold a treat between your thumb and fingers just an inch or so above his head and let him sniff it.

Don't let your fingers and the treat get much further away or you might have trouble getting him to move his body into a sitting position. In fact, if your dog jumps up when you try to guide him into the Sit, you're probably holding your hand too far away from his nose. If your dog backs up, you can practise with a wall behind him.

As he reaches up to sniff it, move the treat upwards and back over the dog towards his tail at the same time as saying *"Sit."* Most dogs will track the treat with their eyes and follow it with their noses, causing their noses to point straight up.

As his head moves up toward the treat, his rear end should automatically go down towards the floor. TaDa! (drum roll!).

The second he sits, say *"Yes!"*. Give him the treat and tell your dog he's a good boy/girl. Stroke and praise him for as long as he stays in the sitting position. If he jumps up on his back legs and paws you while you are moving the treat, be patient and start all over again. At this stage, don't expect your bouncy little pupil to sit for more than a nanosecond!

NOTE: For positive reinforcement, use the words *Yes! Good Boy!* or *Good Girl!*

Another method is to put one hand on his chest and with your other hand, gently push down on his rear end until he is sitting, while saying *"Sit."* Give him a treat and praise; even though you have made him do it, he will eventually associate the position with the word "sit."

Once your dog catches on, leave the treat in your pocket (or have it in your other hand). Repeat the sequence, but this time your dog will just follow your empty hand. Say *"Sit"* and bring your empty hand in front of your dog's nose, holding your fingers as if you had a treat. Move your hand exactly as you did when you held the treat. When your dog sits, say *"Yes!"* and then give him a treat from your other hand or your pocket.

Gradually lessen the amount of movement with your hand. First, say *"Sit"* then hold your hand eight to 10 inches above your dog's face and wait a moment. Most likely, he will sit. If he doesn't, help him by moving your hand back over his head, like you did before, but make a smaller movement this time. Then try again. Your goal is to eventually just say *"Sit"* without having to move or extend your hand at all.

Once your dog reliably sits on cue, you can ask him to sit whenever you meet and people (it may not work straight away, but it might help to calm him down a bit). The key is anticipation. Give your dog the cue before he gets too excited to hear you and before he starts jumping up on the person just arrived. Generously reward him the instant he sits. Say *"Yes"* and give treats/praise every few seconds while he holds the Sit. Dog trainer Lisa Cole has more advice on this in the next chapter.

....

The Stay

This is a very useful command, but it's not so easy to teach a lively and distracted young Dachshund pup to stay still for any length of time. Here is a simple method to get your dog to stay; if you are training a young dog, don't ask him to stay for more than a few seconds at the beginning.

This requires concentration from your dog, so pick a time when he's relaxed and well exercised, or just after a game or mealtimes – but not too exhausted to concentrate.

1. Tell your dog to sit or lie down, but instead of giving a treat as soon as he hits the floor, hold off for one second. Then say *"Yes!"* in an enthusiastic voice and give him a treat. If your dog bounces up again instantly, have two treats ready. Feed one right away, before he has time to move; then say *"Yes!"* and feed the second treat.

2. You need a release word or phrase. It might be *"Free!"* or *"Here!"* or a word that you only use to release your dog from this command. Once you've given the treat, immediately give your release cue and encourage your dog to get up. Then repeat the exercise, a few times gradually waiting a tiny bit longer before releasing the treat. (You can delay the first treat for a moment if your dog bounces up).

3. A common mistake is to hold the treat high and then give the reward slowly. As your dog doesn't know the command yet, he sees the treat coming and gets up to meet the food. Instead, bring the treat toward your dog quickly – the best place to deliver it is right between his front paws. If you're working on a Sit-Stay, give the treat at chest height.

4. When your dog can stay for several seconds, start to add a little distance. At first, you'll walk backwards, because your dog is more likely to get up to follow you if you turn away from him. Take one single step away, then step back towards your dog and say *"Yes!"* and give the treat. Give him the signal to get up immediately, even if five seconds haven't passed.

5. Remember **DISTANCE, DURATION, DISTRACTION.** For best success in teaching a Stay, work on one factor at a time. Whenever you make one factor more difficult, such as distance, ease up on the others, then build them back up. So, when you take that first step back from your dog, adding distance, cut the duration of the stay.

6. Once he's mastered the Stay with you alone, move the training on so that he learns to do the same with distractions. Have someone walk into the room, or squeak a toy or bounce a ball once. A rock-solid stay is mostly a matter of working slowly and patiently to start with. Don't go too fast. If he does get up, take a breather and then give him a short refresher, starting at a point easier than whatever you were working on when he cracked.

If you think he's tired or had enough, leave it for the day and come back later – just finish off on a positive note by giving one very easy command you know he will obey, followed by a reward.

Don't use the Stay command in situations where it is unpleasant for your dog. For instance, avoid telling him to stay as you close the door behind you on your way to work. Finally, don't use Stay to keep a dog in a scary situation.

....

Down

There are a number of different ways to teach this command, which here means for the dog to lie down. (If you are teaching this command, then use the *"Off"* command to teach your dog not to jump up). This does not come naturally to a young pup, so it may take a little while to master the Down command.

Don't make it a battle of wills and, although you may gently push him down, don't physically force him down against his will. This will be seen as you asserting dominance in an aggressive manner and your Dachshund will not like it.

1. Give the Sit command.

2. When your dog sits, don't give him the treat immediately, but keep it in your closed hand. Slowly move your hand straight down toward the floor, between his front legs. As your dog's nose follows the treat, just like a magnet, his head will bend all the way down to the floor.

3. When the treat is on the floor between your dog's paws, start to move it away from him, like you're drawing a line along the floor. (The entire luring motion forms an L-shape).

4. At the same time say *"Down"* in a firm manner.

5. To continue to follow the treat, your dog will probably ease himself into the Down position. The instant his elbows touch the floor, say *"Yes!"* and immediately let him eat the treat. If your dog doesn't automatically stand up after eating the treat, just move a step or two away to encourage him to move out of the Down position. Then repeat the sequence above several times. Aim for two short sessions of five minutes per day.

If your dog's back end pops up when you try to lure him into a Down, quickly snatch the treat away. Then immediately ask your dog to sit and try again. It may help to let your dog nibble on the treat as you move it toward the floor. If you've tried to lure your dog into a Down, but he still seems confused or reluctant, try this trick:

1. Sit down on the floor with your legs straight out in front of you. Your dog should be at your side. Keeping your legs together and your feet on the floor, bend your knees to make a 'tent' shape.

2. Hold a treat right in front of your dog's nose. As he licks and sniffs the treat, slowly move it down to the floor and then underneath your legs. Continue to lure him until he has to crouch down to keep following the treat.

3. The instant his belly touches the floor, say *"Yes!"* and let him eat the treat. If your dog seems nervous about following the treat under your legs, make a trail of treats for him to eat along the way.

Some dogs find it easier to follow a treat into the Down from a standing position.

- 🐾 Hold the treat right in front of your dog's nose, and then slowly move it straight down to the floor, right between his front paws. His nose will follow the treat

- 🐾 If you let him lick the treat as you continue to hold it still on the floor, your dog will probably plop into the Down position

- 🐾 The moment he does, say *"Yes!"* and let him eat the treat (some dogs are reluctant to lie on a cold, hard surface. It may be easier to teach yours to lie down on a carpet). The next step is to introduce a hand signal. You'll still reward him with treats, though, so keep them nearby or hidden behind your back.

1. Start with your dog in a Sit.

2. Say *"Down."*

3. Without a treat in your fingers, use the same hand motion you did before.

Photo of the beautifully-trained GCHB Kenmar's Force Awakens "Sky" aged three, courtesy of Marianne McCullough, Kenmar Hounds, Florida.

4. As soon as your dog's elbows touch the floor, say *"Yes!"* and immediately get a treat to give him. Important: Even though you're not using a treat to lure your dog into position, you must still give him a reward when he lies down. You want your dog to learn that he doesn't have to see a treat to get one.

5. Clap your hands or take a few steps away to encourage him to stand up. Then repeat the sequence from the beginning several times for a week or two. When your dog readily lies down as soon as you say the cue and use your new hand signal, you're ready for the next step. To stop bending all the way down to the floor every time, you can gradually shrink the signal to a smaller movement. To make sure your dog continues to understand what you want him to do, progress slowly.

6. Repeat the hand signal, but instead of moving your hand all the way to the floor, move it ALMOST all the way down. Stop when it's an inch or two above the floor. Practise the Down for a day or two, using this slightly smaller hand signal. Then you can make your movement an inch or two smaller, stopping your hand three or four inches above the floor.

7. After practising for another couple of days, shrink the signal again. As you continue to gradually stop your hand signal farther and farther from the floor, you'll bend over less and less. Eventually, you won't have to bend over at all. You'll be able to stand up straight, say *"Down,"* and then just point to the floor.

Your next job is a bit harder - it's to practise your dog's new skill in many different situations and locations. Start in calm places at first, like different rooms in your house or your garden/yard when there's no one around. Then increase the distractions; so, do some sessions at home when family members are moving around, on walks and then at friends' houses, too.

Basic Recall

This basic command is perhaps the most important of all and one that you can teach right from the beginning. You are limiting both your lives if your dog won't come back to you. A dog who obeys the recall enjoys freedoms that other dogs cannot. Dachshunds love to run free, but don't allow that until he has learned some recall. Trainer Lisa Cole has more in-depth advice in the next chapter for owners of Dachshunds that love to chase.

Tip Whether you have a puppy or an older dog, the first step is always to establish that coming to you is the BEST thing he can do. Any time your dog comes to you - whether you've called him or not - acknowledge that you appreciate it with praise, affection, play or treats. This consistent reinforcement ensures that your dog will continue to "check in" with you frequently.

1. Start off a short distance away from your dog.

2. Say your dog's name followed by the command *"Come!"* in an enthusiastic voice. You'll usually be more successful if you walk or run away from him while you call. Dogs find it hard to resist chasing after a running person, especially their owner.

3. He should run towards you!

4. A young dog will often start running towards you but then get distracted and head off in another direction. Pre-empt this situation by praising your puppy and cheering him on when he starts to come to you and **before** he has a chance to get distracted.

   Your praise will keep him focused so that he'll be more likely to come all the way to you. If he stops or turns away, you can give him feedback by saying *"Oh-oh!"* or *"Hey!"* in a different tone of voice (displeased or unpleasantly surprised). When he looks at you again, smile, call him and praise him as he approaches you.

5. When your puppy comes to you, give him the treat BEFORE he sits down or he may think that the treat was earned for sitting, not coming to you.

6. Another method is to use two people. You hold the treats and let your dog sniff them while the accomplice holds on to the dog by his harness. When you are about 10 or 15 yards away, get your helper to let the dog go, and once he is running towards you, say *"COME!"* loudly and enthusiastically. When he reaches you, stop, bend down and make a fuss of him before giving a treat. Do this several times. The next step is to give the Come command just BEFORE you get your helper to release the dog, and by doing this repetitively, the dog begins to associate the command with the action.

Tip "Come" or a similar word is better than "Here" if you intend using the "Heel" command, as "Here" and "Heel" sound very similar.

Progress your dog's training in baby steps. If he's learned to come when called in your kitchen, you can't expect him to do it straight away at the park, in the woods or on the beach when surrounded by distractions. When you first use the recall outdoors, make sure there's no one around to distract your dog. It's a good idea to consider using a long training lead - or to do the training within a safe, fenced area. Only when your dog has mastered the recall in a number of locations and in the face of various distractions can you expect him to come to you regularly.

Collar, Harness and Lead (Leash) Training

You have to train your dog to get used to a collar and lead (leash) and a harness if you decide to use one, then teach him to walk nicely beside you. This can be challenging with young Dachshunds, who don't necessarily want to walk at the same pace as you - some might even slump to the ground and refuse to move in the beginning!

All dogs will pull on a lead initially. It's not because they want to show you who's boss, it's simply that they are excited to be out and are forging ahead. Teaching a Dachshund NOT to pull on a lead is time well spent, as it will reduce strain on his back when out on walks.

Another option is to start your dog on a small lightweight collar and then change to a harness once he has learned some lead etiquette. Some dogs don't mind collars, some will try to fight them, while others will lie on the floor! You need to be patient and calm and proceed at a pace comfortable to him; don't fight your dog and don't force the collar on.

1. Start your puppy off with a small, lightweight collar, - not one he is going to grow into. You can buy one with clips to start with, just put it on and clip it together, rather than fiddling with buckles, which can be scary when he's wearing a collar for the first time. Stick to the principle of positive reward-based training and give a treat or praise once the collar is on, not after you have taken it off. Then gradually increase the length of time you leave the collar on.

 If you leave your dog in a crate, or leave him alone in the house, take off the collar and tags. He is not used to it and it may get caught, causing panic or injury.

2. Put the collar on when there are other things that will occupy him, like when he is going outside to be with you, or in the home when you are interacting with him. Or put it on at mealtimes or when you are doing some basic training. Don't put the collar on too tight, you want him to forget it's there; **you should be able to get two fingers underneath.**

   Some pups may react as if you've hung a two-ton weight around their necks, while others will be more compliant. If yours scratches the collar, get his attention by encouraging him to follow you or play with a toy to forget the irritation.

3. Once your puppy is happy wearing the collar, introduce the lead. Many owners prefer an extending or retractable lead for their Dachshund, but consider a fixed-length one to start training him to walk close to you. Begin in the house or garden; don't try to go out and about straight away.

Think of the lead as a safety device to stop him running off, not something to drag him around with. You want a dog that doesn't pull, so don't start by pulling him around.

4. Attach the lead and give him a treat while you put it on. Use the treats (instead of pulling on the lead) to lure him beside you, so that he gets used to walking with the collar and lead on. You can also make good use of toys to do exactly the same thing - especially if your dog has a favourite. Walk around the house with the lead on and lure him forwards with the toy.

It might feel a bit odd but it's a good way for your pup to develop a positive relationship with the collar and lead with the minimum of fuss. Act as though it's the most natural thing in the world for you to walk around the house with your dog on a lead – and just hope the neighbours aren't watching!

Some dogs react the moment you attach the lead and they feel some tension on it – a bit like when a horse is being broken for the first time. Drop the lead and allow him to run around the house or yard, dragging it behind, but be careful he doesn't get tangled and hurt himself. Try to make him forget about it by playing or starting a short fun training routine with treats, which are a huge distraction for most young dogs. While he is concentrating on the new task, occasionally pick up the lead and call him to you. Do it gently and in an encouraging tone.

5. **Don't yank on the lead.** If it gets tight, just lure him back beside you with a treat or a toy. Remember to keep the hand holding the treat or toy down, so your dog doesn't get the habit of jumping up at you. If you feel he is getting stressed, try putting treats along the route you'll be taking to turn this into a rewarding game: good times are ahead... and he learns to focus on what's ahead of him with curiosity, not fear.

 Take collar and lead training slowly. Let him gain confidence in you, the lead and himself. Some dogs sit and decide not to move! If this happens, walk a few steps away, go down on one knee and encourage him to come to you, then walk off again.

For some pups, the collar and lead can be restricting and they will react with resistance. Some dogs are perfectly happy to walk alongside you off-lead, but behave differently when they have one on. Others may become more aggressive on a lead once they gain their confidence when their *Fight-or-Flight* instinct kicks in. Again, there is further advice on this in the next chapter.

Proceed in tiny steps if that is what your puppy is happy with, don't over face him, but stick at it if you are met with resistance.

Walking on a Lead (Leash)

There are different methods, but we have found the following one to be successful for quick results. Initially, the lead should be kept fairly loose. Have a treat in your hand as you walk, it will encourage your dog to sniff the treat as he walks alongside. He should not pull ahead as he will want to remain near the treat.

Give the command *"Walk"* or *"Heel"* and then proceed with the treat in your hand, keep giving him a treat every few steps initially, then gradually extend the time between treats. Eventually, you

should be able to walk with your hand comfortably at your side, periodically (every minute or so) reaching into your pocket to grab a treat to reward your dog.

If your dog starts pulling ahead, first give him a warning, by saying *"No"* or *"Steady"* or a similar command. If he slows down, give him a treat. But if he continues to pull ahead so that your arm becomes fully extended, stop walking and ignore your dog. Wait for him to stop pulling and to look up at you. At this point reward him for good behaviour before carrying on your walk.

If your pup refuses to budge, DON'T drag him. This will ultimately achieve nothing as he will learn to resent the lead. Coax him along with praise and, if necessary, treats so that when he moves forward with you, it is because HE wants to and not because he has been dragged by somebody several times bigger.

Be sure to quickly reward your dog any time he doesn't pull and walks with you with the lead slack. If you have a lively young pup who is dashing all over the place on the lead, try starting training when he is already a little tired, after a play or exercise session – but not exhausted.

Another method is what dog trainer Victoria Stillwell describes as the **"Reverse Direction Technique."** When your dog pulls, say **"Let's Go!"** in an encouraging manner, then turn away from him and walk off in the other direction, without jerking on the lead. When he is following you and the lead is slack, turn back and continue on your original way.

It may take a few repetitions, but your words and body language will make it clear that pulling will not get your dog anywhere, whereas walking calmly by your side - or even slightly in front of you - on a loose lead will get him where he wants to go.

There is an excellent video (in front of her beautiful house!) which shows Victoria demonstrating this technique and highlights just how easy it is with a dog that's keen to please. It only lasts three minutes: https://positively.com/dog-behavior/basic-cues/loose-leash-walking

 **With patience and training, your puppy will learn to walk nicely on a lead; it is a question of when, not if!**

Harnesses

Harnesses take the pressure away from the dog's sensitive neck area and distribute it more evenly around the body. Many breeders recommend them and lots of owners prefer them. However, Dachshund Breed Council research found that dogs over the age of three that were exercised in harnesses were 2.3 times more likely to have suffered an IVDD incident, compared with those exercised in collars.

There is **no evidence** that harnesses caused the problems. It could be that owners preferred harnesses to collars following the injury; more research is needed. Certainly, harnesses ARE a good idea if your dog has had a neck injury such as Cervical IVDD. There are several different options:

- **Front-clip or training harness -** this has a lead attachment in front of the harness at the centre of your dog's chest. Dog trainers often choose this type as it helps to discourage your dog from pulling on the lead by turning him around

- **Back-clip –** this is generally the easiest for most dogs to get used to and useful for small dogs with delicate throats that are easily irritated by collars. This type is for calm dogs or ones that have already been trained not to pull on the lead

- **Comfort wrap or step-in harness -** lay the harness on the ground, have your dog step in, pull the harness up and around his shoulders and then clip him in; simple!

- **Soft or vest harness** - typically made of mesh and comes in a range of colours and patterns. Some slip over the head and some can be stepped into

- **No-pull harness** - similar to a training harness, designed to help discourage your dog from pulling. The lead attachment ring is at the centre of the dog's chest and the harness tightens pressure if the dog pulls, encouraging him to stay closer to you. Some styles also tighten around the dog's legs

- **Auto or car harness** - these are designed for car travel and have an attachment that hooks into a seat belt

When choosing a harness, decide what its primary purpose will be – is it instead of or in addition to a collar? Do you need one that will help to train your dog, or will a back-clip harness do the job?

You want to make sure that it is a snug fit, and if it's a front clip, that it hangs high on your dog's chest. If it dangles too low, it can't help control forward momentum. Make sure the harness isn't too tight or too difficult to get on. It shouldn't rub under your dog's armpits or anywhere else. If possible, take your dog to try on a few options before buying one for the first time.

 If you've never used a harness before, it's easy to get tangled up while your pup is bouncing around, excited at the prospect of a walk. It's a good idea to have a few "dry runs" without the dog!

Lay the harness on the floor and familiarise yourself with it. Learn which bits the legs go through, which parts fit where and how it clicks together once the dog is in. If you can train your Dachshund to step into the harness, then even better...!

Dealing with Common Problems

Puppy Biting and Chewing

All puppies spend a great deal of time chewing, playing, and investigating objects. And it's natural for them to explore the world with their mouths and needle-sharp teeth. When puppies play with people, they often bite, chew, nip and mouthe on people's hands, limbs and clothing. Play biting is normal for puppies; they do it all the time with their littermates. They also bite moving targets with their sharp teeth; it's a great game.

FACT › Most dogs originally bred to work, like the Dachshund, are mouthy as pups.

But when they arrive in your home, they have to be taught that human skin is sensitive and body parts are not suitable biting material. Biting is not acceptable, not even from a puppy, and can be a real problem initially, especially if you have children.

When your puppy bites you or the kids, he is playing and investigating; he is NOT being aggressive. A lively young pup can easily get carried away with energy and excitement.

Puppy biting should be dealt with from the get-go. Every time you have a play session, have a soft toy nearby and when he starts to chew your hand or feet, clench your fingers (or toes!) to make it more difficult and distract him with a soft toy in your other hand.

Keep the game interesting by moving the toy around or rolling it around in front of him. (He may be too young to fetch it back if you throw it). He may continue to chew you, but will eventually realise that the toy is far more interesting and livelier than your boring hand.

If he becomes over-excited and too aggressive with the toy, if he growls a lot, stop playing and walk away. When you walk away, don't say anything or make eye or physical contact with your puppy. Simply ignore him, this is usually extremely effective and often works within a few days.

If your pup is more persistent and tries to bite your legs as you walk away, thinking this is another fantastic game, stand still and ignore him. If he still persists, say *"No!"* in a very stern voice, then praise him when he lets go. If you have to physically remove him from your trouser leg or shoe, leave him alone in the room for a while and ignore all demands for your attention.

 Try not to put your pup in a crate when he is being naughty, or he will associate the crate with punishment. Remove yourself or the pup from the room instead - or put him in a pen. Wait until he has stopped being naughty before you put him in his crate.

Although you might find it quite cute and funny if your puppy bites your fingers or toes, it should be discouraged at all costs. You don't want biting and nipping to get out of hand; as an adolescent or adult dog, he could inadvertently cause real injury, especially to children.

Here are some tips to deal with puppy biting:

- Puppies growl and bite more when they are excited. Don't allow things to escalate, so remove your pup from the situation before he gets too excited by putting him in a crate or pen

- Don't put your hand or finger into your pup's mouth to nibble on; this promotes puppy biting

- Limit your children's play time with pup - and always supervise the sessions in the beginning. Teach them to gently play with and stroke your puppy, not to wind him up

- Don't let the kids (or adults) run around the house with the puppy chasing – this is an open invitation to nip at the ankles

- If your puppy does bite, remove him from the situation and people – never smack him

Dachshunds are very affectionate and another tried and tested method is to make a sharp cry of "OUCH!" when your pup bites your hand – even when it doesn't hurt.

This has worked very well for us. Most pups will jump back in amazement, surprised to have hurt you. Divert your attention from your puppy to your hand. He will probably try to get your attention or lick you as a way of saying sorry. Praise him for stopping biting and continue with the game. If he bites you again, repeat the process. A sensitive dog should stop biting you.

You may also think about keeping special toys you use to play with your puppy separate from other toys he chews alone. That way he can associate certain toys with having fun with you and may work harder to please you. Dachshunds are playful and you can use this to your advantage by teaching your dog how to play nicely with you and the toy, and then by using play time as a reward for good behaviour.

As well as biting, puppies also chew, chewing is that it is a normal part of the teething process. Some adolescent and adult dogs chew because they are bored - usually due to lack of exercise and/or mental stimulation. If puppy chewing is a problem it is because your pup is chewing on something you don't want him to.

So, the trick is to keep him, his mouth and sharp little teeth occupied with something he CAN chew on, such as a durable toy – see **Chapter 4. Bringing Puppy Home** for more information.

 Photo: Playing with his favourite toy is this handsome puppy from Lisa Lindfield, Zabannah Dachshunds, Cambridgeshire, UK.

You might also consider freezing peanut butter and/or a liquid inside a Kong toy. Put the Kong into a mug, plug the small end with peanut butter and fill it with gravy before putting it into the freezer. (Check it doesn't contain the sweetener xylitol as this is harmful to dogs). Don't leave the Kong and your Dachshund on your precious Oriental rug! This will keep your pup occupied for quite a long time.

It is also worth giving the dog a frozen Kong or Lickimat when you leave the house if your dog suffers from Separation Anxiety. There are lots of doggie recipes for Kongs and other treats online.

Excessive Barking

Dachshunds are hounds and there's no getting away from the fact that they are vocal - with a whine or scream that cuts right through you! If you want a dog that hardly barks, consider a Bulldog or a Greyhound.

You DO want your Dachshund to bark. He will alert you to approaching strangers or potential dangers before you have heard a thing. The trick is to get him to bark at the right times and then to stop, as incessant barking will drive you and your neighbours nuts.

Dogs, especially youngsters, sometimes behave in ways you might not want them to until they learn that this type of unwanted behaviour doesn't earn any rewards. Young Dachshunds can become overly-fond of the sound of their own voices - until they learn that when they stop their indiscriminate barking, good things happen, such as treats, praise, a game.

 The problem often develops during adolescence when a dog becomes more confident. Also, puppies teethe until about seven or eight months of age, so make sure yours has hardy chews, and perhaps a bone with supervision, to keep him occupied and gnawing. Give these when he's quiet, not when he is barking.

Is your dog getting enough exercise and mental stimulation? Barking can be a way of letting off steam. Or he may be lonely, bored, attention-seeking, possessive or over-protective.

Sometimes it is the Dachshund's alert system going into overdrive. Is he barking at people he can see through the window or coming to the door? You want an alert bark, but not a constant bark.

Your behaviour can also encourage excessive barking. If your dog barks his head off and you give him a treat to quieten down, he associates his barking with getting a nice treat.

 Tone of voice is very important. Do not use a high-pitched or semi-hysterical STOP!! or NO!! Use low, firm commands.

One method is to set up a situation where you know he is going to bark, such as somebody arriving at your house, and put him on a lead beforehand. When he has barked several times, give a short, sharp tug on the lead and the **"Quiet"** command - spoken, not shouted. Reward him when he **stops** barking, not before.

If he's barking to get your attention, ignore him. If that doesn't work, leave the room and don't allow him to follow, so you deprive him of your attention. Do this as well if his barking and attention-seeking turns to nipping. Tell him to **"Stop"** in a firm voice, or use the **"ACK!"** sound, remove your hand or leg and, if necessary, leave the room.

FACT ❯ As humans, we use our voice in many different ways: to express happiness or anger, to scold, to shout a warning, and so on. Dogs are the same; different barks and whines give out different messages.

LISTEN to your dog and try and get an understanding of Dachshund language. Learn to recognise the difference between an alert bark, an excited bark, a demanding bark, a fearful, high pitched bark, an aggressive bark or a plain *"I'm barking 'coz I can bark"* bark!

Speak and Shush!

The Speak and Shush technique teaches your dog or puppy to bark and be quiet on command. When your dog barks at an arrival at your house, gently praise him after the first few barks. If he persists, tell him **"Quiet."**

Get a friend to stand outside your front door and say **"Speak"** or **"Alert."** This is the cue for your accomplice to knock on the door or ring the bell – don't worry if you both feel like idiots, it will be worth the embarrassment!

When your dog barks, say **"Speak"** and praise him profusely. After a few good barks, say **"Shush"** or **"Quiet"** and then dangle a tasty treat in front of his nose. If he is food-motivated, he will stop barking as soon as he sniffs the treat, because it is **physically impossible for a dog to sniff and woof at the same time.**

Praise your dog again as he sniffs quietly and give him the treat. Repeat this routine a few times a day and your Dachshund will quickly learn to bark whenever the doorbell rings and you ask him to **"Speak."** Eventually your dog will bark AFTER your request but BEFORE the doorbell rings, meaning he has learned to bark on command. Even better, he will learn to anticipate the likelihood of getting a treat following your **"Shush"** request and will also be quiet on command.

With Speak and Shush training, progressively increase the length of required shush time before offering a treat - at first just a couple of seconds, then three, five, 10, 20, and so on. By alternating instructions to speak and shush, the dog is praised and rewarded for barking on request and also for stopping barking on request.

In the unlikely event that you have a Dachshund that is silent when somebody approached the house, you can use the following method to get him to bark on the command of **"Speak."** This is also a useful command to teach if you walk your dog alone, especially at night; the Dachshund's surprisingly loud and deep bark will help keep you safe:

1. Have some treats at the ready, waiting for that rare bark.

2. Wait until he barks - for whatever reason - then say **"Speak"** or whatever word you want to use.

3. Praise him and give a treat. At this stage, he won't know why he is receiving the treat.

4. Keep praising him every time he barks and give a treat.

5. After you've done this for several days, hold a treat in your hand in front of his face and say **"Speak."**

6. Your dog will probably still not know what to do, but will eventually get so frustrated at not getting the treat that he will bark.

7. At which point, praise him and give the treat.

We trained a quiet Labrador to do this in a week and then, like clockwork, he barked enthusiastically every time anybody came to the door or whenever we gave him the "Speak" command, knowing he would get a treat for stopping.

Aggression

With aggression, the problem often lies with owners who have not socialised or trained their Dachshund in order to manage the breed's natural wariness of strangers and desire to protect. Given certain situations, any dog can growl, bark or even bite.

Sometimes a Dachshund learns unwanted behaviour from another dog or dogs, but more often it is because the dog either feels insecure, or has become too territorial or protective.

 **FACT** ❯ Puppy biting is not aggression; all puppies bite; they explore the world with their mouths and noses.

To treat aggression, you first have to understand the cause. There are many known types of aggression, and often an aggressive dog has more than one issue. Most are rooted in either fear or dominance:

- Growling or barking at people - this may be **territorial aggression**
- Snarling or lunging at other dogs - **dog-on-dog aggression**
- Snarling and lunging on the leash - **dog-on-dog aggression, which may be rooted in fear**
- Growling or biting if you or another pet goes near his food - **resource guarding**
- Growling if you pet or show attention to another animal – **possessive aggression**
- Marking territory by urinating inside the house, usually males - **dominance**
- Being possessive with toys or food - **possessive aggression**
- Chasing things that move – birds, cats, cars, joggers, strangers, etc. - **prey aggression**
- Standing in your way, blocking your path - **dominance**

Raging hormones can be another reason; a male dog could be asserting his dominance due to high levels of testosterone. If that is the case, consider getting him neutered (if he is over two or three years old). A levelling-off of hormones can lead to a more laid-back dog.

Dachshunds are naturally territorial. If yours has not been socialised enough around other animals and people, he may become over-protective of his people, toys, food or other animals. Or he may be nervous and feel threatened. Rather than being comfortable with new situations, dogs or intrusions, he responds using *"the best form of defence is attack"* philosophy and displays aggressive behaviour to anything or anyone he is not sure about and therefore perceives as a threat.

Tip As well as snarling, lunging, barking or biting, look out for other physical signs such as raised hackles, top lip curled back to bare teeth, ears back or tail raised.

An owner's treatment of a dog can be a further cause. If the owner has been too harsh with the dog, shouting or reprimanding too often or even using physical violence, this in turn causes poor behaviour. Dachshunds are surprisingly sensitive and **aggression breeds aggression.**

And if you haven't bothered to lay down any house rules, your Dachshund will! He may come to believe that he rules the roost and start to throw his weight around. He may start to display bad behaviour or aggression towards you or other members of the family. This should not be tolerated under any circumstances

Start to re-establish your leadership by putting in lots of time on the training front. There is no quick fix — if you love your Dachshund, spend the time to train him.

Dogs can also become aggressive if they are consistently left alone, cooped up, under-fed or under-exercised. A bad experience with another dog or dogs can also be a cause. Some dogs are more combative on the lead. Fight or flight. They know they can't escape, so they make themselves as frightening as possible and warn off the other dog or person.

If your dog **suddenly** shows a change of behaviour or becomes aggressive, ask:

- 🐾 Is he getting enough exercise?
- 🐾 Is he mentally bored?

If the answer to these questions is YES followed by NO, consider getting him checked out by a vet to rule out any underlying medical reason for the crankiness, such as earache or toothache.

A further reason is because a dog has been spoiled by his owner and has come to believe that the world revolves around him. Not spoiling your dog, teaching him what is acceptable behaviour in the first place is the best preventative measure. Early training, especially during puppyhood and adolescence before he develops unwanted habits can save a lot of trouble in the future.

Aggression Towards People

Desensitisation is the most common method of treating aggression. It starts by breaking down the triggers for the behaviour one small step at a time. The aim is to get the dog to associate pleasant things with the trigger, i.e. people or a specific person whom he previously feared or regarded as a threat.

This is done through using positive reinforcement, such as praise or rewards. Successful desensitisation takes time, patience and knowledge. If your dog is starting to growl at people, there are a couple of techniques you can try to break him of this bad habit while he is still young – and before it develops into full-blown biting.

Arrange for friends to come around, one at a time. When one arrives at your house, get her to scatter kibble on the floor in front of him, so your dog associates the arrival of people with tasty treats. As she moves into the house and your dog eats the kibble, praise him for being a good boy.

If your Dachshund is at all anxious around children, separate them or carefully supervise their time together. Children typically react enthusiastically to dogs and some less confident dogs may regard this as frightening or an invasion of their space.

A crate is also a useful tool for removing an aggressive dog from the situation for short periods of time, but should not be used as a regular form of punishment or imprisonment.

We strongly recommend that all new owners book their puppy or rescue dog on to a basic obedience training course, where your Dachshund will also learn to socialise with other dogs. It is also a great, inexpensive way for owners to learn how to train their dog properly. Many local veterinary clinics now run puppy training classes.

If your dog exhibits persistent behavioural problems, particularly if he or she is aggressive towards people or other dogs, consider getting help from a reputable canine behaviourist, such as those listed the Association of Professional Dog Trainers at www.apdt.co.uk (UK), https://apdt.com (US), or www.capdt.ca in Canada.

Check they use positive training methods.

9. Tips From a Trainer

Lisa Cole's life has always revolved around animals. She has worked with dogs for 40 years and bred shaded red Standard Long-Haired Dachshunds with the Foosayo prefix for the past 14. Over the decades she has worked at kennels, veterinary practices, boarding kennels and Greyhound rescue. While working in rescue, Lisa saw the difference time and training could make to an individual dog and this set her on her path to dog training.

Here Lisa shares insights on understanding and training your dog and offers advice on dealing with some common behaviour problems.

Each dog and each trainer learn and teach in a different way, this is why there are so many different training methods, books and ideas.

I can quickly teach a dog to sit on a Monday with no problem, yet a different dog trained with the same technique on a Tuesday just does not understand what I am asking. This is not because the dog is stupid or untrainable; it's because he learns in a slightly different way. All dogs can be taught at all ages, but the methods used to get different dogs to the same point can vary quite dramatically. Before we start, it helps to understand how dogs think, process information and communicate with us and other dogs.

Dogs cannot talk, but they do bark, which usually indicates excitement or a perceived threat. A bark can mean Go away, Someone is at the door, Mums' home, Leave me alone. All of these are alert sounds, but there is so much more than the bark. Dogs' conversations are also done with posture, ear and tail placement, and even making the fur rise so they seem bigger when needed.

We can change how our dog acts with just a little understanding of how he or she thinks.

....

Factors Affecting Behaviour

Natural instincts affect behaviour, so when choosing a pet dog, always research the breed and Breed Group. There are seven Breed Groups: Gundog, Pastoral, (Herding in the US), Working, Hound, Utility (Non-Sporting in the US), Terrier and Toy.

All Dachshunds are in the Hound Group - or The Noisy Group! Hounds just love to alert you. There are over 30 dogs in this group that, on the surface, do not appear to have much in common. The Dachshund, Irish Wolfhound, Saluki, Finnish Spitz, Rhodesian Ridgeback and Whippet are all members. What they do have in common, however, is they all use sight or scent to hunt their prey.

Typically, hounds chase and they will dig if they find a scent to follow. Most are very loyal and get along with children, but can be harder to train or to call back when a hare has just taken off across the field. If you do not have the time to train these dogs and walk them on a good hour's walk at least once a day, then they are not for you. The upside is when they have walked, they are the laziest dogs of all!

Another extremely important factor affecting behaviour is *socialisation,* or dogs meeting other dogs of all sizes, shapes and colours, and people with different smells, colours and moods. Socialisation is so important for a dog's happiness and mental health. If you buy a dog and he never goes out, never sees other dogs, cats, cars, bikes, people or buses, when he does go out, he is very frightened by all these moving things. Your dog may walk quietly by your side, but if he's not socialised, there is an increased risk of him showing aggression if someone approaches.

Imagine you are born and everything is blue. You are blue, your mum is blue, all your brothers and sisters are blue, and you are all happy in a safe, warm, blue home. Then one day a pink person arrives and takes you away from your safe blue home. You are thrust into a world of red, yellow, green, orange, pink – it's scary! But if you were introduced slowly to the other colours a little at a time, you'd be far less afraid.

Socialisation also helps your dog to speak *"Dog."* All day every day your dog is learning the sounds from his owners and trying to respond. When meeting other dogs, he also learns how to behave with them. There is nothing worse than a dog trying to be friendly and, because he does not know what to do, gets the messages mixed up and the other dog takes it as a threat. Fights can happen.

If you become the owner of a dog that has had no socialisation and/or a bad experience, he will be full of fear. It's embarrassing on walks when he lunges and barks at almost everything. With you at home, he is happy, kind and placid, but taking him out is a nightmare. Many owners stop walking their dogs completely or return the dog to the rescue. Sadly, many dogs are returned time and time again before they find the right home.

Common Scenarios

Before any training or behaviour work is done, you need to understand some of the thought processes going through a dog's mind:

Scenario 1: A lovely, happy dog is put in his bed every morning. After the owner leaves the dog starts to bark. WOOF, WOOF, WOOF, this goes on all day every day - poor neighbours. As soon as the owner returns, the happy dog greets the owner and settles down quietly all evening. Why?

From the dog's point of view, the owner gets up and lets the dog out for a wee and leaves. The dog wants the owner to come back, so the only thing he can think of is to shout as loud as he can so the owner will hear him and return. So, WOOF, WOOF, WOOF! And, of course, the owner returns - only the owner knows he was coming back anyway. In the dog's eyes it worked, so tomorrow when he is left alone, he barks all day again.

Scenario 2: The postman comes to the house and posts some letters through your letterbox. Your dog goes bananas, rushing to the front door and barking in a crazy manner. Then after a short time your dog returns to being the happy calm dog he was before the postman arrived. Why?

In the dog's eyes, he's snoozing on the sofa loving life then suddenly a man comes up to the house and is trying to get in through the hole in the door. WOOF WOOF WOOF! Then the man goes away. It worked, he has frightened the man away, so tomorrow guess what will happen...

Scenario 3: The owner is out for a walk with his dog on a lead. His neighbour is heading straight towards him with his dog on a lead. The first dog becomes stiff, staring straight at the approaching dog. In a seemingly aggressive manner he starts barking, lunging forward, pulling at the lead trying to get to the neighbour's dog. He only calms down after the neighbour and dog have passed by.

The following day both neighbours are in the park with their dogs off-lead. The dogs see each other, run over with tails wagging and start to play together.

This can happen for a few reasons, but the biggest cause of this type of on-lead behaviour is US! Having the dog on the lead means the dogs must greet face to face, which is an aggressive posture in the canine world, so the dog feels the need to protect himself and you. He is feeling scared, excited and protective all at the same time - resulting in barking and lunging.

So, armed with a little knowledge about your dog's behaviour and why it might be happening, we can start training. Five to 10 minutes in a whole day is all that is needed, but these short training sessions are especially important, and if you do not go through with them, your dog will not learn.

It's important to do a little bit every day, not 60 minutes one day and nothing for the rest of the week, otherwise your dog will learn a little but not achieve what you want.

....

Taking Control

The first step towards being in control of a dog is by training him to listen to us.

The Clicker

I believe it's important to have a tool that bridges the language barrier of man and dog, and **the clicker** is a simple and highly effective way of letting your dog understand that what he has just done is **exactly** the thing you are asking for. Dogs love to please using a clicker, and it enforces the fact that he is doing it right. It is important that the click happens at the right moment as it means: Well done! He's done what you asked.

One example is teaching the Sit. With the clicker in your hand and treats in your pocket or in a bowl out of reach, ask your dog for a Sit. The moment his bottom touches the floor, CLICK. After the click has happened, take out a treat and give your dog his prize.

If you are too slow, he will think you are praising him for getting up out of a Sit - or if it is too soon, you will be praising him for looking at you.

NOTE: If the clicker goes off randomly it can confuse your dog and the training will not be as effective. You can practise getting used to a clicker (out of your dog's hearing) by bouncing a ball and clicking every time it hits the floor.

The Hierarchy of Treats

Treats are different things to different dogs. A treat is something the dog likes, so it could be food, a toy or just the fact the owner is pleased and happy. Treats are anything that the dog loves to have that does not take up too much time. Most Dachshunds are highly motivated by food treats! Different treats have different values and using them at the right time will help you to get the best out of your dog:

1. **High Value Food** is human food - usually animal-based - such as sausage, ham, chicken, liver and cheese. All should be cooked if raw and cut into pea-sized treats — you're looking to reward your dog, not feed him. Place the tiny treats in a freezer bag in the freezer, which keeps them fresh, then you can grab a handful when you go out training. There's not much water content and they quickly thaw.

   When training, we want our dog to want more High Value Food. He smells and tastes it on his tongue but it is gone in a flash, leaving him wanting more. *So, all treats should be only as large as a pea - even if you're training a Great Dane!*

2. **Medium Value Food** such as moist pet shop treats or a healthy alternative like sliced apple or carrot.

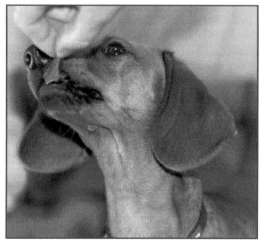

3. **Low Value Food** such as kibble. Use your dog's own food if you feed dry, or buy a small bag if not.

IMPORTANT: Whenever you are asking your dog **to do something new,** make it worth his while. Offer a High Value treat like liver. Once your dog understands what you are asking, you can move down to Medium Value treat. When he does it every time use Low Value... reducing the frequency after a while and then only give it every other time... then only occasionally until you have slowly stopped giving any treat treating when asking for that task.

The aim at this point is to start getting you in control of your dog. And, most importantly, we want your dog to want to be controlled, as control brings good things.

Call My Name (Recall)

For no more than two minutes at a time and spread randomly through the day, practise the *Call My Name* game. With the clicker in your hand ready and treats in your pocket or nearby, wait until your dog is busy doing something or falling asleep. Then in a clear voice - but not shouting - just call your dog's name once.

If your dog shows any interest by moving his ear, looking over or even coming over, CLICK then throw a treat over to him. This is the start of good recall; we want the dog to come so always throw the treat.

 Don't get over-excited when your dog gets it right! We want him to be in control and not rushing around the room in excitement. Stay calm and give a "Good Boy."

Repeat and practise. Very soon your dog will hear you calling his name and come running every time. Perfect, just what we want - but take it one more step. When you have called your dog's name and your dog runs over, hold the treat and in your head count to 10. Your dog should sit nicely in front of you. When you get to 10, CLICK then treat. Good boy!

Instead of calling your dog's name, you can use a whistle in two short blasts. Then CLICK and throw the treat.

The dog should very quickly understand if you follow the Call My Name instructions but blow the whistle instead, he should come to you and sit in front of you nicely.

Look at Me (Focus)

This next exercise also needs to be done randomly during the day. Now we are getting your dog to focus on you, and to do so on command if needed.

Hold a treat in your right hand and clicker in the left. Call your dog over and he should sit. Allow the dog the knowledge you have a treat in your right hand - the treat should be held between your thumb and middle finger leaving your index finger free.

Move your hand up towards your face and with your index finger point to the outside of your right eye (or left, if you are left-handed). Hold it there and use the command word "LOOK." If your dog is looking towards your face, CLICK and give the treat.

Once your dog understands what you are asking, repeat the exercise - but this time keep the treat in your pocket. Just raise your hand and point to the corner of your eye and say "LOOK." If your dog stays looking at you, CLICK and give the treat.

Your visual command for this exercise is to point to your eye while looking at your dog and the command word is "LOOK." Practise this indoors, in the garden and while on a walk. Repeat each day until your dog understands the exercise, and then do it only occasionally.

Once your dog has learned to focus on you and you have started to take control, you can teach him the commands outlined in the previous chapter on **Basic Training.**

 **FACT** Training is teaching a dog to sit or give paw, etc. Behaviour work is trying to change something the dog already does.

You cannot untrain a dog. Once you have taught him to sit, you cannot stop him from sitting - but you can change the Sit into something else. This is not straight forward and can take a little longer than regular training, but with dedication from the owner it can be done. Here are few of the common behavioural problems I come across:

How to Stop Your Dog From Jumping Up

This common behaviour problem is something your dog has learned during puppyhood, and it can be the last thing in the world you want after a busy day at work. Dogs that do this are annoying to some and dangerous to others, such as small children, the elderly or people with disabilities.

So, you walk through the door and your dog, who has missed your company, goes manic and is leaping around the room. You are pushing him off, yelling at him, saying "Get down!"

You are trying to scold him, but the truth is that negative attention is better than no attention, so you are rewarding your dog for his behaviour every time this happens.

Tip ATTENTION = REWARD, so the trick here is to give a bigger, better reward for keeping all four paws on the ground.

For this exercise you need patience and persistence. If you are not prepared to put the effort in, then stay with a dog who jumps up and leave it at that! However, if you are prepared to put the time in and be consistent, your reward will be your best friend keeping all four paws firmly on the floor.

Part 1 - We stop giving attention - positive and negative – this is VERY important. As soon as your dog jumps up, turn your back. Cross your arms over your chest and do not speak to your dog or look at him.

If he runs around trying to get your attention and keeps jumping up, keep turning away from him. BUT DO NOT SAY ANYTHING OR LOOK AT HIM. Or, you could try leaving the room. Again, do not say anything or look at him, but as soon as he jumps up, you leave. Wait a moment, then step back inside and repeat until the dog is calm enough to stop jumping up.

Part 2 - Reward good behaviour. Make sure you always have High Value treats to hand. As soon as your dog is in front of you with all four paws on the ground, throw him a treat. You can praise him, but keep all speech and praise low key; we do not want to excite him.

Then, practise, practise. Set up situations to practise with your dog. If jumping happens when you come home, spend a little time coming and going from the house. Do not make a big fuss and step outside if he jumps up. ONLY REWARD WHEN ALL FOUR PAWS ARE ON THE FLOOR.

Part 3 - Add the Sit. Once your dog is keeping his paws on the floor for a few seconds or more, ask for a sit. Walk into the room through the front door and say "SIT." As soon as the dog sits, give a treat (high value). Practise with a lot of repetitions and your dog WILL start to sit when you walk through the door.

Part 4 - Practise with other people. Use friends, neighbours, family, in fact anyone who is willing to help with training! If you do not, your dog may learn that it's not OK to jump on you, but it's OK to jump on other people. So, when anyone enters the room he must sit. This is your goal.

FACT ❯ We have replaced the Jump with the Sit. Your dog still knows how to jump up; we cannot delete this from his brain, but we can make him feel that doing something else is much better.

This exercise can be achieved with a little effort and practice. However, the next example is much harder - but still doable. Practice, repeats and determination are essential, and the regime must be stuck to, otherwise it will not work or only partially work:

How Do I Stop My Dog Chasing?

All dogs inherit certain behaviour traits, which give them *internal reinforcement.* An easy example of this is that dogs dig. Nobody teaches them to do it. They just do it and they enjoy doing it, so they keep on digging.

The strength of the inherited instinct varies from one bloodline to another and from one dog to the next. Chasing behaviour is part of what is inherited; it is genetically hard-wired into the dog. Dogs in the wild inherit enough behaviour traits to stay alive, whereas my working Cocker tends to have exaggerated bits of chasing or stalking; her inherited behaviour is never in balance, causing exaggerated reactions to any target.

We know that with inherited behaviour traits, the behaviour itself is rewarding and the reward is internal. Good endorphins are released and the dog feels good. So how on earth can we stop a dog chasing if he is rewarded just by doing it? Well, here is what to do...

We can use **external reinforcement,** such as treats, to train dogs. Some dog trainers will tell you the chase problem is due to the dog having poor Recall. Well, working on the Recall may help a little, but the chase urge is often a lot deeper set than that. Understanding the dog's motivation to chase is especially important. When changing a dog's behaviour pattern, you must try to understand what your dog is seeing and feeling.

There are several reasons a dog wants to chase. All of these motivations are quite different and any solution needs to be tailor-made for the individual dog. However, true chasing is a predatory behaviour. This checklist is a guide - if you tick two, plus the last one - your dog is a predatory chaser!

- 🐾 The dog tries to chase more than one target – e.g. cars, bikes, runners, cats and birds
- 🐾 The dog is always looking for the opportunity to chase
- 🐾 The dog gets excited at the smell, sight or sound of the target
- 🐾 The dog may show signs of stalking or searching
- 🐾 The dog can do this anywhere
- 🐾 The dog will want to chase if the target is moving; the faster the target, the more excited the dog becomes
- 🐾 The dog appears to enjoy chasing more than anything

First Steps

Look at the environment you are in. Look for anything that could make your dog anxious and remove or reduce any background anxieties before looking at controlling his behaviour. Go somewhere where there are as few "targets" as possible and introduce as many **emotional improvers** as possible. Possible triggers are fear, noise, phobias, separation and social problems. Improvers are chew toys, praise and treats.

To stop your dog chasing, we may first have to address some things that may seem completely unrelated, e.g. fear. If your dog fears something, he will have very negative feelings and may chase to make himself feel a lot better. If all targets and problems cannot be removed, then add more positive actions to balance the negative emotions thereby reducing the need to chase.

Many owners make the mistake of trying to train their dog when he is chasing. DON'T DO THIS AS IT WON'T WORK! It only reinforces the behaviour. Start to gain control. The chasing behaviour arises because you have no control over his behaviour, so we are going to now control the dog's primary target.

We cannot control cats, rabbits, squirrels or birds, so we need to change the primary target to one we CAN control.

Start as you mean to go on. Your dog must not at any time get the opportunity to chase anything at all. This is essential, because every time he chases, he gets a brain boost. So, do not take your dog anywhere where they can continue their addictive behaviour.

Changing the Target

Buy your dog a toy that is exciting. It could squeak, have a bell, rustle, you could hide treats in it. It must not resemble anything your dog has chased, so no squeaky rabbits, ducks, fluffy things that can be torn apart. Play in areas where there are none of the old targets.

Many dogs will chase a ball, but some dogs may be so focused on their primary target that they ignore toys. This is the time for you to get inventive to make the new target inviting. If speed or movement is something your dog chases, a ball is perfect as it can be thrown and it moves quickly. Put food into the toy.

Photo: Lisa

Play with the target only a few steps away from your dog before starting to throw it further to bring on new brain connections, which will be aimed at the new "target" or toy.

All training bouts should be short but frequent, with no other distractions. Always stop before your dog gets bored and always end the games with the toy in your possession. All of this builds the neural connections between the Got to Chase and the new toy: "play, play, play."

Once you have your dog's attention, work on teaching retrieve. **Do not allow access to the toy at any other time than when you are training.** This is the special treat and chase ball. Your dog will eventually become happy to play with this ball if you have banished all his old targets.

Practise, practise, practise with no distractions until your dog is desperate to play the game. Playing like this will make your dog's chasing drive high, but it will all be focussed on the game.

Now we must use the command word, so let us call it "TOY." Say it in a high tone to make it clear and happy. Use it every time you throw the toy. Very quickly the dog will associate the vocal sound "TOY" with the actual toy you are throwing.

Now the dog is understanding that TOY = GAME. So, we need to move the new training up a notch or two. Please remember to work in a place with no distractions. Buy another identical toy. Perhaps buy several for future uses.

Take both identical toys with you for your training. Ask your dog for a Sit Stay (if he won't, then hold the collar) and throw one of the balls as far as you can **without** using the verbal command "TOY."

Count to five in your head then give your dog the "FETCH" command and let go of the collar. Then immediately call "TOY" and throw the other toy past your dog. As the second toy is still moving, your dog should choose to chase it as it bounces past him. Collect the toys and repeat.

If your dog does go after the first ball and ignores the second one, change the first thing you throw to something much less interesting. Do not worry if your dog goes in search of the first ball after they have retrieved the second. You will have already achieved your goal by getting your dog to focus on the second ball.

After a little while your dog will start waiting for the second ball to be thrown. If this happens call "TOY" for the first one thrown then start again.

Next Step

Throw the first one then call "TOY," but do not throw it immediately. Wave the toy above your head for your dog to see and when he comes back to you, reward him by throwing the toy. If your dog stops running for the first toy, remember to call "TOY" on occasions for that first throw. Even stop the retrieve and just play with the toy and your dog with no calling at all.

All play ends with the toy in your possession. Do not be manipulated by your dog. If he will not let you have the toy the game ends.

The next step is to start to leave it a bit later and later before you call "TOY!" The aim is to throw the first toy, immediately send your dog and wait until he is almost there and then call "TOY" and wait for him to come back before you throw the second toy.

You have worked extremely hard to get to this point and your dog will be doing well, now we need to start adding some distractions. We do not throw in cats, rabbits and so on just yet but we can add things like other dogs and people.

So, take your dog to a place where there is not much chance of a fluffy bunny turning up but does have dog walkers, and play the game while the distractions are there. If you are feeling nervous or you feel your dog might run off, buy a 10 or 20ft lead and tie the loop end to a tree or something solid. When you feel ready to progress you can untie the line, but remember to repeat, repeat, repeat. Try to do it once a day every day.

Eventually the neural connections between **chase and toy** will be stronger than with **chase and old target.** The time it takes will vary with each dog and how much reinforcement, or inherited behaviour, they have received, but persistence will pay off.

When your dog is spinning around looking eagerly for a game every time you call "TOY," you are ready to test how well he is doing where there are rabbits, cats and birds. Look at your dog, watch him, as soon as he even looks in the direction of a cat or squirrel, immediately call "TOY" and play the game in the opposite direction from his old target.

Over time, very slowly edge closer and closer until your dog ignores his old targets. You will never be able to give up the reinforcement and the game, as if you do not satisfy your dog's chase needs they will find their own targets.

And finally, whatever the issue, remember that without control you will have no chance of stopping any behaviour issues.

Training is not just about getting your dog to do what you want him to do or correcting unwanted behaviour; it is an important part of building a lifelong partnership. Done properly with love and patience, training is a very rewarding experience for both dog and owner.

10. Exercise and Socialising

One thing all dogs have in common – including every Dachshund ever born - is that they need daily exercise. Even if you have a large garden or back yard where your dog can run free, there are still lots of benefits to getting out and about.

Dachshunds love going for walks, but are happy to lounge around at home as well. Don't think that because they are happy to snuggle up on the sofa, they don't need regular exercise – THEY DO.

Daily exercise helps to keep your Dachshund happy and healthy. It:

- Strengthens respiratory and circulatory systems
- Helps get oxygen to tissue cells
- Helps keep a healthy heart
- Wards off obesity
- Keeps muscles toned and joints flexible
- Aids digestion
- Releases endorphins that trigger positive feelings
- Helps to keep dogs mentally stimulated and socialised

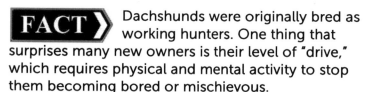 **FACT** ▶ Dachshunds were originally bred as working hunters. One thing that surprises many new owners is their level of "drive," which requires physical and mental activity to stop them becoming bored or mischievous.

If you have the time and interest, an excellent way of keeping your Dachshund's mind and body exercised is to take part in an activity, such as those suggested in **Chapter 11.**

How Much Exercise?

The amount of exercise each adult Dachshund needs varies tremendously from one dog to the next. It depends on various factors, including:

- Temperament
- Natural energy levels
- Bloodline
- Your living conditions
- Whether your dog is kept with other dogs
- What she gets used to

One of the advantages of Dachshunds is that they are happy to fit in with your lifestyle. They are known for being very playful and enjoy toys and games. Some of your dog's natural temperament and energy level will depend on the bloodline - ask the breeder how much exercise he or she recommends.

A minimum of an hour a day spread over at least two walks will keep your Dachshund fit and stimulated. Those with strong hounding instincts will take a lot more exercise, even all-day hikes, once they have built up to it.

The Dachshund Breed Council recommends an hour a day for all types of Dachshunds. Chairman Ian Seath says: "Some people think that Dachshunds don't need a lot of exercise, but they are, after all, hounds, and we recommend an hour a day, even for Miniatures. Of course, that is only once they are fully grown; over 12 months.

"Puppies need to build their exercise regime gradually; typically allowing five minutes of formal on-lead exercise per month of age, each day (i.e. 15 minutes for a three-month puppy, per day). They get the best physical and mental stimulation if they can be exercised off the lead, safely."

Owning more than one dog - or having friends with dogs - is a great way for Dachshunds to get more exercise. A couple of dogs running around together will get far more exercise than one on her own.

A fenced garden or yard is a definite advantage, but should not be seen as a replacement for daily exercise away from the home, where a dog can experience new places, scents, other people and dogs. If you live in an apartment, you may have no outside space, so it is especially important to make time for daily walks.

Your Dachshund will enjoy going for walks on the lead (leash), but will enjoy life much more when she is allowed to run free, following a scent or chasing a ball. If your dog is happy just to amble along beside you, think about playing some games to raise her heartbeat, build muscle and get her fit.

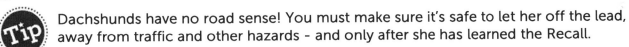 **Dachshunds have no road sense! You must make sure it's safe to let her off the lead, away from traffic and other hazards - and only after she has learned the Recall.**

There are also reports in both the UK and North America about increasing numbers of dog attacks, even in dog parks and public parks. If you are at all worried, avoid popular dog walking areas and find other places where your dog can exercise safely.

If you want to hike or take part in canine competitions with your dog, build up time and distance gradually. Always exercise within your dog's limits - on both land and water - this loyal breed does not know her own limits, but you don't want your beloved pooch to struggle.

Mental Stimulation

Without mental challenges, dogs can become bored, destructive, attention-seeking and/or depressed. Dachshunds are playful and love a game or challenge. If this "drive" is not channelled in a positive manner, it can turn to naughtiness. If you return home to find your favourite cushions shredded or the contents of the kitchen bin strewn around the floor, ask yourself: *"Is she getting enough exercise?"* and *"Am I leaving her alone for too long?"* Have toys and chews, and factor in regular play time with your Dachshund – even gentle play time for old dogs.

A washable *Snuffle Mat, pictured,* is an interesting toy, as it can help to satisfy a Dachshund's hunting instinct, reduce boredom and even help fussy eaters. Hide a treat, toy or food in there and let your Dachshund work out how to get it. NOTE: Always use under supervision.

Most Dachshunds are chasers; they love running after birds, other dogs, squirrels, and especially a ball or toy – some even get obsessed with them. You can make *Fetch* more challenging by hiding the ball or toy and training your dog to find it.

FACT ▷ Sticks can splinter in a dog's mouth or stomach, and jumping up for a Frisbee can cause back damage to Dachshunds.

A Dachshund at the heart of the family getting regular exercise and mental challenges is a happy dog and an affectionate snuggle bug second to none.

Dachshunds and Water

I could write a whole chapter on this subject alone. As far as Dachshund are concerned, there are at least FOUR types of water:

- 🐾 The wet stuff that falls from the sky
- 🐾 The wet stuff that's already fallen from their sky and is under their feet and belly
- 🐾 The wet stuff that's in the bath
- 🐾 The big wet stuff in ponds, lakes, the sea, etc.

As far as the first two go, most Dachshunds HATE them! A lot of Dachshunds also hate having a bath, although some do enjoy the attention. And finally, many Dachshunds – but by no means all - enjoy splashing about and even short swims in the big wet stuff.

The different types of Dachshund have been developed by introducing different breeds somewhere
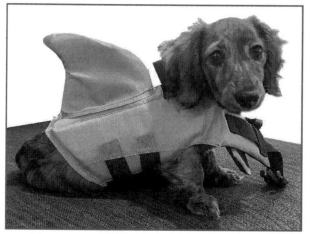
along the line. Do Long-Haireds have some Spaniel (a water dog) in them, Wire-Haireds a pinch of Terrier (many of which are not natural water dogs) and Smooths a lot of Hound genes? We don't 100% know, but could it be that some Dachshunds have *"the water gene?"*

If your Dachshund is one of those who enjoys water, allow her to build up confidence. DON'T repeatedly throw a ball or toy into water for her to retrieve. Dachshunds' heavy bodies and short legs mean they have no stamina for swimming more than a few minutes. They don't know that, so you have to monitor their activity near water.

Pictured sporting his shark lifejacket at home is CunAnnun Win Hands Down, "Tigger," who enjoys rowing with his owner, Freya Parry.

 A paddling pool is one way of allowing your dog to enjoy water safely - many Dachshunds LOVE their paddling pools in warm weather! And if yours is to spend a lot of time on or near water, a doggie lifejacket is a good investment.

Tigger's breeder Stefanie Millington says: "Some of mine hate water and then there is a couple who absolutely love swimming and adore their paddling pool in the summer. With the couple who like swimming, I usually let them swim for about 10 minutes at a time, and they swim in the local river when we are on our daily walk. However, some dislike water to the point where you have difficulty getting them out of the house for their toilet when it rains."

Lisa Lindfield, of Zabannah Dachshunds, says: "My Mini Wires and Mini Longs don't like water, but the Mini Smooths love it - they're manic! I have three Dachshunds that paddle and love water, but they don't swim. They have a paddling pool too. In hot weather they love getting squirted by the hose pipe or soaked with a watering can, and they scream with excitement when I water the garden!

"If I did let them swim it would probably only be for 10 minutes as they have little legs. I'm not sure how long hydrotherapy sessions are, as dogs with IVDD often have hydrotherapy when recovering."

Pauline Cheeseman, Colraed Miniature (Smooth) Dachshunds: "I have one Dachshund, Annie, who is a total water baby. She swims everywhere, including the sea, and this love of water has been passed on to a few of her puppies. One goes paddle boarding with her owners and wears a lifejacket, but the rest of mine will just paddle, and swim if it gets too deep."

Lisa Cole, Foosayo (Standard Longhaired) Dachshunds: "Mine love water; the dirtier and bigger the better! Ponds, lakes and rivers are perfect - they love to paddle and swim. Ruby loves the sea and is often wading out with waves crashing over her. I use life jackets for river, sea or lake; they keep the dog safe, even if they tire.

"At first, I only let them swim for five minutes maximum, then build them up over time. Swimming is great exercise and builds up muscle and stamina, but be careful not to do too much too soon. I also have a couple that would jump in a lake and swim, but don't like going out in the rain."

Sandra Robertson, Hartlebury Miniature (Smooth) Dachshunds: "All three of mine prefer to paddle and be on dry land. Occasionally, they can have a little swim. I find after a couple of minutes they can get tired, due to their heavy bodies and short legs, so I tend to watch over them all time near water and stick to the shallows."

Melissa Sworab, Rabows Dachshunds: "Dachshunds are very finicky and will refuse to go out in the rain and be problematic for those who don't work with them as puppies to appreciate a gentle rain. My advice is to go out in gentle rain with your puppy and show them that the rain isn't bad - but be warned, they are very observant and if you take an umbrella, they know you're lying!

Pictured is Ella, swimming under Melissa's supervision in her pool at home.

"One in 10 or so would not go out if it was raining or even misting - and one in particular would hold a paw up in protest like it was just utterly beneath her to be out there and completely insulting to 'Her Highness'!

"I recommend an early introduction (six to 12 weeks) to a supervised shallow kiddie pool. Apple slices are a great way to show them water isn't bad and also make it fun. After 16 weeks, it's probably too late to try this as they are pretty set in their ways already in regards to water."

"For the ones who love the water, we use a kiddie pool in the hot Texas heat to keep them cooler on trips outside. We let them swim, supervised, for five minutes to a half hour depending upon their

ability and ambition level. Some of ours love it so much they will dive and fetch over and over again and don't know when to quit, so you have to be the adult with those."

Photo of Melissa's Mitch and Claire relaxing at the pool.

"I have never used a lifejacket with ours, but we've always been in our private pool and never in an open lake with our Dachshunds. The pool was circular, so getting to a dog that needed assistance bringing a waterlogged toy out of the pool was always fast and easy."

Ian Seath, Sunsong Dachshunds, added: "None of ours ever really like to get their feet wet."

If you live near water or want your dog to enjoy it, introduce her while still a puppy, but never force a dog into water. Like a child, if a young dog gets frightened of water or loses confidence, she is unlikely to want to swim as an adult. And remember that swimming is a lot more strenuous than any other activity for a Dachshund.

If your dog does enjoy swimming, it is an excellent way to exercise; many veterinary clinics now use water tanks not only for remedial and IVDD therapy, but also for canine recreation.

....

Routine

Establish an exercise regime early in your dog's life. If possible, get your dog used to a walk or walks at similar times every day and gradually build that up as the puppy reaches adulthood. Start out with a regime you know you can continue with, as your dog will come to expect it and will not be happy if the walks suddenly stop.

 If you haven't enough time to give your Dachshund the exercise she needs, consider employing a daily dog walker, if you can afford it, or take her to doggie day care once or twice a week. As well as the exercise, she will love the interaction with other dogs.

Dachshunds are bold and curious and love investigating new scents and places, which is why you need to plug every little gap in your fence – they will be off given half a chance!

Older dogs still need exercise to keep their body, joints and systems functioning properly. They need a less strenuous regime – they are usually happier with shorter walks, but still enough to keep them physically and mentally active. Again, every dog is different; some are willing and able to keep on running to the end of their lives, others slow right down.

If your old or sick dog is struggling, she will show you she's not up to it by stopping and looking at you or sitting/lying down and refusing to move. If she's healthy and does this, she is just being lazy!

Regular exercise can add months or even years to a dog's life.

Some Dachshunds love snow, but snow and ice can clump on paws, ears, legs and tummy. Salt or de-icing products on roads and pathways contain chemicals that can be poisonous to dogs and cause irritation – particularly if she tries to lick it off. If your dog gets iced up, bathe paws and other affected areas in lukewarm - NOT HOT - water.

Exercising Puppies

There are strict guidelines for puppies. It's important not to over-exercise young pups as their bones and joints are still soft and cannot tolerate a lot of stress. Too much impact can cause permanent damage. So, playing Fetch or Frisbee for hours on end with your young Dachshund is definitely not a good plan, nor is allowing a pup to freely run up and down stairs in your home. You'll end up with an injured dog and a pile of vet's bills.

Just like babies, puppies have different temperaments and energy levels; some need more exercise than others. Start slowly and build it up. The worst combination is over-exercise and overweight.

Don't take your pup out of the yard or garden until the all-clear after the vaccinations - unless you carry her around to start the socialisation process. Begin with daily short walks on the lead. Get yours used to being outside the home environment and experiencing new situations as soon as possible. The general guideline for exercise is:

Five minutes of on-lead exercise every day per month of age

So, a total of 15 minutes per day when three months (13 weeks) old

30 minutes per day when six months (26 weeks) old, etc.

This applies until around one year to 18 months old, when most of their growing has finished. Slowly increase the time as she gets used to being exercised and this will gradually build up muscles and stamina.

 It is OK for your young pup to have free run of your garden or yard, provided it has a soft surface such as grass. This does not count in the five minutes per month rule.

If the yard is stone or concrete, limit the time your dog runs around on it, as the hard surface will impact joints. It is also fine for your pup to run freely around the house to burn off energy - although not up and down stairs or jumping on and off furniture.

Photo of this young pup enjoying life courtesy of Pauline Cheeseman. Credit: RSA Photography.

A pup will take things at her own pace and stop to sniff or rest. If you have other dogs, restrict the time pup is allowed to play with them, as she won't know when she's had enough. When older, your dog can go out for much longer walks.

One breeder added: "For the first 18 months whilst the puppy's bones are soft and developing, it's best not to over-exert and put strain on the joints. Daily gentle walking is great, just not constant fast and hard running/chasing in the puppy stage, as too much is a big strain."

And when your little pup has grown into a beautiful adult Dachshund with a skeleton capable of carrying her through a long and healthy life, it will have been worth all the effort:

A long, healthy life is best started slowly

Walkies!

We asked a number of Dachshund breeders how much exercise their dogs get and if they took part in any canine activities, starting in the UK with Stefanie Millington (Mini Longs): "Most people are surprised when they realise how much exercise Dachshunds can handle. My Mini Longs get an hour's walk in the morning and an hour in the afternoon. In between they run around the yard and garden - or dig to Australia! I show all my dogs; I enjoy it and so do most of them."

Lisa Cole (Standard Longs): "I do an off-lead walk either in the woods or along the river bank twice a day. They love it, running back and forth up and down the bank. Sometimes it's a half-hour, but it could be a two-hour walk; it depends on the weather and what else I have to fit in the day. Standard Dachshunds are not small. They weigh up to 14kg and are about the length of a Cocker Spaniel, but on short legs. We also show all year. This year we were placed 4th and 5th at Cruft's, so we were thrilled."

Judith Carruthers (Standard Wires): "They get an hour's field exercise twice a day and half an hour lead exercise daily. They're a hound, so need an outlet for both their physical and psychological needs. I show my dogs, but they're primarily our pets."

Bastiaan Smit (Standard Wires): "Together with my German Shepherd, our first Dachshund, Beau, accompanied me while I was riding my horse. We easily made 10km without any signs of fatigue. Beau was on a lead to avoid her following the trails of wild animals!"

Hannah Norton (Standard and Miniature Smooths): "My dogs get between two and four hours' exercise on my land each day. They could, however, stay out much longer. I participate in local shows and enjoy my local Ringcraft classes."

Lisa Lindfield (all three types of Mini): "I exercise mine for 30 minutes three times a day and the dogs have access to the garden all day long, so they can lay out and sunbathe or chase each other around the trees!"

Pauline Cheeseman (Mini Smooths): "They get a minimum of an hour a day, usually a lot more. I take part in Hoopers, Scentwork and Mantrailing."

Sandra Robertson (Mini Smooths): "Our Miniature Dachshunds are often out and about on our two acres of land. They follow me round when I'm feeding or cleaning poultry or horses. Although they are classed as small hunting dogs, ours have been raised with animals and other pets and they are absolutely fabulous around them - but they can be a wary of chicks.

"We also take them for an hour-long walk morning and evening, keeping them mingled in society by meeting other dogs and people. I foster children and we have let our looked-after children enter our dogs in fun shows. It's lovely to see them win rosettes and meet other dog owners."

And now for the USA, starting with Pame Bates (Mini Longs): "Our dogs have lots of outdoors activities, we are building them a playground at present, with a pool, see-saw and other fun play equipment. They will play all day at the lake, swimming, chasing a ball and running in the woods."

Melissa Sworab (Mini Longs): "Our dogs get to run a half-acre multiple times a day and they play in the house, but we generally don't do a lot of hard road work with them. We keep them at a very healthy weight so they don't have a bunch of weight to carry. Diet is the key. We don't do a lot of commercial treats; we do fresh veggies. Our dogs have been in conformation, rally, barn hunt, tracking, scent, freestyle dance and earth dog. A couple have done agility, but many question how hard it is on their backs. Most athletes have joint problems later in life, so it makes sense."

Marianne McCullough (Mini Longs): "Miniature Dachshunds make great companions for walking and hiking. But like anyone, build the endurance slowly and don't do too much prior to one year of age. I take part in lots of activities with my dogs. Conformation shows are very important to help determine the best dogs to breed. In addition, my dogs have competed and earned titles in obedience, rally, earth dog, dock diving, barn hunt and agility."

Kristin Cihos-Williams (Standard Smooths) has bred almost 50 AKC conformation champions, including Grand Champions, and also regularly takes part in Field Trials in California: "My dogs self-exercise when we are at home. I have 11-year old dogs who constantly hunt and keep themselves active. When we are at Field Trials, some of my field champions may go five miles or more in a day, since the field trials in California involve the entire gallery beating for rabbits, and if rabbits are scarce, the dogs are all out for many hours.

"In general, when not competing with field champions, it is more appropriate for a Standard Dachshund adult to walk perhaps one to three miles. However, a properly conditioned field dog can hold up for much more than that in intense competition."

Dachshund Exercise Tips

- Don't over-exercise puppies

- Don't allow them to run up and down stairs or jump on and off furniture

- Aim for at least one walk away from the house every day

- Vary your exercise route – it will be more interesting for both of you

- Triple check the fencing around your garden or yard to prevent The Great Escape

- Do not throw a ball or toy repeatedly if your dog shows signs of over-exertion. Dachshunds are brave and tenacious with no sense of their own limitations. Stop the activity after a while - no matter how much she begs you to throw it again

- The same goes for swimming; ensure any exercise is within your dog's capabilities – look out for heavy panting

- Don't strenuously exercise your dog straight after or within an hour of a meal as this can cause Bloat, which mainly affects deep-chested dogs. Canine Bloat is extremely serious, if not fatal. See **Chapter 6. Feeding a Dachshund** for details

- Dachshunds have "drive" and need play time as well as walk time to keep their fertile minds engaged – and they love the interaction with their beloved owner

- In hot weather, exercise your dog early morning or in the evening

- Exercise old dogs more gently - especially in cold weather when it is harder to get their bodies moving. Have a cool-down period after exercise to reduce stiffness and soreness; it helps to remove lactic acids - our 13-year-old loves a body rub

- Make sure your dog has constant access to fresh water. Dogs can only sweat a tiny amount through the pads of their paws, they need to drink water to cool down

Admittedly, when it is raining, freezing cold or scorching hot, the last thing you want to do is to venture outdoors with your dog. And your Dachshund may not be too keen either!

But make the effort; the lows are more than compensated for by the highs. Don't let your dog dictate if she doesn't want to go out, it will only make her lazier and less sociable with others. Exercise helps you bond with your dog, keep fit, see different places and meet new companions - both canine and human. In short, it enhances both your lives.

Socialisation

Your adult dog's character will depend largely on two things: inherited temperament and environment, or **NATURE AND NURTURE**. And one absolutely essential aspect of nurture for all dogs, but especially Dachshunds, is socialisation.

FACT ❯ Scientists now realise the importance that socialisation plays in a dog's life. There is a fairly small window regarded as the optimum time for socialisation - and this is up to the age of four to five months.

Socialisation means *"learning to be part of society,"* or *"integration."* This means helping dogs become comfortable within a human society by getting them used to different people, environments, traffic, sights, noises, smells, animals, other dogs, etc.

It actually begins from the moment the puppy is born, and the importance of picking a good breeder cannot be over-emphasised. Not only will he or she breed for good temperament and health, but the dam (puppy's mother) will be well-balanced, friendly and unstressed, and the pup will learn a lot in this positive environment.

Learning When Young Is Easiest

Most young animals, including dogs, are naturally able to get used to their everyday environment until they reach a certain age. When they reach this age, they become much more suspicious of things they haven't yet experienced. This is why it often takes longer to train an older dog.

When you think about it, humans are not so different. Babies and children have a tremendous capacity to learn, we call this early period our *"formative years."* As we age, we can still learn, but not at the speed we absorbed things when very young. Also, as we get older, we are often less receptive to new ideas or new ways of doing things.

This age-specific natural development allows a puppy to get comfortable with the normal sights, sounds, people and animals that will be a part of her life. It ensures that she doesn't spend her life jumping in fright, barking or growling at every blowing leaf.

The suspicion that dogs develop later also ensures that they react with a healthy dose of caution to new things that could really be dangerous - Mother Nature is clever!

It is essential that your dog's introductions to new things are all **positive**. Negative experiences lead to a dog becoming fearful and untrusting.

Your dog may already have a wonderful temperament, but she still needs socialising to avoid her thinking that the world is tiny and it revolves around her. Dachshunds can be very demanding of your attention - don't let yours develop a *"Little Emperor"* complex!

Good socialisation gives confidence and helps puppies – whether bold or timid – to learn their place in society. The ultimate goal is to have a happy, well-adjusted Dachshund you can take anywhere - and one that doesn't spend her entire life barking at anything and everything.

Ever seen a therapy dog in action and noticed how incredibly well-adjusted to life they are? This is no coincidence. These dogs have been extensively socialised and are ready and able to deal in a calm manner with whatever situation they encounter. They are relaxed and comfortable in their own skin - just like you want your dog to be.

 **Spend as much time as you can socialising your dog when young. It's just as important as training.**

Start as soon as you bring your puppy home. Regular socialisation should continue until your dog is around 18 months of age.

After that, don't just forget about it; socialisation isn't only for puppies, it should continue throughout life. As with any skill, if it is not practised, your dog will become less proficient at interacting with other people, animals, noises and new situations.

Developing the Well-Rounded Adult

Dogs that have not been properly integrated are more likely to react with fear or aggression to unfamiliar people, animals and experiences. Dachshunds who are relaxed around strangers, dogs, cats and other animals, honking horns, cyclists, joggers, veterinary examinations, traffic, crowds and noise are easier to live with than dogs who find these situations challenging or frightening. And if you are planning on taking part in canine competitions, get yours socialised and used to the buzz of these events early on.

Well-socialised dogs live more relaxed, peaceful and happy lives than dogs that are constantly stressed by their environment.

Socialisation isn't an *"all or nothing"* project. You can socialise a puppy a bit, a lot, or a whole lot. The wider the range of positive experiences you expose her to (positively) when young, the better. Socialisation should never be forced, but approached systematically and in a manner that builds confidence and curious interaction.

If your pup finds a new experience frightening, take a step back, introduce her to the scary situation much more gradually, and make a big effort to do something she loves during the situation or right afterwards.

For example, if your puppy seems to be frightened by noise and vehicles at a busy road, a good method would be to go to a quiet road, sit with the dog away from - but within sight of - the traffic. Every time she looks towards the traffic say *"YES!"* and reward her with a treat.

If she is still stressed, you need to move further away. When your dog takes the food in a calm manner, she is becoming more relaxed and getting used to traffic sounds, so you can edge a bit nearer - but still just for short periods until she becomes totally relaxed. Keep each session short and **POSITIVE**.

Meeting Other Dogs

When you take your gorgeous and vulnerable little pup out with other dogs for the first few times, you are bound to be a bit apprehensive. To begin with, introduce your puppy to just one other dog — one that you know to be friendly, rather than taking her straight to the park where there are lots of dogs of all sizes racing around, which might frighten the life out of your timid little darling.

On the other hand, your pup might be full of confidence right from the off, but you still need to approach things slowly. If your puppy is too cocksure, she may get a warning bite from an older dog, which could make her more anxious when approaching new dogs in the future.

 Always make initial introductions on neutral ground, so as not to trigger territorial behaviour. You want your Dachshund to approach other dogs with friendliness, not fear.

From the first meeting, help both dogs experience good things when they're in each other's presence. Let them sniff each other briefly, which is normal canine greeting behaviour. As they do, talk to them in a happy, friendly tone of voice; never use a threatening tone.

Don't allow them to sniff each other for too long as this may escalate to an aggressive response. After a short time, get the attention of both dogs and give each a treat in return for obeying a simple command, e.g. *"Sit"* or *"Stay."* Continue with the *"happy talk,"* and rewards.

Learn to spot the difference between normal rough and tumble play and interaction that may develop into fear or aggression. Here are some signs of fear to look out for when your dog interacts with other canines:

- Running away or freezing on the spot
- Licking the lips or lips pulled back
- Trembling or panting, which can be a sign of stress or pain
- Frantic/nervous behaviour, e.g. excessive sniffing, drinking or playing frenetically with a toy
- A lowered body stance or crouching
- Lying on her back with paws in the air — this is submissive, as is submissive urination
- Lowering of the head or turning the head away, when you may see the whites of the eyes as the dog tries to keep eyes on the perceived threat
- Growling and/or hair raised on her back (raised hackles)
- Tail lifted in the air or ears high on the head

Some of these responses are normal. A pup may well crouch on the ground or roll on to her back to show other dogs she's not a threat. If the situation looks like escalating, calmly distract the dogs or remove your puppy — don't shout or shriek. Dogs will pick up on your fear.

Another sign to look out for is *eyeballing.* In the canine world, staring a dog in the eyes is a challenge and may cause an aggressive response.

NOTE: whereas we might look someone in the eye when we are first introduced, it is normal for dogs to sniff the scent glands in another dog's bottom!

 Your puppy has to learn to interact with other dogs. Don't be too quick to pick her up; she will sense your anxiety, lose confidence and become less independent. The same is true when walking on a lead – don't be nervous every time you seen another dog – your Dachshund will pick up on it and may react by barking, lunging or snapping.

Always follow up a socialisation experience with praise, petting, a fun game or a special treat. One positive sign from a dog is the *"play bow"* when she goes down on to her front elbows but keeps her backside up in the air. This is a sign that she's feeling friendly towards the other dog and wants to play. Relaxed ear and body position and wagging tail are other positive signs.

Although Dachshunds are not naturally aggressive dogs, aggression is often grounded in fear, and a dog that mixes easily is less likely to be combative. Similarly, without frequent and new experiences, some Dachshunds can become timid and nervous.

Take your new dog everywhere you can. You want her to feel relaxed and calm in any situation, even noisy and crowded ones. Take treats with you and praise her when she reacts calmly to new situations.

Once settled into your home, introduce her to your friends and teach her not to jump up. If you have young children, it is not only the dog that needs socialising! Youngsters also need training on how to act around dogs, so both parties learn to respect the other.

An excellent way of getting your new puppy to meet other dogs in a safe environment is at a puppy class. We highly recommend this for all puppies. Ask around locally if any classes are being run. Some vets and dog trainers run classes for very junior pups who have had all their vaccinations. These help pups get used to other dogs of a similar age.

Breeders on Socialisation

American breeder Kristin Cihos-Williams says: "Early socialization and training is imperative with this breed. I have taken early socialization seminars at our national specialty and understand the importance of exposure to new people and places during the first 11 crucial weeks of development.

"With early childhood in humans, there is something called Critical Period Theory, which essentially states that failure to acquire language, through exposure to other humans and early education, by a certain age tends to mean that language acquisition may never be achieved.

"The same is true in dogs. A puppy that is neglected and not exposed by a certain age or stage to new experiences and a variety of new people and dogs may always be suspicious of new experiences and unable to function in public."

Pictured living up to his name is Kinderteckel's Hollywood Handsome, bred by Kristin, aged just five weeks.

"It is the responsibility of the breeder to make sure early socialization is achieved during the first 11 weeks of development with puppies. Puppies hit a fear period at age eight weeks, so a responsible breeder holds on to puppies longer, allowing them to learn from their mother and siblings and acquire *"doggie manners."*

"A puppy sold too young and then not exposed appropriately to new sights and sounds by its new owner during the remainder of the Critical Period, is especially at risk of behaviour issues."

Other comments from the US: "Socialization is extremely important as dogs are social animals and they need to figure out themselves it also helps animals gain confidence. Good breeders will have started foundational socialization. Training is important too because it builds respect between dog and owner."

"Socializing EARLY is so very beneficial for a breed that is very protective; it's almost mandatory to have a friendly dog for your guests who might only visit once a year. Lack of socialization can lead to a dog that will NOT allow visitors, mailmen, etc. - and possibly a bite lawsuit."

UK dog trainer Lisa Cole says: "Socialisation is very, very important. I deal with adult dogs with little or no socialisation or formal training. These dogs bark, lunge and squeal as they do not know what to do when facing other dogs or other people. They are scared, excited and protective all at the same time. Training is also very important not only does it leave you with a dog you can control and communicate with, it also creates a strong bond."

Other comments from UK breeders: "Dachshunds are hugely protective of their home and very protective generally. Through early socialisation they accept strangers into their lives, if their owners say it's OK."

"Socialisation is incredibly important so the pup has confidence as it grows up. The last thing you need is a highly strung dog that screams and barks all the time. I introduce mine to the family, my friends and neighbours etc. They also meet other dogs before they leave us. Training ensures a pup knows its boundaries and stays safe. It makes the pup a safer dog in the long run, it means it doesn't bark the neighbourhood down and knows what it can and cannot do. Without decent training, dogs end up in rescue centres."

"It's very important but should be done in the correct manner. Don't throw them into puppy parties, which are free-for-alls."

"Socialisation is critical. It helps your dog have a happy well-balanced life. It teaches your dog to be friendly, make friends and listen to others. Exercise, if fun, helps very much with transitioning and change, and helps to take away stress and loneliness. A dog that as not socialised is often very fearful."

"Training and socialisation are the cornerstones in responsible pet-keeping, and I keep a socialisation chart and advice for puppy owners to carry on with, as well as them going to puppy training classes."

Photo of this handsome duo courtesy of Brenna Carlisle and Laura Potash, Heritage Hounds, Alabama. Marty (left) is six months old and Wilbur (AKC GCH UKC CH INT CH Heritage First In Flight) is five years old.

11. Dachshund Activities

To people not familiar with the breed, the Dachshund is a cute and comical canine companion. He is – but he is considerably more than that. No matter how small, the Dachshund is pure hound, full of instinct, bravery, drive and intelligence, with a strong mind and a muscular body.

All of this adds up to the Dachshund being one of THE most versatile breeds. While they love to snuggle up with you in bed or on the sofa, they are capable of so much more. In this chapter, three breeders tell personal stories of activities with their Dachshunds and give advice on how you can get involved with yours.

We start with Pauline Cheeseman, of Colraed Miniature Smooth Dachshunds, in Surrey, UK:

....

Scentwork

I got my first Dachshund over 15 years ago when I made the swap from German Shepherds. I was attracted to Dachshunds because, as a hound, they wouldn't be a lap dog, they'd be capable of long family walks and have a strong character like bigger dogs. I wasn't wrong - they have such strong personalities and are so loyal.

I had competed quite successfully in Working Trials with my German Shepherds, but it wasn't quite the right activity for Miniature Dachshunds. Mind you, I think they could quite happily do the Nosework (tracking a human scent) or even scale the six-foot obstacle!

I'm a great believer in all dogs benefitting from some form of activity in their daily lives. I first attended normal Obedience classes with my Dachshunds with a small amount of success, but both me and the dogs struggled with the repetitive nature of the exercises. It wasn't really our thing, so I started to look around to see what we could do.

We started Scentwork, which is a great activity for using the Dachshund's best asset – his nose. In Scentwork, a dog uses his sense of smell to identify and locate a specific scent. They start with simple scents - such as food! – which are placed in cones, and then move onto clothes scented with cloves, also in cones.

Once they have mastered these finds, they progress to search for particular scents in objects such as cases. When they grasp what they are looking for, you move on to searching rooms, tables and chairs, even cars for a particular scent.

Dogs have a highly sensitive nose, which is vastly superior to our own. We can't even smell the small amounts of scent used during these exercises, so we have to learn to listen and to trust our dog.

Photo: Bonnie searching cones for a small, scented cloth and indicating her find by standing.

I'd strongly advise joining a class or even having a one-to-one with a trainer to get you started. Then you can practise at home and, once you and your instructor feel you dog has an idea of what to do, you can attend Scentwork Trials, which are held all over the country. Look in the *Find a Trainer* section on www.scentworkuk.com

You start at Level 1. To pass this test, your dog has to recognise one odour in three out of four search areas and gets three minutes per search. In Levels 1 and 2, the odour is always clove oil, with gun oil and truffle oil being added at higher levels.

You can progress all the way up to Level 8, when the dog must find 90 out of 120 scents! To make it even more difficult, the judge can hide up to 24 scented articles throughout the three search areas; two of which are interior and one is exterior. Points are allocated for each find up to 120. The handler is not told how many scents are in each area, which also contains one unscented decoy.

You can then progress through the levels at your own speed or stay at Level 1 as long as you like, gaining points towards an Excellent title. Each level has slightly different objectives. The aim is progression and to help participants focus on their training by achieving small steps in their dog training journey. Annie and I are at Level 3 and I've just started Bonnie at Level 1.

All my dogs enjoy Scentwork, it's such a positive experience for them as, in the beginning, they always succeed. They engage so well, their tails never stop wagging and the bond between you and your dog just builds as you learn to read your dog.

My Annie gives a very subtle indication; we are still working on her standing next to the scent. At the moment, she will glance where the scent is as she walks by, so I have to be in tune with her! It's as if she says: "It's there," and if I miss her indication with my "YES," she will continue and walk out of the area. All my other dogs will stand and indicate, but with Annie, it's: "It's there, I told you and you missed it. I've done my job!"

The trials are relaxed and usually behind closed doors, so just you, the dog and judge. I don't find it nerve racking; you just have to learn to trust your dog. Take a look at www.scentworkuk.com to see all levels and to find your closest trainer.

In the USA, it is known as K9 Nose Work. Visit www.k9nosework.com for more information. Another American activity where the Dachshund uses his hunting instincts is Earthdog. Tests involve dogs navigating man-made tunnels on the scent of the quarry, usually two rats, which are protected by wooden bars at the end of the tunnel.

Hoopers

Another area I briefly attended was **Tricks Training** classes, which Annie took to quite well. There

are also lots of online videos that are easy to follow. **Agility** was another one I looked at for my Miniature Dachshunds. They did enjoy it, but I was concerned at the pressure it put on their backs.

Don't get me wrong, I'm a great believer in the stronger and fitter they are, and not carrying extra weight, the better for their backs. But there's a lot of impact on joints with Agility, so I searched for something else and found **Hoopers**.

Derek navigates the barrel at his own pace! Photo courtesy of Sunshine Canine
www.facebook.com/Sunshine.Canine.Hoopers.Agility

Hoopers has been described as "Croquet with dogs!" It uses a simple set of equipment: large hoops, big barrels and straight tunnels. Dogs are introduced to each using positive rewards and lots of praise.

I signed up with Anna Richardson of Sunshine Canine, who is an accredited Canine Hoopers UK instructor. Off I went with my Annie, who isn't too comfortable around other dogs. I needn't have worried, Hoopers was brilliant as it is so geared up for nervous, reactive dogs.

Hoopers was first registered in the UK in 2012 and has grown steadily since then. It's similar to Agility, but suitable for every Dachshund, due to it being safe, low impact and totally inclusive for all sizes, ages and shapes of dog. Anna herself has two tiny Dachshunds, a nervous Wolfgang, and Wilhelm, an IVDD-recovering hero. Both qualified for the National Hoopers Finals.

As in Agility, dogs are handled and directed from distance. They are trained to wait before racing off around courses set out safely with no tight turns, through hoops and tunnels, across mats and round barrels.

Annie got the gist of the classes quickly. Just to prove how inclusive it is, there was a lovely little Dachshund called Hercules there, *pictured,* born with three legs, who had just qualified for the National Finals! Hoopers is judged not only on speed, but also on points gained for clear rounds. We also trained with Lily, another IVDD survivor.

I spoke to Hercules's owner, she said: "Hercules is three, he was born a tripaw. He does hydrotherapy as well as exercise to take pressure off his legs but maintain his strength. He has been doing Hoopers classes since he was eight months old, so he does the block of training terms each year, but not training every single week. Hoopers made him switch on with his general training. Once we started Hoopers, his obedience and listening skills increased, he became more willing to learn and to work and now Hoopers is one of his favourite things!"

Anna added: "Hercules has grown in confidence and ability. When he sees a hoop, he's off - there's no stopping him! He's already earned a Bronze Good Hooper's Award."

I had to stop attending Sunshine classes as it was little bit too far to travel. But during the Covid lockdown, the governing body put together an online programme. Through that I found the lovely Tracey from TJ's Dog Training and enrolled with great success, with Annie passing the Foundation and Bronze Awards and is now working on her Silver Award. www.caninehoopersuk.co.uk

To compete in Hoopers you first have to first join CHUK (Canine Hoopers UK) and you can then work your way through the four levels. You can also enter their Tri Score Tournaments; all courses are run in fully enclosed areas, so are ideal for nervous or reactive dogs.

My Annie loves Hoopers. The hardest thing for me is standing back and letting your dog learn to run without too many signals, so they learn freethinking, I hope to take part in some competitions soon, but am happy to continue with the online awards at the moment.

Mantrailing

Mantrailing is where the dog follows a scent to find someone. It is utilised by search and rescue teams to find missing people, but is also an established sport in several countries and is establishing itself as an exciting new dog sport in the UK. Dogs have such

incredible noses and what fun for your dog to use theirs. It is a low impact sport and highly suitable for Dachshunds.

As well as providing physical exercise, Mantrailing engages the olfactory (smell) senses, which gives the dogs an intense mental and stimulating session along the way - and it's fantastic to watch the dog's confidence grow as he gets used to following the scent.

There are currently three levels of Mantrailing, starting with a 200m-400m trail length in fields or woods. I am doing my Level 1 with Cassie at the moment and we are both loving it. You have to fully trust your dog, and learn to read their signals when they are on a trail - and when they lose it too.

They "cast around" at the start and at junctions - this is zigzagging or circling around just after they have taken scent from the dropped article from the Misper (missing person) to find the scent pool and the direction they have walked.

Mantrailing is fully accessible, and dogs are always worked alone, so it's fantastic for reactive dogs. I find it immense fun - it's such a thrill to get a successful search. **Photo shows Cassie Mantrailing.**

There are many instructors springing up around the country, and instructors' courses to so take a look at www.mantrailinguk.com and other websites for instructors in your area. I train with www.mantraillingscentdogs.co.uk

I believe to work and train your dogs in these sporting activities is good for both our mental health. Scentwork on any level is great fun as a training activity, it builds such a partnership, and watching your dog's confidence grow along with your own cements such a bond. You can participate for fun or go on and compete. It's suitable for all breeds, but hounds like the Dachshund are born to work.

Showing

Melissa Sworab, of Rabows Dachshunds, Texas, has Dachshund champion descendants on several continents. Here she explains how she got involved in showing and shares tips on starting out.

The first step to dog showing, is simply going to a show! It is the ONLY sport where novices can compete alongside professionals. After 24 years of Dachshunds as pets, I decided it was time for another, and found a breeder that wanted to meet at a dog show. I was a complete novice, never having been before, but was willing to learn.

I videoed the breezy outdoor show and talked to anyone and everyone who had a minute to spare. The air was buzzing with excitement and the barks of hundreds of dogs of all breeds.

I exchanged contact information with several breeders and, to my surprise, got a call later that night: "We are short a person tomorrow, would you help take a puppy in the ring?" Panic ensued and I spent all night watching the videos I'd just taken.... I had no idea how to show a dog!

The next morning, a breeder handed me the show puppy, and I ventured nervously into the ring. People outside the ring were waving their arms trying to make me aware that I had put the puppy on the table at the wrong time! It was intense, but I tried to pay attention to the ring procedure, watching how others pick up and place their dogs on the table, and watching the judge carefully go over each dog with his hands.

Despite my comical first minutes in the ring, the dog show world had me hooked. I could not wait to do it again and haphazardly bought two "show puppies" from a so-called-expert. They were eight weeks old, which, I am now aware, was a big red flag.

Showing these two champion-pedigreed "show-prospects" proved disastrous – third place out of two entries - the judge considered neither entry worthy of first place! Not long after, AKC found an anomaly in a DNA parentage test and cancelled one pup's registration papers.

With a new-found commitment to improve, I needed more information. I studied *"The ABC's of Dog Breeding"* and later *"Practical Canine Anatomy and Movement,"* both by Claudia Orlandi.

I also found two well-respected Australian breeders with 30 years' experience and success in the ring. This mother/daughter team offered guidance on subjects like what to look and feel for in a show dog, and what health issues to look out for. They did it with patience not pressure. I learned it is NOT about the number of Champions in a pedigree, but the consistency in the line. They became my mentors for life.

We communicated online for months, studying pedigrees and photos of their biggest winners. Eventually, I visited their home in Australia, where I learned grooming and showing tips. I brought back two fully-grown show dogs, and a week's worth of notes and video! This method had much better results - my next trip in the ring produced a Champion so fast it felt surreal!

In my experience, showing costs can be tailored to fit most budgets, and quality food, supplements and grooming are similar for pet and show dogs. A few weeks before a show, a more detailed grooming with weekly baths and coat conditioning begins, and weight is monitored. Show expenses do, however, start to add up with travel, hotels, entry fees, and lots of show photos, but you can go slow and show locally to save money.

Some competitors hire a handler - they are great and go to more shows, but at a cost, and you lose experience and may not develop an eye for a good show dog. The "eye" was key to my finding Ehren. Even though four different show breeders advised that Ehren was just a pet, I saw something in him. He became American Norwegian IABCA International Champion Burdachs Brown Eyed Handsome Man ROMX, and produced Champions in four countries, including a Best in Show daughter, Australian Champion Rabows Charmed One.

Photo: Best-In-Show Specialty Competition Victoria KC, Australia, by Ibiza Photoz.

So, can anyone do it? In a nutshell, yes! Training for showing is not difficult...but it is an art. The art to showing is in the presentation. I went to several different handling classes to polish my show skills at my own pace.

In the ring, dogs simply walk on a show lead at heel, except they must do it proudly and slightly ahead and to the left. They then just need to look pretty and stand still for the judge's examination. Puppies should be trained to "stand" on a table for exam starting about five weeks of age - this is much like an exam at a vet - but standing on all four feet with a straight and level back. The judge views them as they stand, checks for a proper bite, confirms coat texture, feels the body condition, grades structure against the Breed Standard, then watches how they move going-around the ring while also observing temperament and attitude.

Photo: Australian BIS Rabows Charmed One "Prue," showing ideal Dachshund movement in the ring. Credit: Mark and Josie Haseldine.

In the USA (AKC) and Canada (CKC), your dog competes against others of the same gender in a class of dogs usually broken down by age, experience level, or other division. First place in each of the classes moves up to "Winners" competition where one winner may earn points depending upon the class count. Unlike in Europe, these dogs do not compete against Champions for points.

One winner of each sex then competes against the Champions for Best of Breed/Variety. Different judges like their own style of Dachshund, so you might win with one judge and get nothing from another. Judges give written critiques at some Specialty shows and most IABCA shows - you learn a LOT about your dog this way.

When you are ready to find a show breeder, choose one who is a member of a breed parent club or multiple clubs, is an AKC Breeder of Merit, a Bred with H.E.A.R.T. member in the US, or Assured Breeder in the UK. All should health test their dogs and supply those results as well as vet and customer references. You also want one who is patient and willing to educate you and matches your personality.

Responsible show breeders meticulously balance Dachshund temperament, performance, health, structure - and add beauty as the icing on the cake. They ideally have finished some of their dogs within the last five years, but good breeders also care about the breed's future and health, not just their own interests or ego. I prefer a breeder that concentrates on one breed, doing all of the breed club's recommended health testing, and going above and beyond with full DNA panels that include hundreds of health tests, ancestry and other genetic data.

They should interview, i.e. interrogate, you and want to know your experience level. They should supply a contract BEFORE taking a deposit, which may include a co-ownership deal. The sire and dam should be available for you to meet and have stable/confident/happy personalities and be of good type and style you like. Most show breeders will have a specific puppy in mind for you, but you can always walk away if you see any caution signs. Know your Breed Standard and visit the puppy on multiple occasions.

Show Puppy Caution Signs

X   Sullen, shy, fearful, aggressive

X Sits a lot/low head/cannot stand still for very long

X Bunny hopping, bouncing, limping

X High rear, compared to shoulders/arched (roached) or sagging back

X 90˚ angle of neck into back or has skin rolls over the shoulder

X Gay curled tail/kinked (bent/broken) tail

X Long hocks /round large eye

X Rare/flashy colors or patterns (harder to finish and groom for a novice)

X Pink pigment (nails, nose, eye rims, footpads)

X Repeat breeding of past litter with zero champions

X Under 16 weeks – still a chance bite will go off or Pes Varus will happen

Show Puppy Good Signs

✓ Energetic, friendly, outgoing, fearless

✓ Stands proudly and for prolonged periods

✓ Moves easily, glides effortlessly

✓ Level back (generally; the shoulder to tail area)

✓ Neck flows gracefully and gradually into spine

✓ Slight or no curl to the tail

✓ Short hocks/small almond eye

✓ Traditional color (red, black and tan) - easier to finish and groom for a novice

✓ Dark eyes and eye rims, black nails, black nose, dark footpads

✓ Repeat breeding of past litter produced multiple champions

✓ Six-month or older puppy: dental malocclusion, patella issues and pes varus risk reduced

Pictured is Burdachs Brown Eyed Handsome Man with Melissa and Judge D. Harrison. Photo CC Photography

Information, education, and experience are keys to finding the best show candidates. Just remember, win or lose, **the best dogs** will be the spoiled ones at home sitting in your lap.

Recommended classes: www.caninecollege.akc.org/collections/courses-for-breeders

Dachshund Field Trials

Dachshund Field Trialling is a fun, bloodless sport in which dogs track game, usually rabbits or hares. It's normally held in a fenced area so the dogs, which compete in pairs called "a brace," don't wander too far. Brush beaters move the quarry from its cover, the Dachshunds are released – exactly when is a skill – and they are judged on how well they track the scent or "line."

Californian Kristin Cihos Williams has bred Standard Smooths for nearly three decades. During that time, her Kinderteckel Dachshunds have won countless show and field trial titles. Some have even won both, making them Dual Champions. This is her field trialling journey:

When I became involved with the sport of dogs nearly 30 years ago, my visualization of the ideal Dachshund was a robust, sufficiently-boned little hound with a gorgeous long head and matching ears. I never thought about what makes a hound a hound, which is the aspect of scent trailing and prey drive.

I immersed myself in conformation shows for years and, because of all the travel involved, never thought I had extra time on the weekends for field trials. Friends who were already involved kept telling me I would really enjoy it if I tried it just once. Still, I never thought it was for me.

But one weekend five years ago, I dragged myself out of bed at 3am and drove the 100 miles to the field trial grounds in Chino, California, to make roll call by 7am. We did not have any idea of what was involved. We borrowed hunt collars and release lines from friends, who probably giggled a little as we tried to figure out the finer points of releasing dogs to follow a scent line.

Some Dachshunds are slow, methodical hunters, while others are fast off the line. They all have their individual styles, but they must track with heads down.

Our dogs were not specifically trained for this event at all. They were AKC champions who had plenty of natural prey drive - as we soon discovered! But they had not been trained with any formal classes or programs, such as Nose Work. As a handler brand new to field trials, I felt overwhelmed with ignorance.

Reading the *AKC Field Trial Rules and Standard Procedure for Dachshunds* did not explain the finer points of releasing dogs from the line smoothly and without getting them tangled in branches! I had many such mishaps, but kept coming back for more, despite the hideously early mornings, because my dogs absolutely loved field trials.

Photo: Absolute winning Dual CH Kinderteckel's Serendipity 3 CHIC # 94857 in the background, Absolute winning GCHS DC Kinderteckel's Lancelot CHIC # 102895 (Lance) in front and field-pointed GCH Kinderteckel's Put My Name In Bold CHIC# 125211, all paddling in the bay at San Diego.

To me, the dogs seemed to get so much more out of their early mornings, alive with the anticipation of rabbits just up ahead, than their two minutes or so in the show ring. One of my girls, who was utterly bored by the show ring absolutely took to field trials and finished her dual championship by achieving wins in the field in just a couple of weekends out.

That inspired me; I wanted to learn to be a better handler in the field. The dogs soon learned that waking up that early meant a field trial weekend, and they would not let me forget that!

One unique challenge we face in California is that our field trial grounds are unfenced. The Chino field trial grounds feature hundreds of acres of old olive tree groves. There are hills, canyons, a densely forested area that is difficult for humans to navigate, a river, and coyotes!

Training recall is important. I especially had a hard time with one of my favourite dogs, Lance, who was a seasoned Grand Champion (#5 Smooth Dachshund in the US in 2015) when he first went to field trials. Initially, he seemed to have little prey drive and refused to leave my side, but his prey drive did eventually kick in.

Unfortunately, this instinct blinded him at field trials, and he refused to recall if he was hot on the scent of a rabbit. This became an embarrassing situation. We had five people out one day looking for him, and it took well over an hour for him to finally decide to come back to me.

Working with him at home on recall, using a 30-foot line, could not overcome the overwhelming excitement he had at field trials when he was hot on a scent line. His quest for his Dual Championship was finally attained, with me actually dampening him down before releasing him on the line. This is the exact opposite approach I take with my dogs normally.

Pictured Absolute winning GCHS DC Kinderteckel's Lancelot, the naughty Dual Champion with little recall, just after he won first place and was still dripping wet from the tall grass.

Every dog is unique, and just when I thought I was finally learning a thing or two about field trials, Lance made me understand that I knew nothing! Each dog has a distinct hunting style out in the field, and I am learning as I go along. So far, despite the fact that I am relatively new to field trials, I have bred five dogs with Dual Championships (AKC conformation championship/grand championship titles, plus AKC field championship titles).

I live a couple of hours from the nearest Nose Work classes, but this type of early formal training works well with Dachshunds to reinforce scent distinction. During winter and spring, I am fortunate to be able to work my dogs on my own property. I have seven acres of old apple trees and an amazing population of cottontail rabbits.

I work young dogs by simply exposing them to game trails and letting their own instincts emerge. If they see a rabbit pop out and they light up, so much the better - as long as they do not learn to sight chase instead of scent track. I currently bring them out with my eight-year-old Dual Champion girl, Absolute winning DC Kinderteckel's Serendipity 3, since she has an extremely accurate nose and will lead the younger pups to a bush and pop the rabbit out for them. I keep her on a 30-foot training line and let her take the lead. Hopefully, seeing her work a tight bush and pop a rabbit out will encourage them to be persistent.

My dogs visibly love working a bush for a rabbit, with tails wagging, and they will eagerly "voice" upon popping a rabbit. My dogs do not "babble," which means constantly barking in a field trial, even if no rabbits have been flushed. However, when they are actively engaged with prey, they will "voice," which is a rapid, sharp yip-bark that they only use when they have flushed a rabbit.

Anyone with an AKC-registered Dachshund may participate in Dachshund field trials in the US. You simply show up with your dog and a completed entry form before the published entry closing time. This information is available in the premium list published by the Dachshund club hosting the field trial, or Google "AKC Dachshund Field Trials" for details of events.

12. Dachshund Health

The Dachshund is generally regarded as a healthy breed with a relatively long lifespan. However, health should always be an important factor when choosing and raising a dog. Firstly, select a puppy from a breeder who produces Dachshunds sound in both body and temperament – and this involves health screening - and secondly, play your role in helping to keep your dog healthy throughout his or her life.

NOTE: This chapter is intended to be used as an encyclopaedia to help you to identify potential health issues and act promptly in the best interests of your dog. Please don't read it thinking your Dachshund will get lots of these ailments – he or she WON'T!

It is becoming increasingly evident that genetics can have a huge influence on a person's health and even life expectancy, with a great deal of time and money currently being devoted to genetic research. A human is more likely to suffer from a hereditary illness if the gene or genes for that disorder is passed on from parents or grandparents. That person is said to have a *"predisposition"* to the ailment if the gene is in the family's bloodline. Well, the same is true of dogs.

There is not a single breed without the potential for some genetic weakness. For example, many Cavalier King Charles Spaniels have heart problems and 25% of all West Highland White Terriers have a hereditary itchy skin disease.

A Dalmatian or a Westie from unscreened parents will be more likely to suffer from these disorders than one from health-tested parents.

The 2015 UK scientific study *The Challenges of Pedigree Dog Health: Approaches to Combating Inherited Disease* states: "The development of (such) pedigree dog breeds can be both a blessing and a curse: desirable features are rigidly retained, but sometimes, undesirable disease-causing genes can be inadvertently fixed within the breed."

In other words, bad genes can be inherited along with good ones.

FACT In the same study, Dachshunds are listed as having 50 inheritable diseases, ranking them 10th highest (worst) out of more than 200 breeds.

To read the full study, type the title into Google and click on Table 1 at the bottom to view individual breed statistics.

With their short legs, all types of Dachshunds can be affected by IVDD, or Intervertebral Disc Disease.

UFAW (Universities Federation for Animal Welfare) www.ufaw.org.uk, says: "Many Dachshunds (approximately 25%), at some point in their lives suffer from damage to the discs in their spines (rather like "slipped discs" in humans). This can cause serious pain that can be of prolonged duration and may lead to severe damage to the spine and paralysis."

The good news is that Dachshunds of all types have a relatively long lifespan, often into their teens. And there is plenty you can do to help yours live a long and healthy life.

Health Certificates for Puppy Buyers

Anyone thinking of getting a Dachshund puppy today can reduce the chance of their dog having a genetic disease by choosing a puppy from healthy bloodlines.

If you're actively searching for a puppy, you might be considering a breeder based on the look or colour of her dogs or their success in the show ring, but consider the health of the puppy's parents and ancestors as well. Could they have passed on unhealthy genes along with the good genes for all those features you are attracted to?

Tip **Check what tests the parents have passed and ask to see original certificates where relevant - a good breeder will be happy to provide them: These are the main tests:**

UK:

1. Cord1 PRA DNA test for all three varieties of Miniature Dachshund (eyes)
2. Lafora DNA test for Miniature Wire-Haired Dachshund (a form of epilepsy)

These first two tests are compulsory for Kennel Club Assured Breeders. The next six are recommended:

3. IVDD X-ray screening for all 6 varieties
4. KC/BVA/ISDS Clinical Eye Examination for all 6 varieties
5. NPHP4 PRA DNA test for Wires and Mini Wires with Scandinavian pedigrees (eyes)
6. Cardiac testing for Standard Wires
7. Patella testing for all Miniatures (knees)
8. Dapple (Merle) gene DNA testing if in doubt about hidden merle breeding

USA:

OFA (Orthopedic Foundation for Animals) recommends the following basic health screening tests for all breeding stock. Dogs meeting these requirements qualify for Canine Health Information Center (CHIC) certification. OFA says: "For potential puppy buyers, CHIC certification is a good indicator the breeder responsibly factors good health into their selection criteria.

"The breed-specific list below represents the basic health screening recommendations. It is not all encompassing. There may be other health screening tests appropriate for this breed. And, there may be other health concerns for which there is no commonly accepted screening protocol available." (One of these others is IVDD).

9. Eye Examination by Ophthalmologist
10. Patellar Luxation
11. PRA, or Progressive Retinal Atrophy (optional)
12. Autoimmune thyroiditis (optional)
13. Congenital Deafness (optional)
14. Cardiac Exam (heart)

All AKC Bred With H.E.A.R.T. breeders must carry out Patella and Ophthalmologist Evaluations and a Cardiac Exam.

The UK Kennel Club has a health monitoring system, called **Breed Watch** with three Categories:

1 Breeds with no current points of concern reported

2 Breeds with Breed Watch points of concern

3 Breeds where some dogs have visible conditions or exaggerations that can cause pain or discomfort

All Dachshunds are in Category 2, with two Points of Concern being added in 2020:

- 🐾 Incorrect hindquarter/unsound movement
- 🐾 Sore eyes or excessive tearing

A further point was added for all three types of Miniatures:

15. Significantly underweight

We asked UK breeders what they believe to be the major health issues affecting Dachshunds. This is what they said: "PRA Cord 1 in all Miniatures, Lafora in Miniature WireHaired, IVDD in all six types. A big issue coming up lately is colour dilution alopecia, very often seen in dogs of so-called rare (unrecognised) colours in adult dogs."

"In Miniature Smooths we are getting on top of PRA cord-1 with testing. Of course, the major health issue is IVDD." "Spinal problems and eye problems, but heath tests can be done to show whether a dog is Clear or a Carrier." "IVDD and PRA." "The back can become an issue if the dog is lifted and handled without precautions."

US breeder Melissa Sworab added: "A major health issue would actually be obesity, since it causes many health issues Dachshunds are prone to, like IVDD, diabetes, thyroid issues, patella issues, elbow issues and neck issues. I see too many overweight puppies too, and that can cause bone growth issues as well as be a risk factor for all the above as well Pes Varus (a curvature of the dwarf limb bones).

"Surprisingly, I have heard of many others' lines with hip dysplasia in the last 10 years, and quite a few come from a specific line it seems, yet the pedigrees are still out there being bred from. A LOT of issues can be prevented with proper care from birth to adult."

 A pedigree certificate from the Kennel Club or AKC does NOT mean that that puppy or its parents have passed any health tests. The only thing a pedigree certificate guarantees is that the puppy's parents can be traced back several generations and that the ancestors were purebred Dachshunds.

As well as asking to see health certificates, prospective buyers should always find out exactly what health guarantees, if any, the breeder is offering with the puppy.

FACT ❯ If a puppy is sold as "Vet Checked," it does not mean that the parents have been health screened. It means that a vet has given the puppy a brief physical and visual examination, worming and vaccinations are up to date, and the pup appears to be in good health on the day of the examination.

If you have already got your dog, don't worry! There is plenty of advice in this book on how to take excellent care of your Dachshund. Taking extra care with a puppy, feeding a quality food, monitoring your dog's weight, regular grooming and check-overs, plenty of exercise and socialisation will all help to keep him in tiptop condition. Good owners can certainly help to extend the life of their Daxie.

Dachshund Insurance

Insurance is another point to consider for a new puppy or adult dog. All puppies from reputable breeders come with four weeks' or 30 days' insurance that can be extended before it expires. If you are getting an older dog, get insurance BEFORE any health issues develop, or you may find any pre-existing conditions are excluded.

If you can afford it, take out life cover. This may be more expensive, but will cover your dog throughout his or her lifetime - including for chronic (recurring and/or long term) ailments, such as joint, heart or eye problems, ear infections, epilepsy and cancer.

Insuring a healthy puppy or adult dog is the only sure-fire way to ensure vets' bills are covered before anything unforeseen happens - and you'd be a rare owner if you didn't use your policy at least once during your dog's lifetime.

Costs in the UK range from around £15 a month for Accident Only to around £30-£50 per month for Lifetime Cover, depending on where you live, how much excess you are willing to pay and the total in pounds covered per year.

I ran a few examples for US pet insurance on a three-month-old Dachshund pup with a deductible of $100-$200 and came back with quotes from $24 to $50, depending on location, the excess and amount of coverage per year in dollars.

With advances in veterinary science, there is so much more vets can do to help an ailing dog - but at a price. Surgical procedures can rack up bills of thousands of pounds or dollars. According to www.PetInsuranceQuotes.com these are some of the most common ailments affecting Dachshunds, and typical treatment costs:

> Intervertebral Disc Disease - $3,000-$9,000, Curvature of the Spine - $6,000-$15,000, Patent Ductus Arteriosus (Dachshunds are 2.5x more likely to get the heart condition PDA than other purebreds) - £2,500-$5,000, Mitral Valve Disease - $1,000-$5,000, Anal Sac Disease - $100-$2,500, Cushing's Disease - $500-$2,000, Eye Problems - $50-$3,000 per eye, Hip Dysplasia - $4,000-$6,000 per hip, Patellar Luxation - $1,500-$3,000, Epilepsy - $200 to $15,000, Achondroplasia (bone growth disorder) – $1,000-$5,000, GDV – $1,500 to $7,500. ($1.3 = approximately £1 at the time of writing).

Of course, if you make a claim, your monthly premium will increase, but if you have a decent insurance policy BEFORE a recurring health problem starts, your dog should continue to be covered if the ailment returns. You have to decide whether insurance is worth the money. On the plus side, you'll have:

1. Peace of mind financially if your beloved Dachshund falls ill, and
2. You know exactly how much hard cash to part with each month, so no nasty surprises.

Three Health Tips

1. **Buy a well-bred puppy** - Good Dachshund breeders select their stock based on:
   - General health and the DNA test of the parents
   - Conformation (physical structure)
   - Temperament

Although well-bred puppies are not cheap, believe it or not, committed Dachshund breeders are not in it for the money, often incurring high bills for health screening, stud fees, veterinary costs, specialised food, etc. Their main concern is to produce healthy, handsome puppies with good temperaments and instincts that are *"fit for function"* – whether from working or show lines.

2. Get pet insurance as soon as you get your dog - Don't wait until your dog has a health issue and needs to see a vet. Most insurers will exclude all pre-existing conditions on their policies. Check the small print to make sure that all conditions are covered and that if the problem is recurring, it will continue to be covered year after year. When working out costs of a dog, factor in annual or monthly pet insurance fees and trips to a vet for check-ups, annual vaccinations, etc. Some breeders provide free insurance for the first few weeks in their Puppy Pack - ask yours if this is the case.

3. Find a good vet who is familiar with dwarf breeds like Dachshunds, Basset Hounds and Corgis - Ask around, rather than just going to the first one you find. A vet that knows your dog from his or her puppy vaccinations and then right through their life is more likely to understand your dog and diagnose quickly and correctly when something is wrong. If you visit a big veterinary practice, ask for the vet by name when you make an appointment.

We all want our dogs to be healthy - so how can you tell if yours is? Well, here are some positive things to look for in a healthy Dachshund:

....

Health Indicators

1. **Movement –** Dachshunds are prone to back problems. A healthy dog will have a fluid, pain-free gait. Look out for warning signs of stiffness, wobbliness, shivering, a reluctance to move, an arched back or the head hung low.

2. **Eyes -** A Dachshund's eyes should be clear with an intelligent, alert expression and no sign of tears, *as shown here by two-year-old Cassie (Hollybirch Gingersnap), courtesy of Pauline Cheeseman, Colraed Miniature Dachshunds, Surrey, UK.*

   These are most commonly dark with dark rims, but dapples can have "wall eyes" and chocolates have lighter eyes and pale rims. Paleness around the eyeball (conjunctiva) could be a sign of underlying problems. A red swelling in the corner of one or both eyes could be cherry eye, and a cloudy eye could be a sign of cataracts. Sometimes the dog's third eyelid (nictating membrane) is visible at the inside corner - this is normal. There should be no thick, green or yellow discharge from the eyes.

3. **Nose –** A dog's nose is an indicator of health. Almost all Dachshunds have a black nose, although chocolates have brown noses, as do some reds. *Dilutes, isabellas* (fawns) and some of the *unaccepted colours* may have liver-coloured, brown or grey noses. A pink nose can be a sign of allergies or other health issues. A pink *"snow nose"* may appear in winter due to a lack of Vitamin D, but usually returns to black during summer. Some dogs'

noses turn pinkish with age, due to them producing less pigment and is not a cause for concern. Regardless of colour, the nose should be moist and cold to the touch as well as free from clear, watery secretions. Any yellow, green or foul-smelling discharge is not normal - in younger dogs this can be a sign of canine distemper.

4. **Ears** – If you are choosing a puppy, gently clap your hands behind the pup (not so loud as to frighten him) to see if he reacts. If not, this may be a sign of deafness (more so in puppies with white on the head or ears). Floppy ears are more susceptible to infections than pricked-up ears. Make sure the ears look clean and smell nice.

5. **Mouth** – Dachshund gums should be black or pink or a mixture. Paleness or whiteness can be a sign of anaemia, Bloat or lack of oxygen due to heart or breathing problems (this is harder to see with black gums). Blue gums or tongue are a sign that your dog is not breathing properly. Red, inflamed gums can be a sign of gingivitis or other tooth disease.

   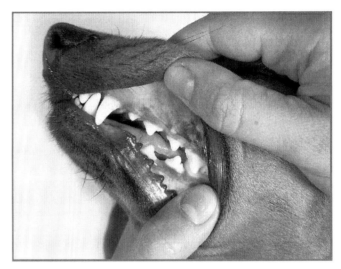

   Young dogs have sparkling white teeth, *pictured,* whereas older dogs have darker teeth, but they should not have any hard white, yellow, green or brown bits. Your dog's breath should smell OK.

6. **Coat and Skin** – These are easy-to-monitor indicators of a healthy dog. A healthy smooth or long coat has a sheen, and a wire coat should not feel brittle. Any dandruff, bald spots, a dull, lifeless, discoloured or oily coat, or one that loses excessive hair, can all be signs that something is amiss. Skin should be smooth without redness or rashes.

   If a dog is scratching, licking or biting a lot, he may have a condition that needs addressing. Open sores, scales, scabs, red patches or growths can be a sign of a skin issue or allergy. Signs of fleas, ticks and other external parasites should be treated immediately; check for small black or dark red specks, which may be fleas or flea poo, on the coat or bedding.

7. **Weight –** Your Dachshund's stomach should be above the bottom of his rib cage when standing, and you should be able to feel his ribs beneath his coat without too much effort. If the stomach is level or hangs below, your dog is overweight - or may have a pot belly, which can also be a symptom of other conditions.

8. **Temperature** – The normal temperature of a dog is 101°F to 102.5°F. (A human's is 98.6°F). Excited or exercising dogs may run a slightly higher temperature. Anything above 103°F or below 100°F should be checked out. The exceptions are female dogs about to give birth that will often have a temperature of 99°F. If you take your dog's temperature, make sure he is relaxed and *always* use a purpose-made canine thermometer.

9. **Stools** - Poo, poop, business, faeces - call it what you will - it's the stuff that comes out of the less appealing end of your Dachshund on a daily basis! It should be mostly firm and brown, not runny, with no signs of blood or worms. Watery stools or a dog not eliminating regularly are both signs of an upset stomach or other ailments. If it continues for a couple of days, consult your vet.

 If puppies have diarrhoea, they need checking out much quicker as they can quickly dehydrate.

10. **Energy** – Dachshunds are bold, alert dogs. Yours should have good amounts of energy with fluid and pain-free movements. Lack of energy or lethargy could be a sign of an underlying problem.

11. **Smell** – If there is a musty, 'off' or generally unpleasant smell coming from your Dachshund's body, it could be a sign of a yeast infection. There can be a number of causes; the ears may require attention or it could be a food allergy. Another not uncommon cause with the breed is an anal sac issue. Whatever the cause, you need to get to the root of the problem quickly before it develops into something more serious.

12. **Attitude** – A generally positive attitude is a sign of good health. Dachshunds are engaged and involved, so symptoms of illness may include one or all of the following: a general lack of interest in his or her surroundings, tail not wagging, lethargy, not eating food and sleeping a lot (more than normal). The important thing is to look out for any behaviour that is out of the ordinary for YOUR Dachshund.

There are many different symptoms that can indicate your canine companion isn't feeling great. If you don't yet know your dog, his habits, temperament and behaviour patterns, then spend some time getting acquainted with them.

What are his normal character and temperament? Lively or calm, playful or serious, a joker or an introvert, bold or nervous, happy to be left alone or loves to be with people, a keen appetite or a fussy eater? How often does he empty his bowels, does he ever vomit? (Dogs will often eat grass to make themselves sick, this is perfectly normal and a natural way of cleansing the digestive system).

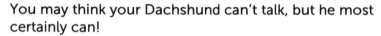

You may think your Dachshund can't talk, but he most certainly can!

If you really know your dog, his character and habits, then he CAN tell you when he's not well. He does this by changing his patterns. Some symptoms are physical, some emotional and others are behavioural. It's important to be able to recognise these changes, as early treatment can be the key to keeping a simple problem from snowballing into something more serious.

If you think your dog is unwell, it is useful to keep an accurate and detailed account of his symptoms to give to the vet, perhaps even take a video of him on your mobile phone. This will help the vet to correctly diagnose and effectively treat your dog.

Four Vital Signs of Illness

16. **Heart Rate** - You can feel your Dachshund's heartbeat by placing your hand on his lower ribcage – just behind the elbow. Don't be alarmed if the heartbeat seems irregular compared to that of a human; it often is in dogs. Your dog will probably love the attention, so it should be quite easy to check his heartbeat. Just lay him on his side and bend his left front leg at the elbow, bring the elbow in to his chest and place your fingers on this area and count the beats. The larger the dog, the slower the heartbeat.

   ❧ Big dogs have a normal resting heart rate of 70 to 120 beats per minute

   ❧ With medium-sized dogs its 80 to 120 beats per minute

- 🐾 Small dogs have a normal rate of 90 to 140 beats per minute
- 🐾 A young puppy has a heartbeat of around 220 beats per minute
- 🐾 An older dog has a slower heartbeat

17. **Temperature -** A new-born puppy has a temperature of 94-97°F. This reaches the normal adult body temperature of around 101°F at four weeks old. A vet takes a dog's temperature reading via the rectum. If you do this, only do it with a special digital rectal thermometer (not glass), get someone to hold the dog and be very careful. Ear thermometers *(pictured)* are now widely available for home use.

    NOTE: Exercise or excitement can cause temperature to rise by 2°F to 3°F when your dog is actually in good health, so wait until he is relaxed before taking his temperature. If it is above or below the norms and the dog seems under par, give your vet a call.

18. **Respiratory Rate -** Another symptom of illness is a change in breathing patterns. This varies a lot depending on the size and weight of the dog. An adult dog will have a respiratory rate of 15-25 breaths per minute when resting. You can easily check this by counting your dog's breaths for a minute with a stopwatch handy. Don't do this if he is panting; it doesn't count.

19. **Behaviour Changes -** Classic symptoms of illness are any inexplicable behaviour changes. If there has NOT been a change in the household atmosphere, such as another new pet, a new baby, moving home, the absence of a family member or the loss of another dog, then the following symptoms may well be a sign that all is not well:

    - 🐾 Depression or lethargy
    - 🐾 Anxiety and/or shivering, which can be a sign of pain
    - 🐾 Falling or stumbling
    - 🐾 Loss of appetite
    - 🐾 Walking in circles
    - 🐾 Being more vocal - grunting, whining or whimpering
    - 🐾 Aggression
    - 🐾 Tiredness - sleeping more than normal or not wanting to exercise
    - 🐾 Abnormal posture

If any of them appear for the first time or worse than usual, you need to keep him under close watch for a few hours or even days. Quite often he will return to normal of his own accord. Like humans, dogs have off-days too.

If he is showing any of the above symptoms, then don't over-exercise him, and avoid stressful situations and hot or cold places. Make sure he has access to clean water. Keep a record and it may be useful to take a fresh stool sample to your vet.

If your dog does need professional medical attention, most vets will want to know:

WHEN the symptoms first appeared in your dog

WHETHER they are getting better or worse, and

HOW FREQUENT the symptoms are - intermittent, continuous or increasing?

IVDD (Intervertebral Disc Disease)

IVDD is the specific name given to a variety of back problems, such as slipped, ruptured, herniated or bulging disk(s), and it's the most common spinal disease in dogs.

The Dachshund is a dwarf breed, having been bred down from larger hounds. It is also *"chondrodystrophic,"* meaning it has short, curved limbs. These factors make the breed prone to back problems, and at some point in their lives, one in four Dachshunds may suffer from IVDD.

Although there is thought to be a genetic link, there is no DNA test to prevent IVDD. However, there is an X-ray scheme to test for calcification (thickening and hardening of the disks) in dogs aged 24 to 48 months.

The UK Kennel Club recommends that ALL Dachshund breeders screen their dogs and any dog showing signs of many calcifications would be considered more of a risk for breeding.

Cartilage is a connective tissue, softer and more elastic than bone, found all over the body, particularly in joints. Intervertebral disks are fibrous cartilage cushions between the vertebrae (series of small bones that form the backbone). The disks allow movement, provide supportive and act as shock absorbers.

There are two main types of IVDD: *Hansen Type 1 and Type 2.* Dachshunds usually suffer from Type 1, also known as a *ruptured disk.* It occurs when the gel-like inner layer of the disk suddenly breaks through the top of the outer layer, causing sudden pressure on the spinal cord. It's sometimes called IVDE (Disk Extrusion) and symptoms are noticeable within one to five days. Type 2, often called a *bulging disk,* happens gradually and more commonly affects older, larger dogs.

According to The Dachshund Breed Council's *DachsLife 2018* health survey, symptoms of IVDD are most likely to show between three and seven years of age, with four being the most common.

FACT › Interestingly, the survey also found that only 13% of unneutered/unspayed dogs over the age of three developed IVDD, compared with 26% of dogs neutered or spayed at 7-12 months old, and 25% of dogs done at 13-18 months.

Symptoms vary according to severity:

Vertebrae in this area have invertebral disks

20. Stiffness of the neck, limbs or back

21. Reluctance to go up or down a step

22. Hanging head when standing

23. Reluctance to lift or lower the head

24. Arched back

25. Knuckling (paws upside down)

26. Swollen or hard abdomen

27. Wobbliness, stumbling, unusual gait – often mainly affecting the hind legs

28. Yelping, either unprovoked or when touched - a sign of pain

29. Trembling, panting or licking the lips

30. Dragging the rear leg(s)

31. In extreme cases: paralysis, loss of bladder control and inability to feel pain

FACT ⟩ Choosing a puppy from bloodlines with no history of back problems and without an overly-exaggerated long back is a good place to start. But if you've already got yours, there's still lots you can do to help keep your Daxie free from back pain:

1. VERY IMPORTANT: Don't let your Dachshund get overweight - it puts strain on the spine.

2. Don't let your dog run up and down stairs or jump on and off furniture.

3. Don't over-exercise puppies.

4. Learn how to handle a Dachshund puppy properly - and teach the kids how to do it.

5. Don't play vigorous games with a young Dachshund - avoid Tug-o-War, Frisbee, etc.

6. Avoid any activity where your dog's spine may twist.

7. Mixing with other dogs is fine, but avoid roughhousing with bigger or boisterous dogs.

8. Hiking and long walks (for healthy <u>adult</u> Dachshunds) help to strengthen muscles around the spine.

Follow this advice and the likelihood is that your Dachshund will remain untroubled by IVDD.

Diagnosis and Treatment

If your dog is showing any of the above signs, get him down to the vet immediately. It's important to get the right diagnosis straight away as a delay may cause a more serious rupturing of the disk(s). Ask if your vet has experience of canine spinal issues; IVDD is sometimes misdiagnosed as arthritis, muscle pain or a gastro problem.

IVDD cannot be diagnosed with normal X-rays or a blood test. A special type of X-ray called a *myelogram* can detect spinal cord problems, but an MRI or CT scan is better. Extensive diagnostic tests and treatment are expensive - another reason to have good pet insurance in place.

If IVDD is confirmed, the vet will give a grading. Grade 1 is the least serious, when a dog is walking normally, but feels some pain. Grade 5 is the most serious, when paralysis and urinary incontinence are evident. Even then, there is a 50%-60% chance that the dog will walk normally again after surgery. With Grades 1 and 2, this can be as high as 95%.

If surgery is decided as the best option, the procedure is often carried out by a veterinary neurologist, rather than a general veterinary surgeon.

Recovery from surgery varies according to severity; the dog can start walking again within anything from one to 12 weeks, although full recovery may take the best part of a year in extreme cases. The owner plays a large part in the dog's return to normal or near-normal, as several weeks of crate rest, carefully-monitored exercise, a healthy diet and bucketloads of patience are all essential.

IVDD is a painful and debilitating condition. If surgery is unsuccessful or the damage is too far gone, it may be kinder to put the dog to sleep, no matter how much you love him.

For all but the most severe cases, there are "*conservative (non-surgical) treatments*" to consider. These may involve painkillers and anti-inflammatories (NSAIDS), crate rest, rehabilitation exercises, massage, acupuncture, hydrotherapy, physiotherapy and even the use of mobility devices, **pictured.**

Tips for Crate Rest

This can be a challenging time for the owner as well as the dog. Here are a few tips:

32. Crate-train your puppy, so if a problem arises later in life, he will be used to a crate

33. Place the crate near the family, don't leave him isolated

34. A recovering dog needs a calm environment

35. Use a Vetbed or folded blanket for him to lie on

36. When you open the crate door, get down to your dog's level and be ready to put on a lead – don't let him dash out

37. Take your dog outside to eliminate on a lead, don't allow him to freely wander

38. If your dog is likely to be mainly in two places, consider getting a second crate

39. DAP (Dog Appeasing Pheromone) diffusers, melatonin, hemp oil and other natural products help some dogs to stay calm and relaxed

40. Some dogs do well with part of their crate covered with a sheet

41. A Kong or puzzle toy may help to stave off boredom, or a drive in the car

42. **Finally - DON'T stop the crate rest too early** – it's a mistake many Dachshund owners make when they see their dog improving. Stick to what the vet says

To read more information and personal experiences from owners of Dachshunds with IVDD, visit the excellent website at www.dachshund-ivdd.uk and Google "*DachsLife 2018*" to see the full health statistics for all types of Dachshund. In the USA there is https://dodgerslist.com

Joint Problems

Luxating Patella

Luxating Patella, also called "*floating kneecap,*" "*loose knee*" or "*slipped stifle,*" can be a painful condition akin to a dislocated kneecap in humans; the most common cause is genetic and it affects some Dachshunds, particularly Miniatures.

A groove in the end of the femur (thigh bone) allows the knee cap to glide up and down when the knee joint is bent, while keeping it in place at the same time. If this groove is too shallow, the knee cap may luxate – or dislocate. It can only return to its natural position when the quadriceps muscle

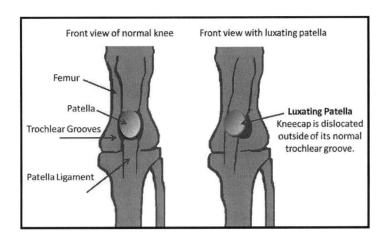

relaxes and increases in length, which is why a dog may have to hold his leg up for some time after the dislocation. Dogs over the age of 12 months can be tested – this is called *patella scoring.* Grade 0 is normal with no problems, while affected dogs score from Grade 1 to Grade 4. In mild cases (Grade 1), the kneecap may pop back into its socket of its own accord, or be manipulated back into place by a vet.

In severe cases, the patella is permanently out of place and the dog has extreme difficulty extending the knees. He may walk with bent knees virtually all the time, often with the whole leg angled and rotated out. The problem can be caused – and is certainly worsened - by obesity. The excess weight puts too much strain on the joint, which is another good reason to keep your Dachshund's weight in check.

Symptoms

You might notice him stretching out a rear leg quite often or *"skipping"* once in a while when walking or running. If the condition is severe, he may hold up the affected leg up for a few days. Another sign might be if your dog suddenly pulls up short when he is running. He might limp on three legs and then after a period of about 10 minutes, drop the affected leg and start to walk normally again.

Dogs that have a luxating patella on both hind legs may change their gait completely, dropping their hindquarters and holding the rear legs further out from the body as they walk. Affected dogs are typically middle-aged with a history of intermittent lameness in the affected rear leg or legs, although the condition may appear as early as four to six months old.

Treatment

If moderate to severe cases are left untreated, the groove will become even shallower and the dog will become progressively lamer, with arthritis prematurely affecting the joint. This will cause a permanently swollen knee and reduce your dog's mobility. It is therefore important to get your dog in for a veterinary check-up ASAP if you suspect patellar luxation.

Surgery is often required for severe luxation. In these cases, known as a *trochlear modification,* the groove at the base of the femur is surgically deepened to better hold the knee cap in place. If your dog is a suitable candidate, the good news is that dogs generally respond well to surgery.

Hip and Elbow Dysplasia

Hip Dysplasia, or *Canine Hip Dysplasia (CHD),* is the most common inherited orthopaedic problem in dogs of all breeds. The hips are the uppermost joints on the rear legs of a dog, either side of the tail, and *"Dysplasia"* means *"abnormal development."* Dogs with this condition develop painful degenerative arthritis of the hip joints.

The hip is a ball and socket joint. Hip dysplasia is caused when the head of the femur, or thigh bone, fits loosely into a shallow and poorly developed socket in the pelvis. The joint carrying the weight of the dog becomes loose and unstable, muscle growth slows and degenerative joint disease often follows.

Symptoms often start to show at five to 18 months of age. Occasionally, an affected dog will have no symptoms at all, while others may experience anything from mild discomfort to extreme pain. Diagnosis is made by X-ray, and an early diagnosis gives a vet the best chance to tackle HD, minimising the chance of arthritis. Symptoms are:

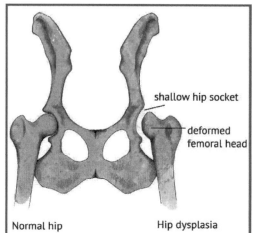

- Hind leg lameness, particularly after exercise
- Difficulty or stiffness when getting up, climbing stairs or walking uphill
- A reluctance to jump, exercise or climb stairs
- A "bunny hop" gait or waddling gait
- A painful reaction to stretching the hind legs, resulting in a short stride
- Side-to-side swaying of the croup (area above the tail)
- Wastage of the thigh muscles

While hip dysplasia is usually inherited, other factors can trigger or worsen it, including:

- Too much exercise, especially while the dog is still growing
- Obesity
- Extended periods without exercise

Prevention and Treatment - There is a system called *hip scoring,* run by the BVA and Kennel Club in the UK and PennHIP or OFA in the USA. A UK dog's hips are X-rayed at a minimum age of 12 months; in the US, dogs must be 24 months old before they can receive their final hip certification.

In the UK, the X-rays are submitted to a specialist panel at the BVA who assess nine features of each hip, giving each feature a score. **The lower the score, the better the hips,** so the range can be from **0** CLEAR to **106** BADLY DYSPLASTIC. A hip certificate shows the individual score for each hip.

It is far better if the dog has evenly matched hips, rather than a low score for one and a high score for the other. Listed here are the American ratings, with the UK ratings in brackets:

Excellent (0-4, with no hip higher than 3)

Good (5-10, with no hip higher than 6)

Fair (11-18)

Borderline (19-25)

Mild (26-35)

Moderate (36-50)

Severe (51-106)

This section of BVA certificate, pictured, shows a hip score of 10

Section C – TO BE COMPLETED BY SCRUTINEERS			
CERTIFICATE OF SCORING			
HIP JOINT	Score Range	Right	Left
Norberg angle	0-6	0	1
Subluxation	0-6	2	3
Cranial acetabular edge	0-6	2	2
Dorsal acetabular edge	0-6	—	
Cranial effective acetabular rim	0-6	—	
Acetabular fossa	0-6	—	
Caudal acetabular edge	0-5	—	
Femoral head/neck exostosis	0-6	—	
Femoral head recontouring	0-6	—	
TOTALS (max possible 53 per column)		4	6	10

There is no 100% guarantee that a puppy from low scoring parents will not develop hip dysplasia, as the condition is caused by a combination of genes, rather than just one. However, the chances are significantly reduced with good hip scores.

Treatment is geared towards preventing the hip joint getting worse. Vets usually recommend restricting exercise, **keeping body weight down** and managing pain with analgesics and anti-inflammatory drugs.

Various medical and surgical treatments are now available to ease discomfort and restore some mobility. They depend on factors such as age, how bad the problem is and, sadly, sometimes how much money you can afford. Cortisone can be injected directly into the affected hip to provide almost immediate relief for a tender, swollen joint. In severe cases, surgery may be an option.

Elbow Dysplasia

The elbow is at the top of a dog's front leg, near the body, and bends backwards. Elbow Dysplasia is a broad term to describe a complex genetic disorder that occurs when cells, tissue or bone don't develop correctly. This causes the joint to form abnormally then to degenerate.

Symptoms begin during puppyhood, typically at four to 10 months of age, although not all young dogs show signs. Look out for:

- Stiffness followed by temporary or permanent lameness aggravated by exercise
- Pain when extending or flexing the elbow
- Holding the affected leg away from the body
- Groaning when getting up
- Swelling around the joint
- In advanced cases, grating of bone and joint when moving

Diagnosis is made by a veterinary examination and X-rays, requiring the dog to be anaesthetised. Treatment depends on age and severity, and may involve Non-steroidal Anti-inflammatory Drugs (NSAIDs) or injections.

Thanks to advances in veterinary medicine, surgery is now an option for many dogs. According to Embrace Pet Insurance, it costs $1,500-$4,000, and results in partial or full improvement in the vast majority of cases.

As with Hip Dysplasia and other joint diseases, feeding the right diet and keeping your dog's weight in check are important. Supplements such as omega-3-fatty acids, glucosamine and chondroitin sulphate can also help to relieve pain and stiffness.

Pes Varus

The name comes from a Latin term meaning *inward-turning foot*. Seen from the back, it looks like the dog has extreme bow leg(s) - or walks like he has a full nappy (diaper)!

Pes Varus, also called **Hock Joint Deformity** or **Bowlegged Syndrome**, affects Dachshunds of all types more than any other breeds - fortunately, less than 1%. The condition, which affects one or both back legs, is genetic and occurs when the outside growth plates of the tibia (lower thigh) grow at a faster rate than the inside ones, causing a deformity and lameness.

Although present from birth, the problem does not become evident until the pup is a few months old, when he may start to swagger around like a cowboy and his leg or legs become noticeably bowed.

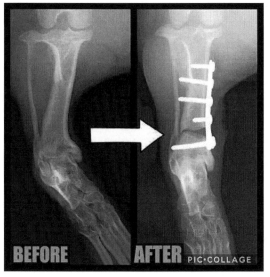

BEFORE | AFTER | PIC·COLLAGE

According to James Tomlinson, DVM, DACVS, Professor of Surgery at the University of Missouri College of Veterinary Medicine: "Dogs that are mildly affected generally have no long-term problems as long as they maintain a reasonable weight. Many moderately affected dogs adapt well with seemingly no pain or limitation in their ability to get around."

Corrective surgery, called an **open wedge osteotomy,** generally produces good to excellent results, with most dogs making a full recovery within eight to 12 weeks.

Early detection and surgery generally lead to a shorter healing time and reduced risk of secondary problems.

Photo showing before and after surgery courtesy of The Dachshund Breed Council and Georgia Wallin.

Eyes

PRA (Progressive Retinal Atrophy)

PRA is the name for several progressive diseases causing degeneration of the retina that lead to blindness. First recognised at the beginning of the 20th century in Gordon Setters, this inherited condition has been documented in over 100 breeds. Miniature Dachshunds are considered high risk, especially Mini Longs.

There are different types of PRA which can affect Dachshunds. There is, however, a DNA test for one particular type that affects the breed called **cord1-PRA,** which stands for Cone-Rod Dystrophy-PRA.

The UK Kennel Club and BVA (British Veterinary Association) recommend that all six types have the relatively inexpensive DNA test for cord1-PRA, and it is compulsory for Assured Breeders of Mini Longs. To qualify for Canine Health Information Center (CHIC) certification in the US, Dachshunds must have an eye exam by an ophthalmologist; screening for PRA is recommended but not compulsory.

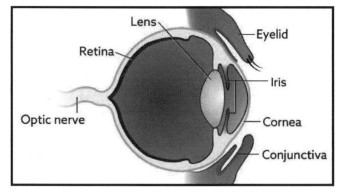

Cord1-PRA first affects the cones in the retina, which are the photoreceptors that detect bright light or daylight. Then the rods, or low-light photoreceptors, begin to degenerate as well. Sadly, there is no cure as yet and most affected dogs eventually go blind.

Some dogs will first show signs at around six months, though the average age of onset is around five years old. A few dogs don't have any symptoms until they are 10 years old.

Cord1-PRA is a genetic disorder associated with a *recessive* mutation in the RPGRIP1 gene. This means that the faulty gene must be inherited *from both parents* in order to cause disease in an offspring.

 The RPGRIP1 gene mutation is Autosomal Recessive. Here are all possible outcomes. They are the same for all other autosomal recessive genetic diseases:

PARENT CLEAR + PARENT CLEAR = pups clear

PARENT CLEAR + PARENT CARRIER = 50% will carry the disease, 50% will be clear

PARENT CLEAR + PARENT AFFECTED = 100% will be carriers

PARENT CARRIER + PARENT CLEAR = 50% will carry disease, 50% will be clear

PARENT CARRIER + PARENT CARRIER = 25% clear, 25% affected and 50% carry disease

PARENT CARRIER + PARENT AFFECTED = 50% affected and 50% carry disease

PARENT AFFECTED + PARENT CLEAR = 100% will carry disease

PARENT AFFECTED + PARENT CARRIER = 50% affected and 50% carry disease

PARENT AFFECTED + PARENT AFFECTED = 100% affected

Although there is no cure, cord1-PRA can be avoided in future generations by DNA testing and not breeding Affected dogs - or Carrier dogs to other Carriers or Affected dogs.

Sight is not as important to dogs as it is to humans as their other senses, such as smell and hearing, are far better than ours. If the deterioration is gradual, many blind dogs learn to live full lives, just as humans learn to live with loss of hearing or smell.

If your Dachshund is affected, it may be helpful to read and share experiences on Facebook at Blind Dog Support or at www.blinddogs.net

 Only proceed with buying a Miniature Dachshund puppy in the UK if one parent has tested CLEAR for cord1-PRA - and if the breeder isn't sure or can't produce the certificate, WALK AWAY. In the US, check exactly which eye tests the parents have undergone, and always ask to see original certificates.

To check if the parents of a UK Miniature puppy have been tested and what the results were, visit www.dachshundhealth.org.uk/eye-disease and scroll down the page to *"The KC's cord1 Results pages are here,"* then follow the link for the relevant breed.

The Kennel Clubs recommend that breeding Dachshunds of all six types have an annual eye exam to check for disorders such as Distichiasis, Entropion and Ectropion, which are explained later in this chapter.

···

Other Eye Conditions

Glaucoma

A normal eye contains a fluid called aqueous humour to maintain its shape. The body constantly adds and removes fluid from inside of the eye to maintain the pressure inside the eye at the correct level. Glaucoma occurs when the pressure inside the eyeball becomes higher than normal.

Just as high blood pressure can damage the heart, high pressure inside the eye can damage the optic nerve, and unless glaucoma is treated QUICKLY, temporary loss of vision or even total blindness can result.

Primary glaucoma is normally inherited and secondary glaucoma means that it is caused by another problem, such as a wound to the eye. Even though a puppy may carry the faulty gene, primary glaucoma does not usually develop until a dog is at least two to three years old. Rarely are both eyes equally affected or at the same time; it usually starts in one eye several months or even years before it affects the second one.

Symptoms - Glaucoma is a serious disease and it's important for an owner to be able to recognise initial symptoms immediately:

43. Pain

44. A dilated pupil or one pupil looks bigger than the other *(Our photo shows an extremely dilated pupil)*

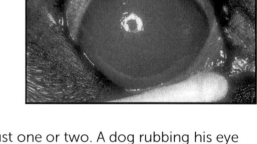

45. Rapid blinking

46. Cloudiness in the cornea at the front of the eye

47. The whites of an eye look bloodshot

48. One eye looks larger or sticks out further than the other one

49. Loss of appetite, which may be due to headaches

50. Change in attitude, less willing to play, etc.

Most dogs will not display all of these signs at first, perhaps just one or two. A dog rubbing his eye with his paw, against the furniture or carpet or your leg is a common - and often unnoticed - early sign. Some dogs will also seem to flutter the eyelids or squint with one eye. The pupil of the affected eye will usually dilate (get bigger) in the early stages. It may still react to all bright light, but only very slowly. If the pupil in one eye is larger than in the other, something is definitely wrong and it could be glaucoma.

If you suspect your dog has glaucoma, get him to the vet as soon as possible, i.e. **immediately,** not the day after. This is a medical emergency. If treatment is not started within a few days - or even hours in some cases - the dog will probably lose sight in that eye. A vet will carry out a manual examination and test your dog's eye pressure using a tonometer on the surface of the eye. There is still a fair chance that the dog may lose sight in the eye, but a much better chance of saving the second eye with the knowledge and preventative measures learned from early intervention.

Treatment – this involves reducing the pressure within the affected eye, draining the aqueous humour and providing pain relief, as this can be very painful for your dog. There are also surgical options for the long-term control of glaucoma. As yet it cannot be cured.

Cataracts

The lens is transparent and its function is to focus rays of light to form an image on the retina. A cataract occurs when the lens becomes cloudy. Less light enters the eye, images become blurry and the dog's sight diminishes as the cataract becomes larger.

If the cataract is small, it won't disturb the dog's vision too much, but owners must monitor cataracts because the thicker and denser they become, the more likely it is they will lead to blindness or glaucoma. Diabetes is a known trigger for cataracts and Dachshunds - particularly overweight ones – are more susceptible to diabetes than many other breeds.

According to health information from the Dachshund Breed Council, 75% of dogs develop cataracts and blindness in both eyes within one year of being diagnosed with diabetes. *Age-related* or *late onset cataracts* can develop any time after the age of eight years and usually have less impact on a dog's vision.

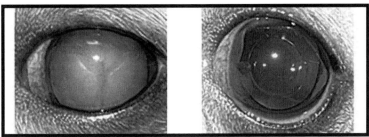

Left: eye with cataracts. Right: same eye with artificial lens

Depending on the cause, severity and type of cataract, surgery is an option for some dogs; the lens is removed and replaced with a plastic substitute. It costs around £2,500-£3,500 per eye (around $2,700-$4,000 in the US), but if the dog is a suitable candidate, it is successful in 90% of cases. In less severe cases, dogs can live a perfectly normal life with daily eye drops and vigilance on the part of the owner.

 Beware of miracle cures! If you do try drops, look for some containing the effective ingredient N-Acetyl Carnosine, or NAC. There is a relatively inexpensive product called Cataract Clear, available from Costcuttersrus.com

As well as a cloudy eye, other signs are the dog bumping into things, especially in dimly-lit situations, squinting or pawing at the eye, eye redness, an inflamed eye socket, or a bulging eye. If you suspect your Dachshund has cataracts, get him to the vet for an examination as soon as possible. Early intervention can prevent complications developing.

Dry Eye (Keratoconjunctivitis sicca)

Keratoconjunctivitis sicca is the technical term for **Dry Eye,** which is caused by not enough tears being produced. With insufficient tears, a dog's eyes can become irritated and the conjunctiva appears red. It's estimated that as many as one in five dogs can suffer from Dry Eye at one time or another in their lives.

Dry Eye causes a dog to blink a lot, the eye or eyes typically develop a thick, yellowy discharge, **pictured,** and the cornea develops a film. Infections are common as tears also have anti-bacterial and cleansing properties, and inadequate lubrication allows dust, pollen and other debris to accumulate. The nerves of these glands may also become damaged.

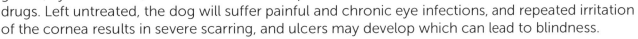

The most common cause is an immune disease that damages the tear glands. Dry eye may also be caused by injuries to the tear glands, eye infections, disease such as distemper or reactions to drugs. Left untreated, the dog will suffer painful and chronic eye infections, and repeated irritation of the cornea results in severe scarring, and ulcers may develop which can lead to blindness.

Early treatment is essential to save the cornea and usually involves drugs: cyclosporine, ophthalmic ointment or drops. In some cases, another eye preparation – Tacrolimus - is also used and may be effective when cyclosporine is not. Sometimes artificial tear solutions are also prescribed.

Treating Dry Eye involves commitment from the owner. Gently cleaning the eyes several times a day with a warm, wet cloth helps a dog feel better and may also help stimulate tear production.

In very severe and rare cases, an operation can be performed to transplant a salivary duct into the upper eyelid, causing saliva to drain into and lubricate the eye.

Eyelash Disorders

Distichiasis, Trichiasis and *Ectopic Cilia* are eyelash disorders that can affect any breed, although Distichiasis is not uncommon in Mini Longs. All three conditions are relatively easy to diagnose.

Distichiasis

This occurs when eyelashes grow from an abnormal spot on the eyelid. (*Trichiasis* is ingrowing eyelashes and *Ectopic Cilia* are single or multiple hairs that grow through the inside of the eyelid - *cilia* are eyelashes).

With distichiasis, an eyelash or eyelashes abnormally grow on the inner surface or the very edge of the eyelid, and both upper and lower eyelids can be affected. The affected eye becomes red, inflamed, and may have a discharge.

The dog typically squints or blinks a lot, just like a human with a hair or other foreign matter in the eye. The dog can make matters worse by rubbing the eye against furniture, other objects or the carpet. In severe cases, the cornea can become ulcerated and it looks blue.

Often, very mild cases require no action, mild cases may require lubricating eye drops and in more severe cases, surgery may be the best option to remove the offending eyelashes and prevent them from regrowing. Left untreated, distichiasis can cause corneal ulcers and infection which can ultimately lead to blindness or loss of the eye.

Entropion and Ectropion

Entropion is rolling in of the eyelids, causing the dog's fur to rub the surface of the eyeball or cornea. This painful condition is thought to be hereditary.

The affected dog scratches at the inflamed, teary eye, which can lead to further injury. Tears typically start off clear and can progress to a thick yellow or green mucus. The dog squints, and signs usually appear before one year of age.

It's important to get your dog to the vet as soon as you suspect Entropion and before the cornea gets scratched. A vet will make the diagnosis after a painless and relatively simple inspection, but he or she will first have to rule out other issues that cause red and itchy eyes, such as allergies. Surgery is the normal option.

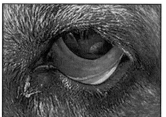

Ectropion, pictured, is where the lower eyelid rolls out loosely away from the eye, making the eye look droopy. It is usually present from birth and is more commonly seen in breeds such as Bloodhounds, Basset Hounds and Bulldogs.

It exposes the delicate tissues that cover the inner eyelids and eyeball, causing them to dry out. This results in conjunctivitis and sometimes inflammation of the cornea. Ectropion can also develop after eye trauma or issues such as hypothyroidism or neuromuscular disease.

Mild cases are treated with drops, while more severe ones may require surgery. You should always discuss all possible options with your vet before proceeding to surgery.

Cherry Eye

This can develop in dogs of all breeds, particularly young dogs. Humans have two eyelids, but dogs have a third eyelid, called a **nictating membrane.** This is a thin, opaque tissue with a tear gland that rests in the inner corner of the eye. It provides extra protection for the eye and spreads tears over the eyeball. Usually it is retracted and therefore you can't see it, although you may notice it when your dog is relaxed and falling asleep.

Cherry Eye, *pictured,* is a collapse of the gland of the third eyelid, thought to be due to a weakness of the fibrous tissue that attaches the gland to the surrounding eye. The gland falls down, exposing it to dry air, irritants and bacteria, when it can become infected and begin to swell.

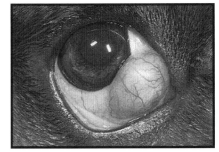

There is sometimes a mucous discharge and if the dog rubs or scratches it, he can further damage the gland and even possibly create an ulcer on the surface of the eye. Although it looks sore, it is not generally painful. Mild cases are treated with a steroid ointment to try and get the gland back to its normal position, and antibiotics to prevent infection. If that doesn't work, surgery to reposition the gland should be considered. A simple stitch or two can tack the gland down into the conjunctiva.

Day Blindness is a rare type of hereditary PRA found in certain bloodlines of Standard and Miniature Wires imported from Scandinavia. *SARDS* (Sudden Acquired Retinal Degeneration Syndrome), is another rare eye disease that can affect all types of Dachshund in later life.

 Eye conditions can be caused or worsened by irritants and injury. Remove or fence off low, spiky plants in your garden or yard. And although it may look super cute when your Dachshund sticks his head out of the open car window with his ears flapping in the wind, bear in mind that dust, insects and dirt particles can hit and damage his eyes.

Epilepsy

Epilepsy means repeated seizures (also called fits or convulsions) due to abnormal electrical activity in the brain. Epilepsy affects around four or five dogs in every 100 across the dog population as whole.

Epilepsy can be classified as *structural,* when an underlying cause can be identified in the brain, or *idiopathic,* when the cause is unknown. The type of epilepsy affecting most dogs of all breeds is *idiopathic epilepsy.* The UK's DachsLife 2018 survey revealed that both Miniature and Standard Longs were three times more likely to have idiopathic epilepsy than the breed average.

In some cases, the gap between seizures is relatively constant, in others it can be very irregular with several occurring over a short period of time, but with long intervals between *"clusters."* Affected dogs behave normally between seizures. If they occur because of a problem somewhere else in the body, such as heart disease (which stops oxygen reaching the brain), this is not epilepsy.

Seizures are not uncommon; however, many dogs only ever have one. If your dog has had more than one, it may be that he is epileptic. Anyone who has witnessed their dog having a seizure knows how frightening it can be. The good news is that, just as with people, there are medications to control epilepsy in dogs, allowing them to live happy lives with normal lifespans.

Symptoms

Some dogs seem to know when they are about to have a seizure and may behave in a certain way. You will come to recognise these signs as meaning that an episode is likely. Often dogs just seek out their owner's company and come to sit beside them. There are two main types of seizure:

❖ **Petit Mal**, also called a Focal or Partial Seizure, which is the lesser of the two as it only affects one half of the brain. This may involve facial twitching, staring into space with a fixed glaze and/or upward eye movement, walking as if drunk, snapping at imaginary flies, and/or running or hiding for no reason. Sometimes this is accompanied by urination. The dog is conscious throughout

- 🐾 **Grand Mal,** or Generalised Seizure, affects both hemispheres of the brain and is more often what we think of when we talk about a seizure. Most dogs become stiff, fall onto their side and make running movements with their legs. Sometimes they will cry out and may lose control of their bowels, bladder or both

FACT ▶ With Grand Mal the dog is unconscious once the seizure starts – he cannot hear or respond to you. While it is distressing to watch, the dog is not in any pain - even if howling.

It's not uncommon for an episode to begin as Petit Mal, but progress into Grand Mal. Sometimes, the progression is pretty clear - there may be twitching or jerking of one body part that gradually increases in intensity and progresses to include the entire body – other times the progression happens very fast.

Lafora Disease (LD) is an aggressive inherited form of structural epilepsy that affects Miniature Wirehaired Dachshunds aged five and older, with six-and-a-half to seven years being the average age of onset.

A genetic defect prevents the dog from efficiently processing starch into sugar, causing insoluble starch platelets to gradually build up in the central nervous system. Typical symptoms are a sudden jerking or shaking of the head, which can be triggered by bright lights (even the TV) or sudden noises or movements, especially near the dog's head. Also, seizures and high-pitched barking or whining.

The disease is progressive, and eventually, wobbliness (ataxia), blindness and dementia can develop, when the dog may have to be put to sleep. Although LD is incurable, medication, a special diet free from starch and sugars, doggie sunglasses and keeping the dog away from flashing/bright lights may slow down the disease.

The faulty gene is recessive, so both parents must have a copy to pass it on to their puppies. There is no cure, but genetic testing has made great strides. In just five years, the proportion of litters bred with a risk of Lafora-affected puppies has been reduced from 55% to under 5%.

If you are buying a Miniature Wirehaired Dachshund, ask to see the Lafora screening certificate, which is compulsory for UK Assured Breeders.

Thanks to Dachshund Health UK, DachsLife 2018

 Most seizures last between one and three minutes - it is worth making a note of the time the seizure starts and ends – or record it on your phone because it often seems to go on for a lot longer than it actually does.

If you are not sure whether or not your dog has had a seizure, look on YouTube, where there are many videos of dogs having epileptic seizures.

Dogs behave in different ways afterwards. Some just get up and carry on with what they were doing, while others appear dazed and confused for up to 24 hours afterwards. Most commonly, dogs will be disorientated for only 10 to 15 minutes before returning to their old self.

FACT ▶ Most seizures occur while the dog is relaxed and resting quietly, often in the evening or at night; it rarely happens during exercise. In a few dogs, seizures can be triggered by particular events or stress.

They often have a set pattern of behaviour that they follow - for example going for a drink of water or asking to go outside to the toilet. If your dog has had more than one seizure, you may well start to notice a pattern of behaviour that is typically repeated.

The most important thing is to **STAY CALM**. Remember that your dog is unconscious during the seizure and is not in pain or distressed. It is probably more distressing for you than for him. Make sure that he is not in a position to injure himself, for example by falling down the stairs, but otherwise do not try to interfere with him. NEVER try to put your hand inside his mouth during a seizure or you are very likely to get bitten.

It is very rare for dogs to injure themselves during a seizure. Occasionally, they may bite their tongue and there may seem to be a lot of blood, but it's unlikely to be serious; your dog will not swallow his tongue.

If it goes on for a very long time (more than 10 minutes), his body temperature will rise, which can cause damage to the liver, kidneys or brain. In very extreme cases, some dogs may be left in a coma after severe seizures. Repeated seizures can cause cumulative brain damage, which can result in early senility (with loss of learned behaviour and housetraining, or behavioural changes).

When Should I Contact the Vet?

Generally, if your dog has a seizure lasting more than five minutes or is having them regularly, you should contact your vet. When your dog starts fitting, make a note of the time. If he comes out of it within five minutes, allow him time to recover quietly before contacting your vet. It is far better for him to recover quietly at home rather than be bundled into the car right away.

If your dog does not come out of the seizure within five minutes, or has repeated seizures close together, contact your vet immediately, as he or she will want to see your dog as soon as possible. Call the vet before setting off to make sure there is someone who can help when you arrive.

The vet may need to run a range of tests to ensure that there is no other cause of the seizures. These may include blood tests, X-rays or an MRI scan of your dog's brain. If no other cause can be found, then a diagnosis of epilepsy may be made. If your Dachshund already has epilepsy, remember these key points:

- Don't change or stop any medication without consulting your vet
- See your vet at least once a year for follow-up visits
- Be sceptical of *"magic cure"* treatments

Treatment

As yet, it is not possible to cure epilepsy, so medication is used to control seizures – in some cases even a well-controlled epileptic may have occasional fits. There are many drugs available; two of the most common are Phenobarbital and Potassium Bromide (some dogs can have negative results with Phenobarbital). There are also a number of holistic remedies advertised, but we have no experience of them or any idea if any are effective.

FACT Factors that have proved useful in some cases are: avoiding dog food containing preservatives, adding vitamins, minerals and/or enzymes to the diet and ensuring drinking water is free of fluoride.

Each epileptic dog is an individual and a treatment plan will be designed specifically for yours, based on the severity and frequency of seizures and how he responds to different medications. Many epileptic dogs require a combination of one or more types of drug for best results.

Keep a record of events in your dog's life, note down dates and times of episodes and record when you have given medication. Each time you visit your vet, take this diary along with you so he or she can see how your dog has been since his last check-up. If seizures are becoming more frequent, it may be necessary to change the medication.

 Owners of epileptic dogs need patience and vigilance. Treatment success often depends on owners keeping a close eye on the dog and reporting any physical or behavioural changes to the vet.

It is also important that medication is given at the same time each day, as he becomes dependent on the levels of drug in his blood to control seizures. If a single dose of treatment is missed, blood levels can drop, which may be enough to trigger a seizure.

It is not common for epileptic dogs to stop having seizures altogether. However, provided your dog is checked regularly by your vet, *there is a good chance that he will live a full and happy life, as most epileptic dogs have far more good days than bad ones.*

LIVE *WITH* EPILEPSY NOT *FOR* EPILEPSY.

Cushing's Disease

This complex ailment, also known as *hyperadrenocorticism,* is caused when a dog produces too much Cortisol hormone. It develops over a period of time, which is why it is more often seen in middle-aged or senior dogs. Dachshunds are more susceptible than some other breeds.

Cortisol is released by the adrenal gland near the kidneys. Normally it is produced during times of stress to prepare the body for strenuous activity. Think of an adrenaline rush. While this hormone is essential for the effective functioning of cells and organs, too much of it can be dangerous. The disease can be difficult to diagnose, as the most common symptoms are similar to those for old age. A dog may display one or more:

- A ravenous appetite
- Drinking excessive amounts of water
- Urinating frequently or urinary incontinence
- Hair loss or recurring skin issues
- Pot belly
- Thin skin
- Muscle wastage
- Insomnia
- Lack of energy, general lethargy
- Panting a lot

Cushing's disease cannot be cured, but it can be successfully managed and controlled with medication, giving the dog a longer,

happier life. Some dogs with mild symptoms do not require treatment, but should be closely monitored for signs of them worsening. Lysodren (mitotane) or Vetoryl (trilostane) are usually prescribed by vets to treat the most common pituitary-dependent Cushing's disease. Both can have a number of side effects – so your dog needs monitoring - and the dog remains on the medication for life.

Immune System Disorders

Certain bloodlines of Long-Haired Dachshunds can suffer from a hereditary auto-immune disease known as **Immune-Mediated Thrombocytopenia** or **IMT.**

Thrombocytes, or platelets, are vital for blood clotting. With IMT the concentration of platelets in the blood is abnormally low as they have been attacked for unknown reasons by the dog's own antibodies (whose normal role is to help guard against infections). Insufficient platelets lead to spontaneous bleeding into tissues.

Visible symptoms are blood spots in hairless and unpigmented parts of the skin, nose bleeds or blood in the urine or faeces. The dog will feel unwell and may have severe pain if internal bleeding is in confined spaces like the eyes, skull or joints.

Around 70% of affected dogs get better with treatment involving immune-suppressant drugs. Some dogs require long-term treatment, and around 30% die or are put to sleep. As yet there is no DNA test for IMT.

Puppy Strangles is an immune disorder that occasionally develops in Standard Smooths, usually between the ages of three weeks and six months when the muzzle, eyelids and face suddenly swell. The cause is uncertain, but there may be a genetic link. The normal treatment is a course of steroids, with antibiotics if the skin has become infected, and the puppy is usually back to normal within a couple of weeks.

....

Diabetes

Diabetes can affect dogs of all breeds, sizes and both genders, as well as obese dogs, although some breeds have a higher than average chance of getting diabetes. These include the Dachshund, Miniature Poodle, Bichons Frise, Pug, Miniature Schnauzer, Beagle, Samoyed and some Terriers. There are two types:

Diabetes insipidus is caused by a lack of vasopressin, a hormone that controls the kidneys' absorption of water.

Diabetes mellitus occurs when the dog's body does not produce enough insulin and therefore cannot successfully process sugars.

Dogs, like us, get their energy by converting the food they eat into sugars, mainly glucose. This travels in the bloodstream and then, using a protein called *insulin,* cells remove some of the glucose from the blood to use for energy. Most diabetic dogs have Type 1 diabetes; their pancreas does not produce any insulin. Without it, the cells can't use the glucose that is in the bloodstream, so they *"starve"* while the glucose level in the blood rises.

Diabetes mellitus (sugar diabetes) is the most common form and affects mostly middle-aged and older dogs. Both males and females can develop it, although unspayed females have a slightly higher risk. Vets take blood and urine samples in order to diagnose diabetes. Early treatment helps to prevent further complications developing.

FACT The condition is treatable and need not shorten a dog's lifespan or interfere greatly with quality of life. Due to advances in veterinary science, diabetic dogs undergoing treatment now have the same life expectancy as non-diabetic dogs of the same age and gender.

Symptoms of Diabetes Mellitus:

- Extreme thirst
- Excessive urination
- Weight loss
- Increased appetite
- Coat in poor condition
- Lethargy
- Vision problems due to cataracts

If left untreated, diabetes can lead to cataracts or other ailments.

Treatment and Exercise

It is EXTREMELY IMPORTANT that Dachshunds are not allowed to get overweight, as obesity is a major trigger for diabetes.

FACT Many cases of canine diabetes can be successfully treated with a combination of a diet low in sugar, fat and carbs (a raw diet is worth considering), alongside a moderate and consistent exercise routine and medication. More severe cases may require insulin injections.

In the newly-diagnosed dog, insulin therapy begins at home after a vet has explained how to prepare and inject insulin. Normally, after a week of treatment, you return to the vet for a series of blood sugar tests over a 12 to 14-hour period to see when the blood glucose peaks and troughs. Adjustments are made to the dosage and timing of the injections. You may also be asked to collect urine samples using a test strip of paper that indicates the glucose levels.

 If your dog is already having insulin injections, beware of a "miracle cure" offered on the internet. It does not exist. There is no diet or vitamin supplement that can reduce a dog's dependence on insulin injections, because vitamins and minerals cannot do what insulin does in the dog's body.

If you think that your dog needs a supplement, discuss it with your vet first to make sure that it does not interfere with any other medication.

Exercise burns up blood glucose the same way that insulin does. If your dog is on insulin, any active exercise on top of the insulin might cause him to have a severe low blood glucose episode, called *"hypoglycaemia."*

Keep your dog on a reasonably consistent exercise routine. Your usual insulin dose will take that amount of exercise into account. If you plan to take your dog out for some demanding exercise, such as running around with other dogs, you may need to reduce his usual insulin dose.

Tips

- Specially-formulated diabetes dog food is available from most vets
- Feed the same type and amount of food at the same times every day

- Most vets recommend twice-a-day feeding for diabetic pets (it's OK if your dog prefers to eat more often)
- Help your dog to achieve the best possible blood glucose control by NOT feeding table scraps or treats between meals
- Watch for signs that your dog is starting to drink more water than usual. Call the vet if you see this happening, as it may mean that the insulin dose needs adjusting

Food raises blood glucose - Insulin and exercise lower blood glucose - Keep them in balance

For more information visit www.caninediabetes.org

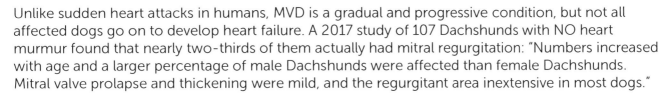

The Heart

Heart issues are relatively common among the canine population in general. Heart failure, or *Congestive Heart Failure (CHF),* occurs when the heart is not able to pump blood around the dog's body properly. The heart is a mechanical pump. It receives blood in one half and forces it through the lungs, then the other half pumps the blood through the entire body.

The most common heart disorder affecting Dachshunds and millions of small dogs is *Mitral Valve Disease (MVD),* which usually affects dogs aged eight and older.

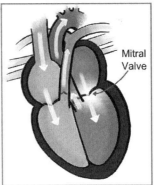

Mitral Valve

The mitral valve acts as a seal on the left side of the heart between the left atrium (the filling chamber, *top right quarter of the diagram)* and the left ventricle (the pumping chamber, *bottom right*). When the ventricle contracts, oxygenated blood is pumped around the body and the mitral valve closes to prevent blood going back into the left atrium.

Mitral valve disease happens slowly over a period of years, causing the edges of the valve to become thick and knobbly and no longer able to provide a good seal. The valve leaks and blood flows backwards, back into the left atrium, which becomes enlarged. This is called *"regurgitation."*

Unlike sudden heart attacks in humans, MVD is a gradual and progressive condition, but not all affected dogs go on to develop heart failure. A 2017 study of 107 Dachshunds with NO heart murmur found that nearly two-thirds of them actually had mitral regurgitation: "Numbers increased with age and a larger percentage of male Dachshunds were affected than female Dachshunds. Mitral valve prolapse and thickening were mild, and the regurgitant area inextensive in most dogs."

In more severe cases, the left chambers of the heart become enlarged causing breathing difficulties due to the lungs filling with fluid. The various medical stages of mitral Valve Disease are:

Stage A: Predisposed breeds without any sign of disease

Stage B1: A heart murmur which can be heard by the vet, but no heart enlargement showing on an echocardiogram, or heart ultrasound

Stage B2: Heart murmur and heart enlargement

Stage C: Symptoms of CHF, such as difficulty breathing

Stage D: Refractory congestive heart failure, i.e. receiving maximum doses of medications but the symptoms are still present

In dogs, hardening of the arteries (arteriosclerosis) and sudden heart attacks are very rare. However, heart disease is quite common. It usually occurs when one chamber or side of the heart is required to do more than it is physically able to do and the muscles "give out" over a long period of time.

Symptoms and Treatment

- 🐾 Tiredness
- 🐾 Decreased activity levels
- 🐾 Restlessness, pacing around instead of settling down to sleep
- 🐾 Intermittent coughing - during exertion or excitement, at night or when he wakes up in the morning - in an attempt to clear the lungs

As the condition progresses, other symptoms may appear:

- 🐾 Lack of appetite
- 🐾 Rapid breathing
- 🐾 Abdominal swelling (due to fluid)
- 🐾 Noticeable loss of weight
- 🐾 Fainting (syncope)
- 🐾 Paleness of gums

A vet will carry out tests that may include listening to the heart, chest X-rays, blood tests, electrocardiogram (a record of your dog's heartbeat) or an echocardiogram. If the heart problem is due to an enlarged heart or valve disease, the condition cannot be reversed.

Treatment focuses on managing exercise and various medications, which may change over time as the condition progresses. The vet may also prescribe a special low salt diet, as sodium determines the amount of water in the blood.

 Pay attention to your Dachshund's oral health, as dental problems can increase the risk of heart disease. There is evidence that fatty acids and other supplements may be beneficial for a heart condition; discuss this with your vet.

The prognosis for dogs with congestive heart failure depends on the cause and severity, as well as their response to treatment. A dog can't recover from congestive heart failure, but once diagnosed, he can live a longer, more comfortable life with the right medication and regular check-ups.

Another form of heart disease is **Dilated Cardiomyopathy (DCM),** also known as **"enlarged heart."** The ventricles, or heart chambers, become larger and the cardiac muscle surrounding them becomes thinner, causing the heart to change shape. This then restricts muscle contractions and the effectiveness of the valves, which can lead to irregular heartbeats and the backflow or leakage of blood through the valves.

NOTE: There is a growing discussion as to whether diet can be a trigger for DCM. You can read more here: www.whole-dog-journal.com/food/diet-dogs-and-dcm

Heart Murmurs

Heart murmurs are not uncommon in dogs and are one of the first signs that something may be amiss. One of our dogs was diagnosed with a Grade 2 murmur several years ago and, of course, your heart sinks when the vet gives you the terrible news. But once the shock is over, it's important to realise that there are several different severities of the condition and, at its mildest, it is no great cause for concern. Our dog lived an active, healthy life and died at the age of 13.

Breeder Melissa Sworab's Smooth Sadie developed a Grade 1 heart murmur around age six. It progressed to Grade 3 when she was 10 - and she went on to live to 18!

Sadie (far right), RIP, relaxing in the garden with friends. Photo by Mark Sworab

Literally, a heart murmur is a specific sound heard through a stethoscope, which results from the blood flowing faster than normal within the heart itself or in one of the two major arteries. Instead of the normal *"lubb dupp"* noise, an additional sound can be heard that can vary from a mild *"pshhh"* to a loud *"whoosh."* The different grades are:

- ❧ **Grade 1 -** barely audible
- ❧ **Grade 2** - soft, but easily heard with a stethoscope
- ❧ **Grade 3** - intermediate loudness; most murmurs that are related to the mechanics of blood circulation are at least Grade 3
- ❧ **Grade 4** - loud murmur that radiates widely, often including opposite side of chest
- ❧ **Grade 5 and Grade 6** - very loud, audible with the stethoscope barely touching the chest; the vibration is strong enough to be felt through the dog's chest wall

Murmurs are caused by a number of factors; it may be a problem with the heart valves or could be due to some other condition, such as hyperthyroidism, anaemia or heartworm.

In puppies, there are two major types of heart murmurs, often detected by a vet at the first or second vaccination visit. The most common type is called an innocent *"flow murmur."* This type of murmur is soft - typically Grade 2 or less - and is not caused by underlying heart disease. An innocent flow murmur typically disappears by four to five months of age.

However, if a puppy has a loud murmur - Grade 3 or louder - or if it is still easily heard with a stethoscope after four or five months of age, it's more likely that the pup has an underlying heart problem. The thought of a puppy having congenital heart disease is worrying, but it is important to remember that the disease will not affect all puppies' life expectancy or quality of life.

....

Canine Cancer

This is the biggest single killer and will claim the lives of one in four dogs, regardless of breed. It is the cause of nearly half the deaths of all dogs aged 10 years and older, according to the American Veterinary Medical Association.

A study of more than 15,000 dogs of different breeds found that the Dachshund is prone to certain types of cancer. One such is *Hemangiosarcoma,* a malignant cancer in the blood vessel walls, most commonly found in the spleen or heart. Symptoms include:

- Pale gums
- Disorientation, tiredness or collapse
- Rapid breathing
- Extreme thirst
- Lack of appetite

Unfortunately, affected Dachshunds can die from internal bleeding or the cancer spreading to other parts of the body. In some cases, however, if the cancer is in the spleen and discovered early, the spleen may be removed before the malignant cells spread to other organs. Symptoms of other types of cancer include:

- Swellings anywhere on the body or around the anus
- Sores that don't heal
- Weight loss
- Lameness, which may be a sign of bone cancer, with or without a visible lump
- Laboured breathing
- Changes in exercise or stamina level
- Change in bowel or bladder habits
- Increased drinking or urination
- Bad breath, which can be a sign of oral cancer
- Poor appetite, difficulty swallowing or excessive drooling
- Vomiting

FACT ❯ There is evidence that the risk of testicular, uterine and mammary cancers decreases with neutering and spaying. However, recent studies also show that Dachshunds may have a higher risk of spinal and other problems after early neutering. See Chapter 15. The Facts of Life for more detailed information.

Treatment and Reducing the Risk

Just because your dog has a skin growth doesn't mean that it's serious. Many older dogs develop fatty lumps, or lipomas, which are often harmless, but it's still advisable to have the first one checked. Your vet will make a diagnosis following an X-ray, scan, blood test, biopsy or combination of these.

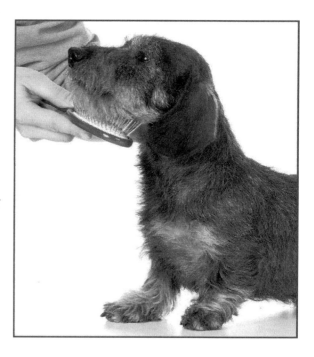

If your dog is diagnosed with cancer, there is hope. Advances in veterinary medicine and technology offer various treatment options, including chemotherapy, radiation and surgery. Unlike with humans, a dog's hair does not fall out with chemotherapy.

We had a happy ending. We had a four-year-old dog develop a lump like a black grape on his anus. We took him down to the vet within a day or so of first noticing it and got the dreaded diagnosis of T-cell lymphoma, a particularly aggressive form of cancer. The vet removed the lump a couple of days later and the dog went on to live into his teens.

 Every time you groom your dog, get into the habit of checking his body for lumps and lift his top lip to check for signs of paleness or whiteness in the gums. As with any illness, early detection often leads to a better outcome.

We have all become aware of the risk factors for human cancer - stopping smoking, protecting ourselves from over-exposure to strong sunlight and eating a healthy, balanced diet all help to reduce cancer rates. We know to keep a close eye on ourselves, go for regular health checks and report any lumps to our doctors as soon as they appear.

The same is true with your dog.

The outcome depends on the type of cancer, treatment used and, importantly, how early the tumour is found. The sooner treatment begins, the greater the chances of success. While it is impossible to completely prevent cancer, the following points can help to reduce the risk:

- Feed a healthy diet with few or no preservatives
- Don't let your Dachshund get overweight
- Consider dietary supplements, such as antioxidants, Vitamins, A, C, E, beta carotene, lycopene or selenium, or coconut oil – check compatibility with any other treatments
- Give pure, filtered or bottled water (fluoride-free) for drinking
- Give your dog regular daily exercise
- Keep your dog away from chemicals, pesticides, cleaning products, etc. around the garden and home
- Avoid passive smoking
- Consider natural flea remedies (check they are working) and avoid unnecessary vaccinations
- Check your dog regularly for lumps and any other physical or behavioural changes
- If you are buying a puppy, ask whether there is any history of cancer among the ancestors

Canine cancer research is currently being conducted all over the world, and medical advances are producing a steady flow of new tests and treatments to improve survival rates and cancer care.

....

With thanks to The Dachshund Breed Council https://dachshundbreedcouncil.wordpress.com and Chairman Ian Seath for assistance with this chapter.

Disclaimer: The author is not a vet. This chapter is intended to give owners an outline of some of the main health issues and symptoms that may affect their Dachshund(s). If you have any concerns regarding your dog's health, our advice is always the same: consult a veterinarian.

13. Skin Conditions

Like many breeds, Dachshunds can be affected by a number of skin issues. Visit any busy veterinary clinic these days – especially in spring and summer – and you'll see itchy dogs. Skin conditions, allergies and intolerances are on the increase in the canine world as well as the human one.

How many children did you hear of having asthma or a peanut allergy when you were at school? Not too many, I'll bet. Yet allergies and adverse reactions are now relatively common – and it's the same with dogs. The reasons are not clear; it could be connected to genetics, diet, environment, over-vaccination – or a combination. As yet, there is no clear scientific evidence to back this up.

The skin is a complicated topic and a whole book could be written on this subject alone. While many dogs have no problems at all, some suffer from sensitive, itchy, dry or oily skin, hot spots, yeast infections or other skin disorders, causing them to scratch, bite or lick themselves excessively. Symptoms vary from mild itchiness to a chronic reaction.

FACT White or light-coloured "double dapple" Dachshunds are susceptible to a number of health issues, including skin disorders.

Canine Skin

The skin is the dog's largest organ. It acts as the protective barrier between your dog's internal organs and the outside world; it also regulates temperature and provides the sense of touch. Surprisingly, a dog's skin is actually thinner than ours, and it is made up of three layers:

1. **Epidermis** or outer layer, the one that bears the brunt of your dog's contact with the outside world.

2. **Dermis** is the extremely tough layer mostly made up of collagen, a strong and fibrous protein. This is where blood vessels deliver nutrients and oxygen to the skin, and it also acts as your dog's thermostat by allowing her body to release or retain heat, depending on the outside temperature and your dog's activity level.

3. **Hypodermis** is a dense layer of fatty tissue that allows your dog's skin to move independently from the muscle layers below it, as well as providing insulation and support for the skin.

FACT Human allergies often trigger a reaction within the respiratory system, causing us to wheeze or sneeze, whereas allergies or hypersensitivities in a dog often cause a reaction in her SKIN.

Skin can be affected from the **INSIDE** by things that your dog eats or drinks

Skin can be affected from the **OUTSIDE** by fleas, parasites, or inhaled and contact allergies triggered by grass, pollen, man-made chemicals, dust, mould, etc.

Some dogs can run through fields, digging holes and rolling around in the grass with no after-effects at all. Others may spend more time indoors and have an excellent diet, but still experience severe itching, hot spots or recurring ear infections. Some dogs can eat anything and everything with no issues at all, while owners of others spend a lot of time trying to find the magic bullet – the ideal food for their dog's sensitive stomach.

It's by no means possible to cover all of the issues and causes in this chapter. The aim here is to give a broad outline of some of the ailments most likely to affect your Dachshund and how to deal with them. We have also included remedies tried with some success by ourselves (we had a dog with skin issues) and other owners of affected dogs, as well as advice from a holistic specialist.

This information is not intended to take the place of professional help; always contact your vet if your dog appears physically unwell or uncomfortable. This is particularly true with skin conditions:

Tip SEEK TREATMENT AS SOON AS POSSIBLE. **If you can find the cause(s) early, you reduce the chances of it taking hold and causing secondary issues and infections.**

Whatever the cause, before a vet can make a diagnosis, you'll have to give details of your dog's diet, exercise regime, habits, medical history and local environment. The vet will then carry out a physical examination, possibly followed by further tests, before a course of treatment can be prescribed. One of the difficulties with skin ailments is that the exact cause is often difficult to diagnose, as the symptoms are similar to other issues.

If environmental allergies are involved, specific and expensive tests are available. You'll have to take your vet's advice on this, as the tests are not always conclusive. And if the answer is dust or pollen, it can be difficult – if not downright impossible - to keep your dog away from the triggers. It is often a question of managing - rather than curing - the condition.

There are many things you as an owner can do to reduce the allergen load – and many natural remedies and supplements that can help as well as veterinary medications. Food allergies and intolerances are dealt with in **Chapter 6. Feeding a Dachshund.**

Types of Allergies

"Canine dermatitis" means inflammation of a dog's skin and it can be triggered by numerous things, but the most common is allergies. Vets estimate that as many as one in four dogs they see has some kind of allergy. Symptoms are:

Chewing her feet

Rubbing her face on the floor

Scratching

Scratching or biting the anus

Itchy ears, head shaking

Hair loss

Mutilated skin with sore or discoloured patches or hot spots

A Dachshund who is allergic to something will show it through skin problems and itching; your vet may call this *"pruritus."* It may seem logical that if a dog is allergic to something inhaled, like certain pollen grains, her nose will run; if she's allergic to something she eats, she may vomit, or if allergic to an insect bite, she may develop a swelling. But in practice this is seldom the case.

Dogs with allergies often chew their feet until they are sore and red. You may see yours rubbing her face on the carpet or couch, or scratching her belly and flanks. Because the ear glands produce too much wax in response to the allergy, ear infections can occur - with bacteria and yeast (which is a fungus) often thriving in the excessive wax and debris.

Digestive health can play an important role. Holistic vet Dr Jodie Gruenstern says: "It's estimated that up to 80% of the immune system resides within the gastrointestinal system; building a healthy gut supports a more appropriate immune response. The importance of choosing fresh proteins and healthy fats over processed, starchy diets (such as kibble) can't be overemphasized. Grains and other starches have a negative impact on gut health, creating insulin resistance and inflammation."

An allergic dog may cause skin lesions or **hot spots** by constant chewing and scratching. Sometimes she will lose hair, which can be patchy, leaving a mottled appearance. The skin itself may be dry and crusty, reddened, swollen or oily, depending on the dog. It is common to get secondary bacterial skin infections due to these self-inflicted wounds.

An allergic dog's body is reacting to certain molecules called **allergens.** These may come from:

   Tree, grass or plant pollens

   Flea bites

   Specific food or food additives, such as a type of meat, grains, colourings or preservatives

   Milk products

   Fabrics, such as wool or nylon

   Rubber and plastics

   House dust and dust mites

   Mould

   Chemical products used around the home or garden

 These allergens may be INHALED as the dog breathes, INGESTED as the dog eats, or caused by CONTACT with the dog's body when she walks or rolls.

Regardless of how they arrive, they all cause the immune system to produce a protein called IgE, which releases irritating chemicals like histamine inside the skin, hence the scratching.

Managing allergies is all about **REDUCING THE ALLERGEN LOAD.**

Inhalant Allergies (Atopy)

Some of the most common allergies in dogs are inhalant and seasonal - at least at first; some allergies may develop and worsen. Substances that can cause an allergic reaction in dogs are similar to those causing problems for humans, and dogs of all breeds can suffer from them.

Look at the timing of the reaction. Does it happen all year round? If so, this may be mould, dust or some other permanent trigger. If the reaction is seasonal, then pollens may well be the culprit. A diagnosis can be made by **allergy testing.**

The most common type is a blood test for antibodies caused by antigens in the dog's blood, and there are two standard tests: a **RAST** and an **ELISA**. Many vets feel that the ELISA test gives more accurate results. The other type of testing is **intradermal skin testing** where a small amount of antigen is injected into the skin of the animal and after a short period of time, the area around the injection site is inspected to see if the dog has had an allergic reaction. This method has been more widely used in the USA than the UK to date.

Our photo shows a Golden Retriever that has undergone intradermal skin testing.

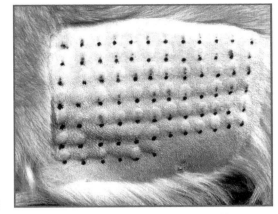

In this case, the dog was tested for more than 70 allergens, which is a lot. In all likelihood, your vet would test for fewer. The injections are in kits. If you consider this option, ask the vet or specialist how many allergens are in the kit. Intradermal skin testing is regarded as *"the gold standard"* of allergy testing for atopy.

The dog is sedated and an area on the flank is shaved down to the skin. A small amount of antigen is injected into the skin on this shaved area. This is done in a specific pattern and order. After a short time, the shaved area is examined to detect which antigens, if any, have created a reaction. It may look pretty drastic, but reactions – the visible round bumps - are only temporary and the hair grows back.

Allergy testing is not particularly expensive, but your dog has to be sedated, and the resulting immunotherapy treatment, or *"hyposensitisation,"* IS expensive. It is a series of injections made specifically for your dog and administered over months (or even years) to make her more tolerant of specific allergens. Vets in the US claim that success rates can be as high as 75%.

Before you get to the stage of considering allergy testing, a vet has to rule out other potential causes, such as fleas or mites, fungal, yeast or bacterial infections and hypothyroidism.

FACT ❯ Skin testing is expensive and time-consuming In practice, vets often treat mild cases of allergies with a combination of avoidance, fatty acids, tablets, and steroid injections for flare-ups.

Many owners of dogs with allergies also consider changing to an unprocessed diet (raw or cooked) and natural alternatives to long-term use of steroids, which can cause other health issues.

Environmental or Contact Irritations

These are a direct reaction to something the dog physically comes into contact with, and the triggers are similar to inhalant allergies. If grass or pollen is the issue, the allergies are often seasonal. An affected dog may be given treatments such as tablets, shampoo or localised cortisone spray for spring and summer – with a steroid injection to control a flare-up - but be perfectly fine the rest of the year. This was the case with our dog with allergies.

If you suspect your Dachshund has outdoor contact allergies, hose her down after walks. Washing her feet and belly will get rid of some of the pollen and other allergens, which then reduces scratching and biting.

The problem may be localised - such as the paws or belly. Symptoms are a general skin irritation or specific hotspots - itching (pruritus) and sometimes hair loss. Readers of our website sometimes report that their dog will incessantly lick one part of the body, often the paws, anus, belly or back.

Flea Bite Allergy

This is a common allergy affecting lots of dogs. It's typically seasonal, worse during summer and autumn - peak time for fleas - and in warmer climates where fleas are prevalent. Unfortunately, some dogs with a flea allergy also have inhalant allergies.

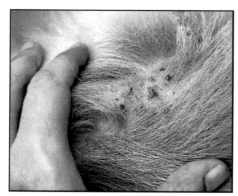 This allergy is not to the flea itself, but to proteins in flea saliva left under the dog's skin when the insect feeds. Just one bite to an allergic dog will cause red, crusty bumps *(pictured)* and intense itching.

An affected dog usually has a rash at the base of her tail and rear legs, and she will bite and scratch the area. Much of the skin damage is done by the dog's scratching, rather than the flea bite, and can result in hair falling out or skin abrasions. Some dogs also develop hot spots, often along the base of the tail and back.

A vet can make a diagnosis with a simple blood test. If fleas are the cause, you'll also have to make sure her bedding and your home are flea-free zones. Most flea bite allergies can be treated with medication, but they can only be totally prevented by keeping all fleas away from the dog. Various flea prevention treatments are available – see the section on **Parasites**.

 **Some Dachshunds can have an adverse reaction to topical (on-the-skin) flea treatments. Tablets or holistic remedies may be a better alternative.**

Acute Moist Dermatitis (Hot Spots)

A hot spot can appear suddenly and is a raw, inflamed and often bleeding area of skin. The area becomes moist and painful and begins spreading due to continual licking and chewing. They can become large, red, irritated lesions in a short pace of time. The cause is often a local reaction to an insect bite.

US breeder Melissa Sworab adds: "Oh how the Dachshund can wick up moisture, being low to the ground! A wet Dachshund may become a yeasty Dachshund and itch and chew themselves into hot spots and have ugly sores and hair loss that may or may not grow back if left untreated. Keep them dry and use a spray for rain-rot meant for horses.

"I spray mine any time they go out in the rain, dive into a puddle and after a bath as a preventative. In the ears we use a product for ears that contains gentian violet, witch hazel or alcohol, boric acid and colloidal silver and it keeps wet ears from getting yeasty."

 Some owners have had good results after dabbing hot spots, interdigital cysts and other skin irritations with an equal mixture of the amber-coloured Original Listerine baby oil and water. US owners have also reported success with Gold Bond Powder.

Once diagnosed and with the right treatment for the underlying cause, hot spots often disappear as soon as they appeared. Treatments may come in the form of injections, tablets or creams – or a combination of all three. The affected area is clipped and cleaned by the vet to help the effectiveness of any spray or ointment.

The dog may also have to wear an E-collar, which is stressful for everybody, as you watch your Dachshund bumping into door frames and furniture. Some dogs can be resistant to the *"Cone of Shame"* - they may slump down like you've hung a 10-ton weight on their neck or sink into a depression. Fortunately, they don't usually have to wear them for more than a few days.

Bacterial infection (Pyoderma)

Pyoderma literally means **pus in the skin** (yuk)! The offending bacteria is staphylococcus, and the condition may also be referred to as a **staph infection.** Early signs are itchy red spots filled with yellow pus, similar to pimples or spots in humans. They can sometimes develop into red, ulcerated skin with dry and crusty patches. Fortunately, the condition is not contagious.

Pyoderma **(pictured)** is caused by several things: a broken skin surface, a skin wound due to chronic exposure to moisture, altered skin bacteria, or poor blood flow to the skin.

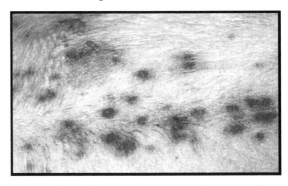

Allergies to fleas, food, parasites, yeast or fungal skin infections, thyroid disease, hormonal imbalances, heredity and some medications can all increase the risk. One of the biggest causes is a dog with a skin disorder excessively licking or biting an itchy patch.

Puppies can develop **puppy pyoderma** in thinly-haired areas, such as the groin and underarms. If you notice symptoms, get to the vet quickly before the condition develops from **superficial pyoderma** into **severe pyoderma**, which is very unpleasant and takes a lot longer to treat.

Superficial and puppy pyoderma are usually treated with a two to six-week course of antibiotic tablets or ointment. Severe or recurring pyoderma looks awful, causes your dog some distress and can take months to completely cure.

Medicated shampoos and regular bathing, as instructed by your vet, are also part of the treatment. It's also important to ensure your dog has clean, dry, padded bedding. Bacterial infection, no matter how bad it may look, usually responds well to medical treatment.

Malassezia Dermatitis and Yeast Infections

Malassezia Dermatitis is a specific type of yeast infection that affects Dachshunds more than many other breeds. **Malassezia** is a yeast, or fungus, that gets into the surface layers of the skin. These organisms cause no harm to the vast majority of animals, but cause inflammation in some dogs when numbers multiply.

While it's not known exactly why the Malassezia spread, we do know that they like humid conditions - so climate can be a factor, and they like warm, damp areas on a dog's body like ear canals and skin folds. Dachshunds that already have poor skin condition, allergies or a hormonal disorder are also more prone to Malassezia infection. Symptoms are:

Itchy, flaky skin at inflamed areas around the lips, ear canals, neck and armpits, between the toes and in skin folds on the face

Greasy or flaky skin

Unpleasant smell

In long-term cases, the skin becomes thicker and darker

Reddish-brown discolouration of the claws

The condition is easily diagnosed with a skin scraping and is often effectively treated with anti-fungal shampoos, wipes and creams, or tablets. If another skin disorder is causing the Malassezia to spread, this will have to be addressed to rid the dog of the problem.

Acanthosis Nigricans

Type 1 or Primary Acanthosis Nigricans is a hereditary canine skin disease that almost exclusively affects Dachshunds. Typical symptoms usually show by the time the dog is one year old and are darkening and thickening of patches of skin, which becomes hairless and leathery or velvety – usually around the armpits or groin. There may also be warty areas.

This type of Acanthosis Nigricans cannot be cured. Although the dark patches are visible, mild cases do not adversely affect the dog. However, if the areas are inflamed, they may become itchy or painful. If it's caught quickly enough, the condition can be successfully treated with antimicrobial shampoos, sprays and ointments.

Type 2 or Secondary Acanthosis Nigricans can develop in any dog. The symptoms are the same - although they are more likely to be inflamed - and triggered by a primary issue such as bacterial or yeast infection, allergies, hypothyroidism, Cushing's or immune disease.

This type is treatable, provided the root cause of the problem can be correctly diagnosed - and this is one of the difficulties facing vets, as symptoms are similar for a range of skin disorders.

Alopecia

Colour Dilution Alopecia (CDA) is a genetic disease that affects only *blue/lilac and isabella (fawn) Dachshunds, also known as dilutes.* It causes patches of thin hair or baldness and often flaky, itchy skin. Dilutes carry a recessive colour gene, dd, as opposed to the DD or Dd gene in normal colours of Dachshunds. They are usually blue or fawn and have blue, blueish grey, lavender, or flesh-coloured lips, noses and eyelids.

Although CDA is genetic, the cause is not fully understood. It's thought that affected dogs have abnormalities in their hair follicles, causing them to self-destruct - and making it impossible to grow new hairs. This also leaves the dog particularly prone to sunburn, infection, dermatitis and cancer.

Symptoms start to appear from around six months to two years of age. The condition needs lifelong treatment or nasty infections will develop. This usually involves shampoos and rinses, and/or ointments to the dry skin, scaling and superficial infections. The vet may prescribe antibiotic tablets to deal with severe skin infections.

 CDA is incurable and the only sure-fire way of avoiding it is not to buy a dilute-coloured Dachshund.

NOTE: The UK Breed Standard states: "The dilute colours isabella and blue are highly undesirable." Gray (blue) and isabella, *pictured*, are accepted by the AKC in the USA. If you choose one of these colours, look at the puppies' and parents' hair and ask if there is CDA in the bloodlines - although many breeders of dilutes are either ignorant of the disease or deny it exists.

Helen Kerfoot, resident geneticist and colour expert on the UK Dachshund Breed Council's Health and Welfare sub-committee says: "At the moment, there is no DNA test for CDA (there is a DNA test for the dilution gene but it cannot differentiate between the version that causes CDA and the version that doesn't).

"Therefore, at the moment there is no 100% safe way to breed dilute colour Dachshunds, and the people who are breeding them who say they don't have CDA in their lines cannot possibly know that for certain, as they haven't been breeding Dachshunds long enough to prove it. They are relying on mainly American breeders and some in Eastern Europe, and I am not convinced I would be trusting them all."

Pinnal Alopecia is another hereditary skin disease, this time affecting some Smooths and Miniature Smooths. Its onset varies - it can come on suddenly and severely within days, or gradually and mildly over years. In some cases, the owner might not even notice until the ears are completely bald. (Pinnal means "of the ear").

There's usually no inflammation or redness and the dog doesn't seem to notice the hair loss. Typical symptoms are the thinning and disappearance of hairs on the ears, with darkening of the affected skin. Diagnosis is usually made with a skin scraping at the vet's. Pinnal Alopecia isn't painful or itchy and doesn't appear to harm the dog, so no treatment is necessary. If an owner does opt for treatment, a four to six-week course of melatonin (a natural hormone made by the body's pineal gland) is the usual prescription.

Seborrhoea

There are two common types of seborrhoea: oily (oleosa) and dry (sicca). With seborrhoea, the dog's skin gives off a smelly, waxy substance that clumps in the ears, under the belly and armpits, elbows, and ankles. Dogs may scratch at the affected areas, causing bleeding, crusting, hair loss and secondary infections.

Primary seborrhoea is genetic-based, while secondary seborrhoea results from injury to the skin caused by things such as parasites, allergies, food disorders and hormonal issues like hypothyroidism.

Normally, the condition cannot be completely cured. Treatment involving anti-seborrheic or tar-based shampoos, may last a lifetime and focusses on managing the symptoms. If there is an underlying cause - such as allergies, then this also has to be tackled, along with any yeast or bacterial infections. Omega-3 fatty acid supplement, such as fish oils, can help. This may seem odd as the dog often already has a greasy coat, but fatty acids are essential for normal skin cell function.

Ear Margin Dermatosis or Seborrhoea causes crustiness at the edge of the ears and is found in some Smooths, Miniature Smooths, and other breeds with long, droopy ears. It can sometimes be misdiagnosed with a visual inspection, but a skin scraping should result in the correct diagnosis.

Typical symptoms are grey to yellow crust and grease along the edges of the ears and, in severe cases, the sores can crack and bleed.

The cause is unknown and it cannot be cured, but it can be treated with ointments and, when necessary, antibiotics. Vitamin A, moisturisers and barriers creams can also help.

···

Interdigital Cysts

If your Dachshund gets a fleshy red lump between the toes that looks like an ulcerated sore or a hairless bump, then it's probably an interdigital cyst - or *interdigital furuncle. These* can be very difficult to cure as they are often not the main problem, but a symptom of some other ailment.

They are not cysts, but the result of *furunculosis*, a skin condition that clogs hair follicles and creates chronic infection. Causes include allergies, obesity, poor foot conformation, mites, yeast infections, ingrowing hairs or other foreign bodies.

 **Bulldogs are the most susceptible breed, but any dog can get them - often the dog also has allergies.**

These nasty-looking bumps are painful, will probably cause a limp and can be a nightmare to get rid of. Vets might recommend a whole range of treatments to get to the root cause, and it can be very expensive to have a barrage of tests or biopsies - even then you're not guaranteed to find the underlying cause.

The vet might recommend an E-collar. If your dog is resistant, try putting socks on the affected foot or feet instead. This works well while your dog sleeps, but you have to watch her like a hawk when she's awake to stop her licking the affected areas. Here are some remedies your vet may suggest:

- 🐾 Antibiotics and/or steroids and/or mite killers
- 🐾 Soaking the feet in Epsom salts
- 🐾 Testing for allergies or thyroid problems
- 🐾 Starting a food trial if food allergies are suspected
- 🐾 Shampooing the feet
- 🐾 Cleaning between the toes with medicated (benzoyl peroxide) wipes
- 🐾 A referral to a veterinary dermatologist
- 🐾 Surgery (this is a last-resort option)

If you suspect your Dachshund has an interdigital cyst, get to the vet for a correct diagnosis and then discuss the various options. A course of antibiotics may be suggested initially, along with switching to a hypoallergenic diet if a food allergy is suspected. If the condition persists, many owners get discouraged, especially when treatment continues for several weeks.

 Be wary of agreeing to a series of steroid injections or repeated courses of antibiotics, as this means that the underlying cause of the furuncle has not been diagnosed. In such cases, it is worth exploring natural diets and remedies – and trying to lower the overall allergen load on your dog.

Before you resort to any drastic action, first try soaking your Dachshund's affected paw in Epsom salts for five or 10 minutes twice a day. After the soaking, clean the area with medicated wipes, which are antiseptic and control inflammation. Surgery is a drastic option. Although it can be effective in solving the immediate issue, it doesn't deal with the underlying problem.

Post-surgery healing is slow and difficult, and the dog does not have the same foot as before. Future orthopaedic issues and more interdigital cysts are a couple of problems that can occur afterwards. All that said, your vet will understand that interdigital cysts are not simple to deal with, but they are always treatable. ***Get the right diagnosis as soon as possible.***

Hormonal Imbalances

These occur in dogs of all breeds, including Dachshunds. They are often difficult to diagnose and occur when a dog is producing either too much (hyper) or too little (hypo) of a particular hormone. One visual sign is often hair loss on both sides of the dog's body, which is not usually itchy. Hormone imbalances can be serious as they are often indicators that glands that affect the dog internally are not working properly. However, some types can be diagnosed by special blood tests and treated effectively.

Hypothyroidism – this can affect Dachshunds of different ages and occurs when the dog does not produce enough thyroid hormone, causing her metabolism to slow. Diagnosis is by blood test and symptoms include:

- Lethargy
- Thickening of the skin
- Increased shedding and hair becoming thin and brittle
- Intolerance to cold or exercise
- Dullness, lack of interest
- Unexplained weight gain

Hypothyroidism is treatable with a lifelong daily dose of thyroxine, a hormone replacement, which is not particularly expensive. The dog may have to be retested once or twice a year and the dose adjusted accordingly.

Hyperthyroidism occurs when a dog produces ***too much*** thyroid hormone, increasing metabolic rate to dangerous levels. This disease is rarely found in dogs; it is much more common in cats.

Parasites

Demodectic Mange

Also known as ***Demodex, red mange, follicular mange*** or ***puppy mange,*** this is caused by the microscopic mite Demodex canis, ***pictured.*** They live inside the hair follicles on the bodies of virtually every adult dog without causing any harm or irritation. In humans, the mites are found in the skin, eyelids and the creases of the nose...try not to think about that!

The Demodex mite spends its entire life on the host dog. Eggs hatch and mature from larvae to nymphs to adults in 20-35 days and the mites transfer directly from mother to puppies within the first week of life. Most puppies have no reaction to the mites.

However, Demodex can develop in pups whose parents have mange, usually at three to six months *Puppy Mange* is not usually serious and most cases disappear when the pup's immune system kicks in at about 12 months old. It can also occur when females have their first season, which may be due to a slight dip in their immune systems.

FACT Adult dogs with healthy immune systems rarely get full-blown Demodex. However, a few with weak immune systems can't combat the mites and the disease spreads to the face and forelimbs or across the dog's whole body. Affected skin turns blue-grey due to the presence of thousands of blackheads or "comedones."

Symptoms — Bald patches, usually accompanied by crusty, red skin that sometimes appears greasy or wet. Hair loss usually begins around the muzzle, eyes and other areas on the head. The lesions may or may not itch.

In *localised mange*, a few circular crusty areas appear, most frequently on the head and front legs of puppies. With *generalised mange* there are bald patches over the entire coat. The skin on the head, side and back is crusty, inflamed and oozes a clear fluid. The skin is often oily to touch and there is usually a secondary bacterial infection.

Tip Some puppies can become quite ill and can develop a fever, lose their appetites and become lethargic. If you suspect your puppy has generalised demodectic mange, (as opposed to local, which only affects the face and front legs), get her to a vet ASAP.

There is also a condition called *pododermatitis,* when the mange affects a puppy's paws. It can cause bacterial infections and be very uncomfortable, even painful. Symptoms include hair loss on the paws, swelling of the paws (especially around the nail beds) and red, hot or inflamed areas that are often infected. Treatment is always recommended, and it can take several rounds to clear it up.

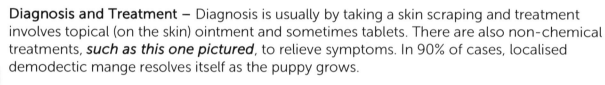

Diagnosis and Treatment — Diagnosis is usually by taking a skin scraping and treatment involves topical (on the skin) ointment and sometimes tablets. There are also non-chemical treatments, *such as this one pictured*, to relieve symptoms. In 90% of cases, localised demodectic mange resolves itself as the puppy grows.

Treatment for generalised demodectic mange can be lengthy and expensive. The vet might prescribe an anti-parasitic dip every two weeks. Owners should always wear rubber gloves when treating their dog, and it should be applied in an area with ventilation. Most dogs with a severe issue need six to 14 dips every two weeks. Dips continue for a month after the mites have disappeared, but dogs are not considered cured until a year after their last treatment.

FACT Some dogs can have a bad reaction to anti-parasitic dips. Check with your vet as to whether an anti-parasitic dip is suitable for your Dachshund.

Other options include the heartworm treatment Ivermectin. This isn't approved by the FDA for treating mange, but is often used to do so. **Again, some dogs react badly to it.** Another drug is Interceptor (Milbemycin oxime), which can be expensive as it has to be given daily. However, it is effective on up to 80% of the dogs who did not respond to dips — but may not be suitable for pups.

Dogs with generalised mange may have underlying skin infections, so antibiotics may be necessary. Because the mite flourishes on dogs with suppressed immune systems, you should try to get to the root cause of immune system disease, especially if your Dachshund is an adult when she first develops demodectic mange.

Cheyletiella (Walking Dandruff)

"My dog appears to have dandruff, there's lots of white scurf in her coat," is a commonly-heard claim. Occasionally, scurf can be caused by a very dry skin or even by shampoo not being thoroughly rinsed out of the coat after a bath, but often, the parasitic Cheyletiella mite is to blame.

There are few symptoms, but a heavy infestation can cause itching, skin scaling and hair loss. The mites, their eggs and the scurf they produce have been called *"walking dandruff,"* which is most frequently seen on the back and sides of the dog. Skin scales are carried through the hair coat by the mites, so **the dandruff appears to be moving along the back of the animal,** hence the nickname!

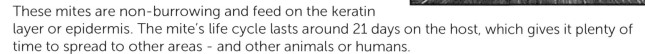

The mite spends its entire life cycle on the dog. Eggs are laid glued to the hair shafts and go on to form larvae, then nymph and then adult mites. They are spread by direct contact with an infected individual or infested bedding.

These mites are non-burrowing and feed on the keratin layer or epidermis. The mite's life cycle lasts around 21 days on the host, which gives it plenty of time to spread to other areas - and other animals or humans.

Most affected dogs respond quite well to treatment, although it can sometimes take a while to completely cure the infestation. Your vet may prescribe a pyrethrin-based shampoo. Frontline spray has also been proved to be effective. Bedding should be treated and be aware that these mites can temporarily infest humans, causing a mild skin irritation and itching.

Sarcoptic Mange (Scabies)

Also known as canine scabies, this is caused by the parasite *Sarcoptes scabiei.* This microscopic mite can cause a range of skin problems, the most common of which is hair loss and severe itching. The mites can infect other animals such as foxes, cats and even humans, but prefer to live their short lives on dogs. Fortunately, there are several good treatments and it can be easily controlled.

In cool, moist environments, the mites live for up to 22 days. At normal room temperature they live from two to six days, preferring to live on parts of the dog with less hair. Diagnosing canine scabies can be somewhat difficult, and it is often mistaken for inhalant allergies.

Once diagnosed, there are a number of effective treatments, including selamectin (Revolution – again, some dogs can have a bad reaction to this), an on-the-skin solution applied once a month which also provides heartworm prevention, flea control and some tick protection. Various Frontline products are also effective – check with your vet for the correct ones.

There is, however, one product recommended by many breeders and gets excellent reviews, both in terms of effectiveness and also the fact that very few dogs have any reaction to it. It is the **Seresto Flea Collar,** *pictured,* which provides full body protection against all fleas, ticks, sarcoptic mange, lice and other bloodsucking critters!

This collar lasts up to eight months and is waterproof. Provided your Dachshund will keep the collar on, I'd recommend it - but it's not cheap, at around £30 in the UK and $50 in the US. There are also holistic remedies for many skin conditions.

Because your dog does not have to come into direct contact with an infected dog to catch scabies, it is difficult to completely protect her. Foxes and their environment can also transmit the mite.

Fleas

When you see your dog scratching and biting, your first thought is probably: *"She's got fleas!"* and you may well be right. Fleas don't fly, but they do have very strong back legs and they will take any opportunity to jump from the ground or another animal into your Dachshund's lovely, warm coat. You can sometimes see the fleas if you part your dog's hair.

And for every flea that you see on your dog, there is the stomach-churning prospect of hundreds of eggs and larvae in your home.... So, if your dog gets fleas, you'll have to treat your environment as well as the dog in order to completely get rid of them. **The best form of cure is prevention.**

Vets recommend giving dogs a preventative flea treatment every four to eight weeks – although the Seresto Flea Collar lasts for eight months. If you do give a regular skin treatment, the frequency depends on your climate, the season - fleas do not breed as quickly in the cold - and how much time your dog spends outdoors.

To apply topical insecticides like Frontline and Advantix, part the skin and apply drops of the liquid on to a small area on your dog's back, usually near the neck. Some kill fleas and ticks, and others just kill fleas - check the details.

It is worth spending the money on a quality treatment, as cheap brands may not rid your Dachshund completely of fleas, ticks and other parasites. There are also holistic and natural alternatives to insecticides, discussed later in this chapter.

One UK breeder added that some breeders are opposed to chemical flea treatments, as they can cause a reaction - in extreme cases some dogs have been known to have seizures. She added that when she found a flea, she simply washed all of her dogs, one after the other, and then washed every last piece of bedding.

One breeder warned of the over-use of chemical preventatives with Dachshunds: "One of our dogs was five years old when he suddenly developed symptoms of IVDD and seizures simultaneously, but had no family history of either disease. I took him back from his owners, temporarily, booked him in with my chiropractor and within three days he was doing great. When I returned him to his owner... the symptoms returned! Then another unrelated pet in their home exhibited the same symptoms.

"It turned out the owner was applying topical MONTHLY flea medication on them EVERY WEEK, causing a chemical toxicity. After stopping the chemical exposure and bathing them multiple times in a regular non-microbial blue dish soap specifically used to strip the chemical out, they were then bathed in a pH-appropriate dog shampoo and conditioner. Neither pet has ever had a seizure or IVDD symptoms again."

NOTE: There is also anecdotal evidence from owners of various breeds that the US flea and worm tablet **Trifexis** may cause severe side effects in some dogs. You can read some owners' comments at: www.max-the-schnauzer.com/trifexis-side-effects-in-schnauzers.html

Ticks

A tick is not an insect, but a member of the arachnid family, like the spider. There are over 850 types, some have a hard shell and some a soft one. Ticks don't have wings, they crawl.

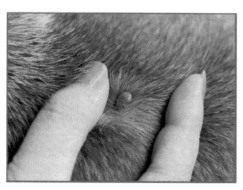

They have a sensor called Haller's organ that detects smell, heat and humidity to help them locate food, which in some cases is a Dachshund. A tick's diet consists of one thing and one thing only – blood! They climb up onto tall grass and when they sense an animal is close, crawl on.

Ticks can pass on a number of diseases to animals and humans, the most well-known of which is **Lyme Disease**, a serious condition that causes lameness and other problems. Dogs that spend a lot of time outdoors in high risk areas, such as woods, can have a vaccination against Lime Disease.

One breeder said: "We get ticks from sand dunes sometimes and, if removed quickly, they're not harmful. We use a tick tool which has instructions in the packet. You put the forked end either side of the tick and twist it till it comes out."

If you do find a tick on your Dachshund's coat and are not sure how to get it out, have it removed by a vet or other expert. Inexpertly pulling it out yourself and leaving a bit of the tick behind can be detrimental to your dog's health.

Tick prevention treatments are similar to those for fleas. If your Dachshund has sensitive skin or allergies, she may well do better with a natural flea or tick remedy.

Heartworm

Heartworm is a serious and potentially fatal disease affecting pets in North America and many other parts of the world, but not the UK. These foot-long worms live in the heart, lungs and blood vessels of affected animals, causing severe lung disease, heart failure and damage to organs. The dog is a natural host for heartworms, enabling the worms living inside a dog to mature into adults, mate and produce offspring. If untreated, their numbers can increase; dogs have been known to harbour several hundred worms in their bodies.

Heartworm disease causes lasting damage to the heart, lungs and arteries, and can affect the dog's health and quality of life long after the parasites are gone. For this reason, **prevention is by far the best option** and treatment - when needed - should be administered as early as possible.

When a mosquito *(pictured)* bites and takes a blood meal from an infected dog, it picks up baby worms that develop and mature into *infective-stage* larvae over 10 to 14 days. Then, when it bites another dog, it spreads the disease.

Once inside a dog, it takes about six months for the larvae to develop into adult heartworms, which can then live for five to seven years in a dog. In the early stages, many dogs show few or no symptoms. The longer the infection persists, the more likely symptoms will develop, including:

- 🐾 A mild persistent cough
- 🐾 Reluctance to exercise
- 🐾 Tiredness after normal activity
- 🐾 Decreased appetite and weight loss

As the disease progresses, dogs can develop a swollen belly due to excess fluid in the abdomen and heart failure. Dogs with large numbers of heartworms can develop the life-threatening caval syndrome, which, without prompt surgery, is often fatal.

Although more common in the south eastern US, heartworm disease has been diagnosed in all 50 states. The American Heartworm Society recommends that you get your dog tested every year and give your dog heartworm preventive treatment for all 12 months of the year. If you live in a risk area, check that your tick and flea medication also prevent heartworm. In the UK, heartworm has only been found in imported dogs.

Thanks to the American Heartworm Society for assistance with the section.

Ringworm

This is not actually a worm, but a fungus and is most commonly seen in puppies and young dogs. It is highly infectious and often found on the face, ears, paws or tail. The ringworm fungus is most prevalent in hot, humid climates but, surprisingly, most cases occur in autumn and winter. But it is

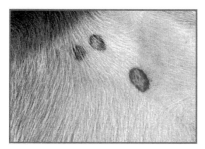

not that common; in one study of dogs with active skin problems, less than 3% had ringworm, *pictured.*

Ringworm is transmitted by spores in the soil and by contact with the infected hair of dogs and cats, typically found on carpets, brushes, combs, toys and furniture. Spores from infected animals can be shed into the environment and live for over 18 months, but most healthy adult dogs have some resistance and never develop symptoms. The fungi live in dead skin, hairs and nails - and the head and legs are the most common areas affected. Tell-tale signs are bald patches with a roughly circular shape. Ringworm is relatively easy to treat with fungicidal shampoos or antibiotics from a vet.

FACT ❯ Humans can catch ringworm from pets, and vice versa. Children are especially susceptible, as are adults with suppressed immune systems and those undergoing chemotherapy. Hygiene is extremely important.

If your dog has ringworm, wear gloves when handling her and wash your hands well afterwards. And if a member of your family catches ringworm, make sure they use separate towels from everyone else or the fungus may spread. As a teenager, I caught ringworm from horses at the local stables where I worked at weekends - much to my mother's horror - and was treated like a leper by the rest of the family until it cleared up!

Ear Infections

Dachshunds have floppy ears; it's a fact! This makes them more susceptible to ear infections than breeds with pricked-up ears, which allow air to circulate inside more easily. Owners of dogs with long hair, like Long-Haired Dachshunds and Spaniels, need to pay particular attention to cleanliness to avoid problems.

FACT ❯ The fact that a dog has recurring ear infections does NOT necessarily mean that the ears are the issue – although they might be. They may also be due to allergies or low thyroid function (hypothyroidism). The underlying problem must be treated or the dog will continue to have ear infections.

The ears themselves can be the cause – a dog's ear canal can be a warm, damp environment much loved by home-hunting bacteria.

Tell-tale signs of an infection include your dog shaking her head, scratching or rubbing her ears a lot, or an unpleasant smell from the ears. If you look inside, you may notice a reddy brown or yellow discharge, it may also be red and inflamed with a lot of wax. Sometimes a dog may appear depressed or irritable; ear infections are painful. In chronic cases, the inside of her ears may become crusty or thickened. Treatment depends on the cause and what – if any - other conditions your dog may have.

Antibiotics are used for bacterial infections and antifungals for yeast infections. Glucocorticoids, such as dexamethasone, are often included in these medications to reduce the inflammation in the ear. Your vet may also flush out and clean the ear with special drops, something you may have to do daily at home until the infection clears.

A dog's ear canal is L-shaped, which means it can be difficult to get medication into the lower, or horizontal, part of the ear. The best method is to hold the dog's ear flap with one hand and put the ointment or drops in with the other, if possible, tilting the dog's head away from you so the liquid flows downwards **with gravity**.

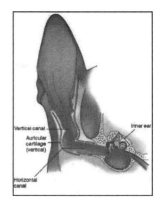

Hold the ear flap down and massage the medication into the horizontal canal before letting go of your dog, as the first thing she will do is shake her head – and if the ointment or drops aren't massaged in, they will fly out.

Nearly all ear infections can be successfully managed if properly diagnosed and treated. But if an underlying problem remains undiagnosed, the ears will continue to become infected.

 Check your Dachshund's ears when grooming, dry them after swimming and get the vet to check inside on routine visits. Long-Haireds may need the hair inside the ears plucking to allow air to flow more easily.

When cleaning or plucking your dog's ears, be very careful not to put anything too far inside. DO NOT use cotton buds inside the ear, they are too small and can cause injury. Visit YouTube to see how to clean ears without injuring them. Some owners recommend regularly cleaning the inside of ears with cotton wool and a mixture of water and white vinegar.

If your dog appears to be in pain, has smelly ears, or if her ear canals look inflamed, contact your vet straight away. If you can nip the first infection in the bud, there is a chance it will not return. If your dog has a ruptured or weakened eardrum, ear cleansers and medications could do more harm than good.

Some Allergy Treatments

Treatments and success rates vary tremendously from dog to dog and from one allergy to another, which is why it is so important to consult a vet at the outset. <u>Earlier diagnosis is more likely to lead to a successful treatment.</u>

Some owners of dogs with recurring skin issues find that a course of antibiotics or steroids works wonders for their dog's sore skin and itching. However, the scratching starts all over again shortly after the treatment stops.

Food allergies require patience, a change or several changes of diet and maybe even a food trial, and the specific trigger is notoriously difficult to isolate – unless you are lucky and hit on the culprit straight away. With inhalant and contact allergies, blood and skin tests are available, followed by hyposensitisation treatment. However, these are expensive and often the specific trigger for many dogs remains unknown. So, the reality for many owners of Dachshunds with allergies is that they manage the condition, rather than curing it completely.

FACT ❯ While a single steroid injection is often highly effective in calming down symptoms almost immediately, frequent or long-term steroid use is not a good option as it can lead to serious side effects.

Our Experience With Max

According to our vet, Graham, more and more dogs are appearing in his waiting room with various types of allergies. Whether this is connected to how we breed or feed our dogs remains to be seen.

Our dog, Max, was perfectly fine until he was about two years old, when he began to scratch a lot. He scratched more in spring and summer, which meant that his allergies were almost certainly inhalant or contact-based and related to pollens, grasses or other outdoor triggers. We decided not to have a lot of tests, not because of the cost, but because the vet said it was highly likely that he was allergic to pollens.

Max was an active dog and if we'd had pollen allergy confirmed, we were not going to stop taking him out for thrice-daily walks.

It's definitely beneficial to have a hose or bath outside to rinse the dog's paws and underbelly after a walk. Regarding medications, Max was at first put on to a tiny dose of Piriton *(pictured),* a cheap antihistamine manufactured in the millions for canine and human hay fever sufferers. For the first few springs and summers, this worked well.

Allergies can change and a dog can build up a tolerance to a treatment, which is why they can be so difficult to treat. Max's symptoms changed from season to season, although the main ones were: general scratching, paw biting and ear infections.

One year he bit the skin under his tail a lot– he would jump around like he had been stung by a bee and bite frenetically. This was treated effectively with a single steroid injection, followed by spraying the area with cortisone once a day at home for a period. Localised spray can be very effective if the itchy area is small, but no good for spraying all over a dog's body.

Over the years we tried a number of treatments, all of which worked for a while, before he came off the medication in October when pollen levels fell. He was perfectly fine the rest of the year without any treatment at all.

Not every owner wants to treat his or her dog with chemicals, nor feed a diet that includes preservatives, which is why this book includes alternatives. Also, 15 years ago, when we were starting out on the *"Allergy Trail,"* there were far fewer options than there are now.

We fed Max a high quality hypoallergenic dry food. If we were starting again from scratch, knowing what we know now, I'd look into a raw or home-cooked diet (which is what he was fed towards the end of his life), if necessary in combination with holistic remedies.

One spring the vet put him on a short course of steroids, which were effective for a season, but steroids are not a long-term solution. Another year we were prescribed the non-steroid Atopica. The active ingredient is **cyclosporine**, which suppresses the immune system - some dogs can get side effects, although ours didn't.

The daily tablet was expensive, but initially extremely effective – so much so that we thought we had cured the problem completely. However, after a couple of seasons on cyclosporine he developed a tolerance to the drug and started scratching again.

A few years ago, he went back on the antihistamine Piriton, a higher dose than when he was two years old, and this was effective.

Apoquel

In 2013 the FDA approved **Apoquel** (oclacitinib) – *pictured* - to control itching and inflammation in allergic dogs. Like most allergy drugs, it acts by suppressing the immune system, rather than addressing the root cause. It has, however, proved to be highly effective in treating countless thousands of dogs

with allergies. It proved so popular in the UK and North America that in the two years after release there was a world shortage, as the manufacturers weren't able to produce it fast enough. We tried Apoquel with excellent results. There was some initial tweaking to get the daily dose right, but it proved highly effective. The tablets are administered according to body weight – it's not cheap, but Apoquel can be a miracle worker for some dogs.

NOTE: Side effects have been reported in some dogs, and holistic practitioners and Dogs Naturally magazine believe that it is harmful to the dog.

Allergies are often complex and difficult to treat; you should weigh up the pros and cons in the best interests of your own dog. Max's allergies were manageable; he loved his food, was full of energy and otherwise healthy, and lived a happy life to the age of 13.

Other Options

Add fish oils, which contain Omega-3 fatty acids, to a daily feed to keep your dog's skin and coat healthy all year round – whether or not she has problems.

A liquid supplement called Yumove, which contains Omegas 3 and 6, golden flax and borage, is a good choice to add to your dog's daily feeds all year round. When the scratching got particularly bad, we also bathed Max in an antiseborrheic shampoo called Malaseb, *pictured,* twice a week for a limited time. This helped, although was not necessary once on Apoquel. Here are some other suggestions from owners:

Use an astringent such as witch hazel or alcohol on affected areas. We have heard of zinc oxide cream being used to some effect on dogs as well as babies' bottoms! In the human world, this is rubbed on to mild skin abrasions and acts as a protective coating. Zinc oxide works as a mild astringent and has some antiseptic properties and is safe to use on dogs, *as long as you do not allow the dog to lick it off*.

Vitamins A and E all also help to make a dog's skin healthy, and lots of owners have tried coconut oil *(pictured)* with some success. Here is a link to an article on the benefits of coconut oils and fish oils, check with your vet first: www.dogsnaturallymagazine.com/the-health-benefits-of-coconut-oil

 If you suspect your dog has a skin problem, ear infection or allergy, get her to the vet straight away. You can hopefully nip it in the bud before secondary infections develop – and save a lot of heartache and money in the long run.

The Holistic Approach

Many owners of dogs with sensitivities find that their dog does well for a time with injections or medication, but then the symptoms slowly start to reappear. More owners are now considering turning to natural foods and remedies. A holistic practitioner looks at finding and treating the root cause of the problem, rather than just treating the symptoms.

Dr Sara Skiwski is a holistic vet working in California. She writes here about canine environmental allergies: "Here in California, with our mild weather and no hard freeze in Winter, environmental allergens can build up and cause nearly year-round issues for our beloved pets.

"Also, seasonal allergies, when left unaddressed, can lead to year-round allergies. Unlike humans, whose allergy symptoms seem to affect mostly the respiratory tract, seasonal allergies in dogs often take the form of skin irritation/inflammation.

"Allergic reactions are produced by the immune system. The way the immune system functions is a result of both genetics and the environment: Nature versus Nurture. Let's look at a typical case. A puppy starts showing mild seasonal allergy symptoms, for instance a red tummy and mild itching in Spring. Off to the vet!

"The treatment prescribed is symptomatic to provide relief, such as a topical spray. The next year when the weather warms up, the patient is back again - same symptoms but more severe this time.

This time the dog has very itchy skin. Again, the treatment is symptomatic - antibiotics, topical spray (hopefully no steroids), until the symptoms resolve with the season change. Fast forward to another Spring...on the third year, the patient is back again but this time the symptoms last longer, (not just Spring but also through most of Summer and into Fall).

"By Year Five, all the symptoms are significantly worse and are occurring year-round. This is what happens with seasonal environmental allergies. The more your pet is exposed to the allergens they are sensitive to, the more the immune system over-reacts and the more intense and long-lasting the allergic response becomes. What to do?

"In my practice, I like to address the potential root cause at the very first sign of an allergic response, which is normally seen between the ages of six to nine months old. I do this to circumvent the escalating response year after year. Since the allergen load your environmentally-sensitive dog is most susceptible to is much heavier outdoors, I recommend two essential steps in managing the condition. They are vigilance in foot care as well as hair care.

"What does this mean? A wipe down of feet and hair, especially the tummy, to remove any pollens or allergens is key. This can be done with a damp cloth, but my favorite method is to get a spray bottle filled with Witch Hazel *(pictured)* and spray these areas.

"First, spray the feet then wipe them off with a cloth, and then spray and wipe down the tummy and sides. This is best done right after the pup has been outside playing or walking. This will help keep your pet from tracking the environmental allergens into the home and into their beds. If the feet end up still being itchy, I suggest adding foot soaks in Epsom salts."

Dr Sara also stresses the importance of keeping the immune system healthy by avoiding unnecessary vaccinations or drugs: "The vaccine stimulates the immune system, which is the last thing your pet with seasonal environmental allergies needs.

"I also will move the pet to an anti-inflammatory diet. Foods that create or worsen inflammation are high in carbohydrates. An allergic pet's diet should be very low in carbohydrates, especially grains. Research has shown that 'leaky gut,' or dysbiosis, is a root cause of immune system overreactions in both dog and cats (and some humans).

"Feed a diet that is not processed, or minimally processed; one that doesn't have grain and takes a little longer to get absorbed and assimilated through the gut. Slowing the assimilation assures that there are not large spikes of nutrients and proteins that come into the body all at once and overtax the pancreas and liver, creating inflammation.

"A lot of commercial diets are too high in grains and carbohydrates. These foods create inflammation that overtaxes the body and leads not just to skin inflammation, but also to other inflammatory conditions, such as colitis, pancreatitis, arthritis, inflammatory bowel disease and ear infections.

"Also, these diets are too low in protein, which is needed to make blood. This causes a decreased blood reserve in the body and in some of these animals this can lead to the skin not being properly nourished, starting a cycle of chronic skin infections which produce more itching."

After looking at diet, check that your dog is free from fleas and then these are some of Dr Sara's suggested supplements:

- ✓ **Raw (Unpasteurised) Local Honey** - an alkaline-forming food containing natural vitamins, enzymes, powerful antioxidants and other important natural nutrients, which are destroyed during the heating and pasteurisation processes. Raw honey has anti-viral, anti-bacterial and anti-fungal properties. It promotes body and digestive health, is a powerful antioxidant, strengthens the immune system, eliminates allergies, and is an excellent remedy for skin wounds and all types of infections. Bees collect pollen from local plants and their honey often acts as an immune booster for dogs living in the locality.

  Dr Sara says: "It may seem odd that straight exposure to pollen often triggers allergies, but that exposure to pollen in the honey usually has the opposite effect. But this is typically what we see. In honey, the allergens are delivered in small, manageable doses and the effect over time is very much like that from undergoing a whole series of allergy immunology injections."

- ✓ **Mushrooms** - make sure you choose the non-poisonous ones! Dogs don't like the taste, so you may have to mask it with another food. Medicinal mushrooms are used to treat and prevent a wide array of illnesses through their use as immune stimulants and modulators, and antioxidants.

  The most well-known and researched are reishi, maitake, cordyceps, blazei, split-gill, turkey tail and shiitake. Histamine is what causes much of the inflammation, redness and irritation in allergies. By helping to control histamine production, the mushrooms can moderate the effects of inflammation and even help prevent allergies in the first place.

WARNING! Mushrooms can interact with some over-the-counter and prescription drugs, so do your research as well as checking with your vet first.

- ✓ **Stinging Nettles** - contain biologically active compounds that reduce inflammation. Nettles can reduce the amount of histamine the body produces in response to an allergen. Nettle tea or extract can help with itching. Nettles not only help directly to decrease the itch, but also work overtime to desensitise the body to allergens.

- ✓ **Quercetin** – is an over-the-counter supplement with anti-inflammatory properties. It is a strong antioxidant and reduces the body's production of histamines.

- ✓ **Omega-3 Fatty Acids** - these help decrease inflammation throughout the body. Adding them into the diet of all pets - particularly those struggling with seasonal environmental allergies – is very beneficial. If your dog has more itching along the top of their back and on their sides, add in a fish oil supplement. Fish oil helps to decrease the itch and heal skin lesions. The best sources of Omega 3s are krill oil, salmon oil, tuna oil, anchovy oil and other fish body oils, as well as raw organic egg yolks. If using an oil alone, it is important to give a vitamin B complex supplement.

✓ **Coconut Oil -** contains lauric acid, which helps decrease the production of yeast, a common opportunistic infection. Using a fish body oil combined with coconut oil before inflammation flares up can help moderate or even suppress your dog's inflammatory response.

Dr Sara adds: "Above are but a few of the over-the-counter remedies I like. In non-responsive cases, Chinese herbs can be used to work with the body to help to decrease the allergy threshold even more than with diet and supplements alone. Most of the animals I work with are on a program of Chinese herbs, diet change and acupuncture.

"So, the next time Fido is showing symptoms of seasonal allergies, consider rethinking your strategy to treat the root cause instead of the symptom."

With thanks to Dr Sara Skiwski, of the Western Dragon Integrated Veterinary Services, San Jose, California, for her kind permission to use her writings as the basis for _The Holistic Approach_.

....

 Massage can stimulate your dog's immune system and help to prevent or reduce allergies. It's also good for improving your dog's circulation and flexibility, reducing muscle and arthritis pain and other age-related problems.

Anybody can do it – we do – and your Dachshund will love the attention!

Holistic practitioners also believe that **acupressure** can specifically help dogs with allergies.

Type _"Acupressure for Dogs"_ into Google to learn about the theory behind it and how to apply pressure at specific points on your dog's body. Acupressure can also help nervous and elderly dogs.

If your Dachshund has a skin issue, seek a professional diagnosis as soon as possible before attempting to treat it yourself and it becomes entrenched. Even if a skin condition cannot be completely cured, most can be successfully managed, allowing your dog to live a happy, pain-free life. Remember:

🐾 A high-quality diet

🐾 Regular grooming and check-overs

🐾 Attention to cleanliness, and

🐾 Maintaining a healthy weight

All go a long way in preventing or managing skin problems in Dachshunds.

....

14. Grooming

Regular grooming, cleaning and check-overs are essential to keep your Dachshund handsome and healthy. The amount of time spent grooming depends on the type of Dachshund you own.

Coat Types and Colours

Few, if any, breeds have as many variations as the Dachshund - you'd have an easier time trying to get to grips with quantum physics than Dachshund coat genetics. To keep it simple, there are three coat types: **Smooth, Wire** and **Long.**

The Smooth coat is short and shiny and the easiest to care for. A weekly check-over and groom with a soft brush, and a wipe down with a soft cloth or occasional bath when dirty is enough to keep the Smooth looking good.

Next is the double-coated Wire, with a softer undercoat and a wiry outer coat that hardly sheds. If you don't know how to hand-strip or clipper a dog, a Wire-Haired Dachshund will require a trip to the groomer's two to three times a year. If you aren't showing your Wire, he can be trimmed with electric clippers, but this will make the coat softer. Clipping is not acceptable for show dogs, which have to be hand-stripped to maintain the wiry outer coat.

The highest maintenance coat is the Long, which needs regular brushing to prevent matts and to keep it looking beautifully silky. Longs also need the hairs between the pads of their feet (as do Wires) and inside their ears kept short. The coat itself does not need trimming. Our breeders have plenty of advice for maintaining the beautiful coat of the Long.

 Early spay or neuter can affect all Dachshunds' coats, but particularly Longs. The coat may become "fuzzy" and brittle, destroying the soft, silky texture. For this and health reasons, many breeders recommend waiting until your Dachshund is one to two years old before considering spaying or neutering.

Other factors affecting coat characteristics include: genetics, skin condition, diet, gender, age, and temperature - a dog kept in a warm, centrally-heated house will shed all year, whereas one in a cool house or kennel may only shed seasonally. The many coat colours are the same for Standards and Miniatures.

FACT ❯ None of the coat types is considered hypoallergenic, or suitable for people with allergies.

The basic colours are:

- 🐾 Red
- 🐾 Black and Tan
- 🐾 Cream
- 🐾 Black and Cream
- 🐾 Chocolate and Tan
- 🐾 Chocolate and Cream

The most common colour for Wire-Haired Dachshunds **is Wild Boar,** *pictured,* (also called

Brindle in the UK), where each hair is individually banded with grey, brown and black. Wild Boar is actually a Sable pattern.

There are also "**Dilutes,**" caused by a dilution gene, which alters Black to Blue or Grey and Chocolate to Isabella (fawn). More commonly seen in America, Dilute Dachshunds are considered "undesirable" by the UK Kennel Club, as they are known to be susceptible to skin diseases such as Colour Dilution Alopecia (CDA), infections and dermatitis.

Then there are the patterns:

- **Dapple,** known as **merle** in Collies and other breeds

- **Brindle** or **Tiger-Striped** (not to be confused with Wild Boar)

- **Sable**

- **Piebald or Pied** (also considered undesirable by the UK Kennel Club)

Plus, combinations of these patterns.

 **The Dapple pattern is very attractive, and Single Dapples,** *pictured,* **are fine. But avoid "Double Dapples,"** which are the result of mating two Dapples, as they have well-documented health issues.

The Dachshund Breed Council says: "Double Dapple puppies will always have white markings, many in the same pattern that you would associate with a Collie-type dog (band around the neck, white on paws, nose, and tail tip). A Double Dapple Dachshund usually has blue eyes, but may have one or both dark eyes.

"The problems associated with the lethal genes in Double Dapples are varying degrees of vision and hearing loss, including missing eyes or "micro eyes." Blindness and/or deafness can be caused by the Double Dapple gene combination. Given the potential health risks associated with Double Dapples, it is considered irresponsible and unacceptable to mate two Dapples together. Remember that Single Dapple Dachshunds **do not** have these lethal health problems."

There are also markings, accepted in the US, such as **ticking or spotting** on Piebalds, which are little spots of colour, such as those seen on Coonhounds and roan Cocker Spaniels.

 If you have set your heart on a favourite colour or pattern, remember to check that the health-testing boxes have been ticked as well.

Benefits of Regular Grooming

Time spent grooming is also time spent bonding; this physical and emotional inter-reliance brings us closer to our dogs. There are facets to grooming that play a part in keeping your dog clean and skin-related issues at bay. Routine grooming sessions also allow you to examine your dog's coat, skin, ears, teeth, eyes, paws and nails for signs of problems and parasites.

Although puppies require fairly minimal brushing, it's very important to get your Dachshund used to being handled and groomed from an early age; an adult will not take kindly to being handled if he's not used to it. Other benefits of regular brushing are that it:

- Removes dead hair and skin – the main source of matts is unremoved dead hair
- Stimulates blood circulation
- Spreads natural oils throughout the coat, helping to keep it in good condition

Tip **Long-Haireds require more grooming than other Dachshunds. It may be worth investing in a grooming table or using a table or bench. Once he is out of his normal environment (floor level) and at your level, he may be more co-operative. Make sure he can't jump off and injure himself.**

A few things to look out for when grooming are:

Dry Skin - A dog's skin can dry out, especially with artificial heat in the winter months. If you spot any dry patches, for example on the inner thighs or armpits, or a cracked nose, massage a little petroleum jelly or baby oil into the dry patch.

A Yeasty Smell – often a sign of infection. Skin and ear infections need prompt treatment before they take a hold. An ear drying agent used after a bath, swim or rain can help reduce yeasty ears.

Eyes - These should be clean and clear. Cloudy eyes, particularly in an older dog, could be early signs of cataracts. Red or swollen tissue in the corner(s) could be a symptom of Cherry Eye, which can affect all breeds. Ingrowing eyelashes is another issue which causes red, watery eyes.

If your dog has an issue, gently bathe the outer eye(s) with warm water and gauze or cotton cloth - never use anything sharp; your dog can suddenly jump forwards or backwards, causing injury. If the eye is red or watering for a few days or more, get it checked out by a vet.

Acne - Little red pimples on a dog's face and chin means he has got acne. A dog can get acne at any age, not just as an adolescent. Plastic bowls can also trigger the condition, which is why stainless steel ones are better. Daily washing followed by an application of an antibiotic cream is usually enough to get rid of the problem.

Breeders' Advice on Grooming and Bathing

Lisa Lindfield (all three types of Miniature): "The Wires have their coat trimmed twice a year. I used to hand-strip, but found it stresses my dogs as it takes a good while (sometimes an hour or two). Once you start using clippers, you can never return to stripping, as it alters the coat. So, I now use clippers, as it's kinder and faster in my opinion. The coat still looks very good.

"The Mini Longs need their paws and paw pads maintaining so they don't get overly fluffy and slippery, for example on laminate floor. They need their toes and paw pads to make contact with the floor. I bath Wires and Smooths every three months and Longs every two months, depending on the weather.

"As they are low to the ground, they may need a dip in the sink in the winter as they can get a wet, muddy tummy (it can be a couple of times a week if the weather is bad). They dislike going out in the rain - it's a Dachshund trait. They fake wees outside if it's raining and then sneak a toilet break in the house!

"Mine don't particularly like the bath, but they adore being clean and zoom around the house afterwards, finding rugs and carpets to roll around on. If you have a Miniature puppy, bath them in the sink and don't fill the sink higher than their armpits, use a jug for rinsing them off. If using the bath, use a rubber bath mat so they don't slip. You don't want an injured back caused by a Dachshund trying to get out."

Sandra Robertson: "We groom our Mini Smooths once or twice a week. We bath them about once every three months (unless they get a bit stinky from the river), using special dog shampoos and always avoiding getting shampoo in their eyes and ears. When I bath them, I put them in our bath with enough water for them to feel comfortable and move about in, as they love water, and I also have the shower running. I use a hairdryer to quickly dry them off, but they do love a good towel rub. I really dry between their paws too.

"We clean eyes and ears separately using gauze, not cotton buds as bits of cotton can break off in their ears, causing irritation and infection. Even though they have a Smooth coat, I run a soft brush over them to feel that I've done a proper job. My dogs wait for the brush as they love the feel. They lie down and relax while I brush them, turning their heads for me to brush all three of them in turn."

Pauline Cheeseman (Mini Smooths): "I only bath mine if they are dirty, usually after they have rolled in nasty stuff. None of mine mind being bathed, I just use the shower above my bath and they all stand in a line, waiting for the shampoo bubbles and I just rinse them off. Being Smooth-Haired, they don't need a lot of grooming, but at least once a week I wipe a cloth over them and check them over for lumps and bumps."

Hannah Norton: "I don't bath my dogs unless they have rolled in something unpleasant. Being Smooth-Haired, they require very little grooming."

Kristin Cihos-Williams: "I have Standard Smooth Dachshunds for good reason! Although I do know how to hand-strip a Wirehair dachshund as I kept a Standard Wirehair show-groomed (he was a top-ranked Best in Specialty Show-winning Grand Champion), I also know that keeping a Wire or a Long coat in tip top show condition is a full-time job!

"I much prefer the wash-and-wear Smooth coat. I do field trials in rain or shine with my dogs. When it is pouring rain and we are out in the field, I am always thankful for a correct Smooth coat - not too thin and silky and properly dense - that can simply be towel-dried after we come in.

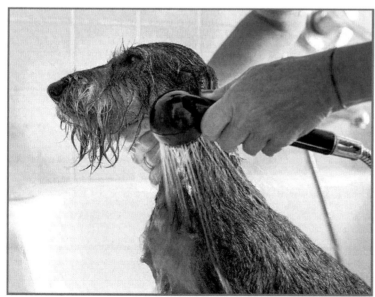

"With the dogs that we show, I am constantly keeping nails short and bathing with a very pure shampoo developed by a professional handler's chemist partner. I have learned that lesser quality shampoos do not rinse clean and will leave residue behind. I do not have dandruff with my dogs, when I use the proper shampoo."

Judith Carruthers (breeder of Wire-Haireds): "Diet and exercise help promote a healthy coat. Smooths need very little, just a bristle brush, Wires need regularly brushing and stripping, and Longs need brushing often - and trimming, particularly between the toes."

"Bathe as often as you think necessary. I advise all owners to get their dog used to having a bath while still a puppy. Place a towel or rubber mat on the base of the shower to prevent puppy from slipping, and use warm water. They do enjoy it if their initial experience is a good one. Use a good quality shampoo - there are some shampoos specifically for wire coats - rinse thoroughly and dry gently.

"Wire-Haireds need regular brushing with a slicker or bristle brush, and combing with a metal comb, particularly furnishings (eyebrows and beard). And unless your WHD is a pin-wire (with a short coat), it will require regular stripping two or three times as year, depending on coat quality and texture. It is kinder to clip a soft-textured coat. A professional groomer can do this or you can learn to do it yourself."

Bastiaan Smit: "Wire-Haireds need to be hand-stripped to maintain the Wire hair, which we do in the spring and autumn. We wash them only when needed – such as when smelling or after accidents. They enjoy playing in the water."

Brenna Carlisle (Standard Long-Haireds): "I bath mine weekly! And I would suggest a force dryer to dry them. Never leave them wet as this can lead to skin issues. Also keep their feet trimmed. The pad of the foot should always be touching the ground; there should never be never hair in between, and their ears should be clipped around as well."

Lisa Cole (Standard Long-Haireds): "Grooming never ends. It's as and when, which is almost daily. Baths are every couple of months, but every two to four weeks when showing, as their coats need to be well looked after. Start young, they feel great when it's over, so doing it on a regular basis means they love it – mine do!

"Long-Haired Dachshunds need to be checked every now and then for knots under their armpits, behind the ears, and in the tail and fluffy bum. They also get long hair growing between the toes which needs to be trimmed every month and, of course, the nails need to be cut once every month or two months - and don't forget to do the dew claws."

Marianne McCullough (Mini Long-Haireds): "I think it is important to address the spay/neuter coat. Early spay and neuter can drastically impact the coat. Once the dog is altered, the texture of the coat softens and it may need a little more trimming of the ends, which become more difficult to maintain. Waiting until the puppy has finished developing and grown its full coat before spaying or neutering will not totally eliminate it, but it helps.

"Pets are bathed as needed, usually every two to three weeks. Dogs being shown are groomed and bathed every five to seven days without fail. I wouldn't say they like it, but they do fine with it. They understand they are expected to behave. I advise bathing them often as puppies so they get used to a routine. Longs require stripping of the undercoat once or twice a year, depending on its thickness. Paw hair needs trimming every two weeks to ensure that they don't slip and slide. Any other trimming is preference, but overall, the coat is beautiful and requires little maintenance."

Stefanie Millington: "My Mini Longs need a bit more work than a Smooth coat, but not quite as much work as Wires, which require hand-stripping to look their best. I bath them quarterly and trim the hair on their feet every two to three weeks., I brush them at least once a week, some twice -

depending on the thickness of their coat - so they don't get knotty, paying special attention to the feathering behind the ears and on the inside of their legs and tail.

"Nails should be clipped monthly and I personally check their teeth regularly to avoid tartar. If there is any, I remove it with a dental scaler. I try not to wash my dogs too often: usually about four times a year unless it's needed more often, for example, with an especially dirty digger. Overbathing can cause the skin to lose its essential oils. Quite frankly, most of mine very much hate a bath!"

Melissa Sworab (Mini Long-Haireds): "Long-Haired pups need a little more grooming than a Smooth. They do great with weekly brushing, a monthly nail trim (although we prefer weekly), and a de-shedding tool like a Furminator twice a year when the seasons change from warm to cold to warm again. We never suggest shaving them, since that removes their natural ability to regulate temperature in hot and cold weather.

"On a Long-Haired, brushing behind the ears and legs is critical to prevent knots. Having someone regularly and carefully remove the fuzzy coat in these areas will help prevent knots from forming. Each dog is different, so some Longhairs will get fuzzy faster than others.

"We do a lot of "wipe downs" on the dogs instead of too many baths, as we feel that if the dog isn't dirty or smelly (yeasty), then they do best with their own natural oils for the most part. A cool water spritz or a damp wash cloth over them, then brushed dry. This is less traumatic than a bath.

"We do baths about once a month or after an "incident," like rolling in mud or something dead! Our dogs usually have a swimming pool in the hotter months and they tend to keep themselves rather clean. If I can smell them, it's bath time, otherwise, with my sensitive nose, I wouldn't be able to sleep in bed with them. Most of my dogs do not like baths for the most part, but tolerate it. Occasionally, you get extremes, like one that takes two people to bathe, or one that will jump into the shower with you and lick the walls dry, but not too often.

"Baths should never be rushed and you should talk to them about what's going on around them. We might say: "The water is running and its nice and warm"...and put your hand in the stream and let them investigate at their own speed the first few times. I find they don't panic that way. With little puppies, I will sometimes put on a swimsuit and get in the tub with them so they understand it's not so scary and they are not alone! Puppies think that's pretty cool and climb on your legs if they get nervous...they remember that for life."

Pame Bates (Mini Long-Haireds): "We bath ours every two to three weeks, and every six months they go to our groomer's for a complete grooming experience. We bath ours up in a high sink that is too deep for them to jump out. We often use a restraining leash to hold them in the sink so they cannot jump out and hurt themselves. Some love it, some are resigned to it and some do not like it at all."

Photo of Lady Black Pearl and Lady Red Rose, courtesy of Pame.

"Longhairs require regular brushing and clipping of the nether regions. One of our dogs, Rose, **(pictured above),** has a curly coat like a lion, the vet calls it a beauty coat. The beauty coat takes some maintenance, but it is worth it."

Nail Trimming

If your Dachshund is regularly exercised on grass or other soft surfaces, his nails may not be getting worn down sufficiently, so they may require clipping or filing.

 FACT ❯ Nails should be kept short for the paws to remain healthy. Overly-long nails interfere with a dog's gait, making walking awkward or painful and putting stress on elbows, shoulder and back. They can also break easily, usually at the base of the nail where blood vessels and nerves are located.

Be prepared: many Dachshunds dislike having their nails trimmed – especially if they are not used to it - so it requires patience and persistence if you do it yourself.

Get your dog used to having his paws inspected from puppyhood; it's also a good opportunity to check for other problems, such as cracked pads or interdigital cysts. (These are swellings between the toes, often due to a bacterial infection).

To trim your dog's nails, use a specially designed clipper. Most have safety guards to prevent you cutting the nails too short. Do it before they get too long.

Tip If you can hear the nails clicking on a hard surface, they're too long.

You want to trim only the ends, before *"the quick,"* which is a blood vessel inside the nail. You can see where the quick ends on a white nail, but not on a dark nail.

Clip only the hook-like part of the nail that turns down. Start trimming gently, a nail or two at a time, and your dog will learn that you're not going to hurt him. If you accidentally cut the quick, stop the bleeding with some styptic powder.

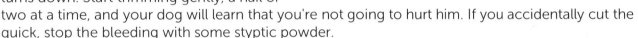

Another option is to file your dog's nails with a nail grinder tool, also called a Dremel. Some Dachshunds have tough nails that are harder to trim and this may be a less stressful method for your dog, with less chance of pain or bleeding. The grinder is like an electric nail file and only removes a small amount of nail at a time. Some owners prefer to use one as there is less chance of cutting the quick, and many dogs prefer them to a clipper. Introduce your dog to the grinder gradually - the noise and vibration take some getting used to.

NOTE: Do not use a Dremel on a Long-Haired Dachshund if the hair is not trimmed first - and keep it away from their coat.

If you find it impossible to clip your dog's nails, or you are at all worried about doing it, take him to a vet or groomer and have it done as part of a routine visit - and get your Dachshund's anal sacs squeezed, or "expressed," while he's there!

Anal Glands

While we're discussing the less appealing end of your Dachshund, let's dive straight in and talk about anal sacs. Sometimes called scent glands, these are a pair of glands located inside your dog's anus that give off a scent when he has a bowel movement. You won't want to hear this, but problems with impacted anal glands are not uncommon in dogs!

When a dog passes firm stools, the glands normally empty themselves, but soft poop or diarrhoea can mean that not enough pressure is exerted to empty the glands, causing discomfort. If they get infected, they become swollen and painful. In extreme cases, one or both anal glands can be removed – we had a dog that lived happily for many years with one anal gland.

If your dog drags himself along on his rear end – *"scooting"* - or tries to lick or scratch his anus, he could well have impacted anal glands that need squeezing, either by you if you know how to do it, your vet or a groomer. (Scooting is also a sign of worms). Either way, it pays to keep an eye on both ends of your dog!

Ear Cleaning

Ear infections affect dogs of all breeds –in general, Dachshunds suffer fewer ear infections than many breeds, but owners of Long-Haireds in particular need to keep an eye out for them. Floppy ears create a warm, moist haven for bacteria and infection. Any dog can get an ear infection, particularly if they suffer from allergies, or have dense hair inside the ear.

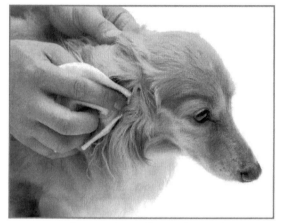

Ear infections are notorious for recurring once they have taken hold, and cause deafness in very severe cases. So, it pays to check your dog's ears regularly while grooming. Many Dachshunds enjoy swimming or paddling. A good habit to get into is to towel dry the ears afterwards or use anear-drying powder, as ear infections can develop if the area inside the ear remains wet.

Keep an eye out for redness or inflammation at the inner base of the ear, or a build-up of dark wax, and if your Dachshund has a particularly long coat with hairy ears, the hair inside the ear should be regularly plucked or trimmed to allow air to circulate more freely.

 Never put anything sharp or narrow - like a cotton bud – inside your dog's ears, as you can cause damage. Typical signs of an ear infection are the dog:

- Shaking his head a lot
- Scratching his ears
- Rubbing his ears on the floor
- An unpleasant smell coming from the ears, which is a sign of a yeast infection

If your dog exhibits any of these signs, consult your vet ASAP, as simple routine cleaning won't solve the problem. Keep your dog's ears clean, dry and free from too much hair right from puppyhood.

Teeth Cleaning

Veterinary studies show that by the of age of three, 80% of dogs show signs of gum or dental disease. Toy and Miniature breeds are particularly susceptible as they have a lot of teeth crammed into a relatively small space.

Symptoms include yellow and brown build-up of tartar along the gum line, red inflamed gums and persistent bad breath (halitosis). And if your dog suddenly stops eating his food, check his mouth and teeth.

Many owners keep their dogs' teeth clean by giving them an occasional raw bone (not chicken as it splinters), or regularly feeding bully sticks, Nylabones, Dentastix, etc. However, it is important to take time to take care of your Dachshund's teeth – regular dental care greatly reduces the onset of gum and tooth decay and infection. If left, problems can quickly escalate.

Without cleaning, plaque coats teeth and within a few days this starts to harden into tartar, often turning into gingivitis (inflammation of the gums). Gingivitis is regularly accompanied by periodontal disease (infections around the teeth).

This can be serious as, in the worst cases, it can lead to infections of the vital organs, such as heart, liver and kidneys. Even if the infection doesn't spread beyond the mouth, bad teeth are very unpleasant for a dog, just as with a human, causing painful toothache and difficulty chewing.

Some owners book their dog in for a professional clean at the local veterinary clinic every year. However, if your Dachshund needs a deep clean, remedial work or teeth removing, he will have to be anaesthetised, a procedure which is to be avoided unless it is absolutely necessary. Prevention is better than cure.

 If your dog has to be anaesthetised for something else, ask the vet to check and clean your dog's teeth while he's under.

One option is to brush your dog's teeth. There are also various tools owners can buy to control plaque, such as dental picks and scrapers.

Start while still a puppy and take things slowly in the beginning, giving lots of praise. Once used to the process, many dogs love the attention - especially if they like the flavour of the toothpaste! Use a pet toothpaste, as the human variety can upset a canine's stomach.

The real benefit comes from the actual action of the brush on the teeth, and various brushes, sponges and pads are available for dogs - the choice depends on factors such as the health of your dog's gums, the size of his mouth and how good you are at teeth cleaning.

Get him used to the toothpaste by letting him lick some off your finger when he is young. If he doesn't like the flavour, try a different one. Continue this until he enjoys licking the paste - it might be instant or it might take days.

Put a small amount on your finger and gently rub it on one of the big canine teeth at the front of his mouth. Then get him used to the toothbrush or dental sponge for several days - praise him when he licks it. The next step is to actually start brushing.

Lift his upper lip gently and place the brush at a 45º angle to the gum line. Gently move the brush backwards and forwards. Start just with his front teeth and then gradually do a few more.

Do the top ones first. Regular brushing shouldn't take more than five minutes - well worth the time and effort when it spares your Dachshund the pain and misery of serious dental or gum disease.

15. The Facts of Life

Judging by the number of questions our website receives, there is a lot of confusion about the canine facts of life. Some ask if, and at what age, they should have their dog spayed or neutered, while others want to know whether they should breed their dog.

Owners of females ask when and how often she will come on heat and how long this will last. Sometimes they want to know how you can tell if a female is pregnant or how long a pregnancy lasts. So here, in a nutshell, is a chapter on the birds and bees as far as Dachshunds are concerned.

Females and Heat

Just like all other female mammals, including humans, a female Dachshund has a menstrual cycle - or to be more accurate, an oestrus cycle *(estrus* in the US). This is when she is ready (and willing!) for mating and is more commonly called **heat**, being **in heat**, **on heat** or **in season**.

Large breeds tend to have their first heat cycle later than small breeds. A Dachshund can have her first cycle any time between six months and 18 months old. We asked some of our breeders when their females typically had their first heat and they said: 7-8 months, 8-15 months, 9 months, 9-11 months, 9-12 months, 10-12 months, and occasionally later.

Kristin Cihos-Williams, of Kinderteckel Standard Smooth Dachshunds, said: "My girls tend to have their first season sometime between 9-12 months. I have occasionally had girls wait until age 14-15 months for their first season. I have noticed that these "late blooming" girls also have seasons every 12 months, once their seasons become established.

"Most of my girls cycle every 8-9 months. I do not have any that cycle every 6 months. I have one girl who cycles every April, and even within a particular week in April, to be precise! She has been like clockwork for the first three years of her life with this pattern."

A Dachshund typically has a heat cycle every six to nine or 10 months. There is no time of the year that corresponds to a breeding season, so the heat could occur during any month.

 Females often follow the patterns of their mother, so ask the breeder at what age the dam had her first heat and then how often they occur.

When a young bitch comes in season, it is normal for her cycles to be somewhat irregular - it can take up to two years for regular cycles to develop. The timescale also becomes more erratic with older, unspayed females. A heat cycle normally lasts 18 to 21 days, but some of our breeders' Dachshunds go on for longer. These last days might be lighter in terms of blood loss - you might not even know that she is still in heat.

Mini Long breeder Stefanie Millington has a few words of caution: "I do ovulation testing occasionally and one of my girls was ovulating as late as Day 23 and standing for the dog until Day 28. So, I would always advise you to be careful for up to FOUR weeks if you are NOT intending to breed from your bitch."

Unlike women, female dogs do not stop menstruating when they reach middle age, although the heat becomes shorter and lighter. However, a litter takes a heavy toll on older females. NOTE: Women cannot get pregnant during their period, while female dogs can ONLY get pregnant during their heat.

There are four stages of the heat cycle:

Proestrus – this is when the bleeding starts and lasts around nine days. Male dogs are attracted to her, but she is not yet interested, so she may hold her tail close to her body. You will notice that her vulva (external sex organ, or pink bit under her tail) becomes swollen. If you're not sure if she's in heat, hold a tissue against her vulva – does it turn pink or red? She will lick the area a lot, which may be your first sign that she is coming into season. The blood is usually light red or brown, turning more straw-coloured after a week or so. She may also urinate more frequently.

Oestrus - this is when eggs are released from ovaries and the optimum time for breeding. Males are extremely interested in her - and the feelings are very much reciprocated. Her hormones are raging and she definitely wants sex! If there is a male around, she may stand for him and *"flag"* her tail (or move it to one side) to allow him to mount her. Oestrus is the time when a female CAN get pregnant and usually lasts a further nine days.

Dioestrus – this is the two-month stage when her body produces the hormone progesterone whether or not she is pregnant. All the hormones are present; even if she hasn't conceived. This can sometimes lead to what is known as a *"false pregnancy."* During this stage she is no longer interested in males.

Anoestrus – this the period of rest when reproductive organs are inactive. It is the longest stage of the cycle and lasts around five-and-a-half months. If she normally lives with a male dog, they can return to living together again - neither will be interested in mating and she cannot get pregnant.

The canine heat cycle is a complex mix of hormonal, behavioural, and physical changes. Each dog is different. Some show behavioural changes, such as becoming more clingy or irritable, going off their food, shedding hair, mounting other dogs or your leg, or sulking in their beds.

The amount of blood varies from one female Dachshund to another. One breeder said: "Some girls are so clean about their cycles; the owners aren't even aware it's happening until suddenly there's a pregnancy and no idea who the father is! And some have to wear doggie panties *(pictured)* to stop staining of furniture."

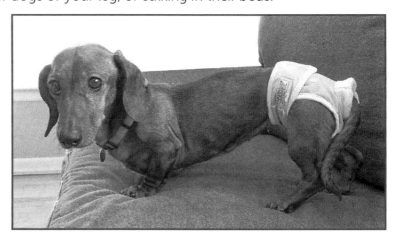

Even with pants on, leakages occasionally occur and a few female Dachshunds will even take advantage and eliminate in them.

When a female is on heat, she produces pheromones that attract male dogs. Because dogs have a sense of smell several hundred times stronger than ours, your girl on heat is a magnet for all the neighbourhood males. It is believed that they can detect the scent of a female on heat up to two miles away!

They may congregate around your house or follow you around the park - if you are brave or foolish enough to venture out there while she is in season - waiting for their chance to prove their manhood (or mutthood in their case).

It is amazing the lengths some intact males will go to impregnate a female on heat. Travelling great distances to follow her scent, digging under fences, jumping over barriers, chewing through doors or walls and sneaking through hedges are just some of the tactics employed by canine Casanovas on the loose.

Love is a powerful thing - and canine lust even more so. A dog living in the same house as a female in heat has even been known to mate with her through the bars of a crate!

To avoid an unwanted pregnancy, you must keep a close eye on her throughout her heat and not allow her to wander unsupervised - and that includes the garden or yard unless you 100% know it is safe. Determined male dogs can jump and scramble over high fences.

Keep her on a lead if you go out on walks and whatever you do, don't let her run free anywhere that you might come across other dogs. You can compensate for the restrictions by playing more games at home to keep her mentally and physically active.

 The instinct to mate will trump all of her training. Her hormones are raging and, during her most fertile days (the Oestrus), she is ready, able and ... VERY willing! If you do have an intact male, you need to physically keep him in a separate place or kennel.

The desire to mate is all-consuming and can be accompanied by howling or "marking" (urinating) indoors from a frustrated Romeo.

You can also buy a spray that masks the natural oestrus scent. Marketed under such attractive names as "*Bitch Spray,*" these lessen, but don't eliminate, the scent. They may reduce the amount of unwanted attention, but are not a complete deterrent.

There is no canine contraceptive, so if your female is unspayed, you need to keep her under supervision during her heat cycle - which may be up to four weeks. There is a *"morning after pill"* – actually a series of oestrogen tablets or an injection - which some vets may administer after an unwanted coupling, but side effects can be severe, including Pyometra (a potentially life-threatening infection of the womb), bone marrow suppression and infertility. Vets usually prefer to let the litter be born as normal and placed as pets if unwanted.

Neutering - Pros and Cons

This is currently a hot potato in the dog world. Dogs kept purely as pets – i.e. not for showing, breeding or working – are often spayed or neutered. There is also the life-threatening risk of *Pyometra* in unspayed middle-aged females.

There is already too much indiscriminate breeding of dogs in the world. However, there's also mounting scientific evidence that early spay/neuter can have a detrimental effect on Dachshunds.

As you will read in **Chapter 16. Dachshund Rescue**, it is estimated that 1,000 dogs are put to sleep every hour in the USA alone. Rescue organisations in North America, the UK and Australia routinely neuter all dogs that they rehome. The RSPCA, along with most UK vets, also promotes the benefits of neutering; it's estimated that more than half of all dogs in the UK are spayed or castrated.

Another point is that you may not have a choice. Some breeders' Puppy Contracts may stipulate that, except in special circumstances, you agree to neuter your Dachshund as a Condition of Sale. Others may state that you need the breeder's permission to breed your dog. While early spay/neuter has been traditionally recommended, there is scientific evidence that for Dachshunds it is better to wait until the dog is through puberty – whatever your vet might recommend.

Timing

The Dachshund breed Council says: "Our position is clear; we do not recommend neutering before the age of 12 months unless there is a clear clinical benefit because of the evidence that it increases the risks of IVDD (Intervertebral Disk Disease).

"The results of our DachsLife 2015 survey showed that the odds of a neutered Dachshund suffering IVDD over the age of is nearly double (1.8x) that of an entire Dachshund. Neutering under the age of 12 months has higher odds of IVDD than neutering over the age of 1. (Note: "neutering" includes castration of males and spaying of females)."

In the DachsLife 2018 survey, the evidence is even stronger:

* For all Dachshunds aged 3-10, those neutered under 24 months were twice as likely to have reported an IVDD incident

* For male Dachshunds aged 3-10, those neutered under 24 months were twice as likely to have reported an IVDD incident

* For female Dachshunds aged 3-10, those neutered under 24 months were four times as likely to have reported an IVDD incident

In simple terms, it is thought that the sex hormones (which are no longer produced after neutering) have other important roles to play in the bodies of growing dogs.

Four UC Davis School of Veterinary Medicine studies involving veterinary records for thousands of Golden Retrievers, Labradors and German Shepherds found that spaying or neutering before the age of one increased the risk of one or more of the following: certain cancers, joint disorders and urinary incontinence. The one area where early neutering was beneficial was mammary cancer, the equivalent of breast cancer in women.

The Dachshund Breed Council adds:

* If you must have your Dachshund neutered, we recommend that you do not have this done before the dog or bitch is fully mature (at least 12 months old)

* Many vets are not aware of the current evidence on the potential negative impacts of neutering; particularly early neutering (before 6 months)

* Because Dachshunds are predisposed to IVDD, it is particularly important that the growth hormones have time to do their vital work on the skeletal frame, ligaments and muscles

* As a breed, Dachshunds have a relatively low risk of cancers and tumours compared with many other breeds, so the argument for neutering to avoid these health issues is weak

There is plenty of information out there, just type *"Dachshunds early spay/neuter"* into an online search engine to do more research. Armed with the facts, it is for individual owners to decide what's best for their dog.

Spaying

Spaying is the term traditionally used to describe the sterilisation of a female dog so that she cannot become pregnant. This is normally done by a procedure called an *"ovariohysterectomy"* and involves the removal of the ovaries and uterus, or womb. Although this is a routine operation, it is major abdominal surgery and she has to be anaesthetised.

One less invasive option offered by some vets is an *"ovariectomy,"* which removes the ovaries, but leaves the womb intact. It requires only a small incision and can even be carried out by laparoscopy, or keyhole surgery. The dog is anaesthetised for a shorter time and there is less risk of infection or excess bleeding during surgery.

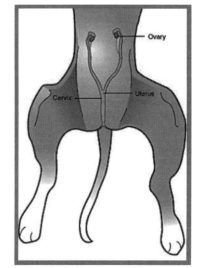

One major reason often given for not opting for an ovariectomy is that the female still runs the risk of **Pyometra** later in life. However, there is currently little or no scientific evidence of females that have undergone an ovariectomy contracting Pyometra afterwards. Traditional spaying considerably reduces the risk of Pyometra.

FACT ❯ Spaying is a much more serious operation for females than neutering is for males. It involves an internal abdominal operation, whereas the neutering procedure is carried out on the male's testicles, which are outside his abdomen.

As with any major procedure, there are pros and cons.

Pros:

- ❧ Spaying prevents infections, cancer and other diseases of the uterus and ovaries. A spayed female will have a greatly reduced risk of mammary cancer

- ❧ Spaying eliminates the risk of Pyometra, which results from hormonal changes in the female's reproductive tract. It also reduces hormonal changes that can interfere with the treatment of diseases like diabetes or epilepsy

- ❧ You no longer have to cope with any potential mess caused by bleeding inside the house during heat cycles

- ❧ You don't have to guard your female against unwanted attention from males

- ❧ Spaying can reduce behaviour problems, such as roaming, aggression towards other dogs, anxiety or fear (not all canine experts agree)

- ❧ A spayed dog does not contribute to the pet overpopulation problem

Cons:

- ❧ Complications can occur, including an abnormal reaction to the anaesthetic, bleeding, stitches breaking and infections; these are not common

- ❧ Occasionally there can be long-term effects connected to hormonal changes. These include weight gain or less stamina, which can occur years after spaying

- Cost. This can range from £100 to £250 in the UK, more for keyhole spaying, and anything from $150 to over $1,000 at a vet's clinic in the USA, or from around $50 at a low-cost clinic, for those that qualify
- Early spay can lead to an increased risk of IVDD and some females may suffer urinary incontinence

One breeder added: "Spaying too early or during a heat cycle can cause life-long incontinence in female puppies."

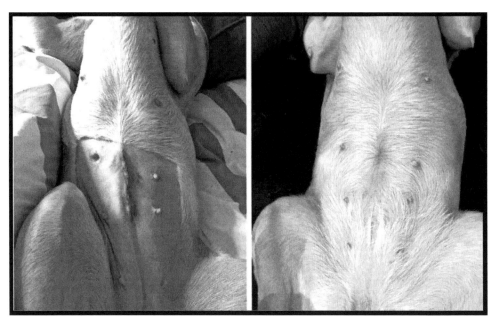

These photographs are reproduced courtesy of Guy Bunce and Chloe Spencer, of Dizzywaltz Labrador Retrievers, Berkshire, England. The left image shows four-year-old Disney shortly after a full spay (ovariohysterectomy). The right one shows Disney several weeks later.

Neutering

Neutering male dogs involves castration, or the removal of the testicles. This can be a difficult decision for some owners, as it causes a drop in the pet's testosterone levels, which some humans — men in particular! - feel affects the quality of their dog's life. Fortunately, dogs do not think like people, and male dogs do not miss their testicles or the loss of sex.

Dogs working in the Services or for charities are often neutered and this does not impair their ability to perform any of their duties.

Technically, neutering can be carried out at any age over eight weeks, provided both testicles have descended. However, recent scientific studies, such as the ones already outlined, are coming down on the side of waiting until the dog is one year or older.

FACT **Dogs neutered before puberty, which is NOT recommended for Dachshunds, tend to grow a little larger than dogs done later. This is because testosterone is involved in the process that stops growth, so the bones grow for longer without testosterone.**

Surgery is relatively straightforward, and complications are less common and less severe than with spaying. Although he will feel tender afterwards, your dog should return to his normal self within a couple of days. When a dog comes out of surgery, his scrotum, or sacs that held the testicles, will be swollen and it may look like nothing has been done. It is normal for these to shrink slowly in the days following surgery. Here are the main pros and cons:

Pros:

* 🐾 Castration is a simple procedure, and dogs usually make a swift recovery afterwards

* 🐾 Behaviour problems such as aggression, marking and roaming can be reduced

* 🐾 Unwanted sexual behaviour, such as mounting people or objects, is usually reduced or eliminated

* 🐾 Testicular problems such as infections, cancer and torsion (painful rotation of the testicle) are eradicated

* 🐾 Prostate disease, common in older male dogs, is less likely to occur

* 🐾 A submissive intact male dog may be targeted by other dogs. After he has been neutered, he will no longer produce testosterone and so will not be regarded as much of a threat by the other males, so he is less likely to be bullied

* 🐾 A neutered dog is not fathering unwanted puppies

Cons:

* 🐾 Studies indicate that Dachshunds neutered before one year old are more likely to get IVDD than those neutered after two years

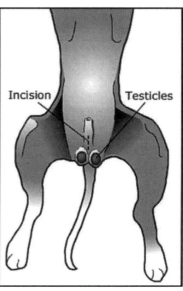

* 🐾 As with any surgery, there can be bleeding afterwards; you should keep an eye on your dog after the procedure. Infections can also occur, generally caused by the dog licking the wound, so try and prevent him doing this. If he persists, use an E-collar. In the **vast majority** of cases, these problems do not occur

* 🐾 Some dogs' coats may be affected; this also applies to spaying. Supplementing the diet with fish oil can compensate for this

* 🐾 Cost - this starts at around £80 in the UK. In the USA this might cost anything from $100 to $1,000 at a private veterinary clinic, depending on your state, or $50-$100 at a low cost or Humane Society clinic

New Techniques

Two other phrases you may hear are *"tubal ligation"* or *"vasectomy." Tubal ligation* is the tying of a female's Fallopian tubes and a *vasectomy* is the clamping shut of the sperm ducts from the male's testicles. Many veterinary papers have been written on these topics, but as yet, not many vets offer them as options.

In both cases, unlike with spaying and neutering, the dog continues to produce hormones, but is unable to get pregnant or father puppies. With further evidence of the positive effects of hormones, these operations could become more common in the future – although more vets will first have to be trained.

There's a new non-surgical procedure to sterilise male dogs called *"Zeutering."* It involves injecting zinc gluconate into the dog's testicles. Dogs are lightly sedated, but not anaesthetised. It's inexpensive, there's little recovery time and no stitches. However, studies show that Zeutering is only 99% effective, and its long-term effects are still being researched. And while it makes dogs sterile, they still retain some of their testosterone.

Therefore, habits that usually disappear with traditional castration, such as marking, roaming, following females on heat and aggression towards other males, remain. Zeutering isn't for every dog, but worth discussing with your vet.

Urban Myths

Neutering or spaying will spoil the dog's character - There is no evidence that any of the positive characteristics of your dog will be altered. He or she will be just as obedient, playful and loyal as before. Neutering may reduce aggression or roaming in male dogs, because they are no longer competing to mate with a female.

A female needs to have at least one litter - There is no proven physical or mental benefit to a female having a litter.

Mating is natural and necessary - We tend to ascribe human emotions to our dogs, but they do not think emotionally about sex or having and raising a family. Unlike humans, their desire to mate or breed is entirely physical, triggered by the chemicals called hormones within their body. Without these hormones – i.e. after neutering or spaying – the desire disappears or is greatly reduced.

Male dogs will behave better if they can mate - This is simply not true; sex does not make a dog behave better. In fact, it can have the opposite effect. Having mated once, a male may show an increased interest in females. He may also consider his status elevated, which may make him harder to control or call back.

 Do your research. Many vets still promote early spay and neuter.

....

Pregnancy

Regardless of how big or small the dog is, a canine pregnancy lasts for 58 to 65 days; 63 days is average. This is true of all breeds of dog from the Chihuahua to the Great Dane. Sometimes pregnancy is referred to as *"the gestation period."*

A female should have a pre-natal check-up after mating. The vet should answer any questions about type of food, supplements and extra care needed, as well as informing the owner about any physical changes likely to occur in your female.

There is a blood test available that measures levels of *relaxin*. This is a hormone produced by the ovary

and the developing placenta, and pregnancy can be detected by monitoring relaxin levels as early as 22 to 27 days after mating. The levels are high throughout pregnancy and then decline rapidly after the female has given birth.

A vet can usually see the puppies (but not how many) using Ultrasound from around the same time. X-rays carried out seven to eight or so weeks into the pregnancy show the puppies' skeletons and give the breeder a good idea of the number of puppies. They can also help to give the vet more information, which is particularly useful if the female has had previous whelping problems. Signs of pregnancy are:

- After mating, many females become more affectionate. However, a few may become uncharacteristically irritable and maybe even a little aggressive!

- She may produce a slight mucous-like discharge from her vagina one month after mating

- Three or four weeks after mating, some females experience morning sickness – if this is the case, feed little and often. She may seem more tired than usual

- She may seem slightly depressed or show a drop in appetite. These signs can also mean there are other problems, so you should consult your vet

- Her teats will become more prominent, pink and erect 25 to 30 days into the pregnancy. Later on, you may notice a fluid coming from them. This first milk (colostrum) is the most important milk a puppy gets on Day One as it contains the mother's immunity.

- Her body weight will noticeably increase about 35 days after mating

- Her abdomen will become noticeably larger from around Day 40, although first-time mums and females carrying few puppies may not show as much

- Many pregnant females' appetite will increase in the second half of pregnancy

- Her nesting instincts will kick in as the delivery date approaches. She may seem restless or scratch her bed or the floor - she may even rip and shred items like your comforter, curtains or carpeting!

- During the last week of pregnancy, females often start to look for a safe place for whelping. Some seem to become confused, wanting to be with their owners and at the same time wanting to prepare their nest. If the female is having a C-section, she should still be allowed to nest in a whelping box with layers of newspaper, which she will scratch and dig as the time approaches

✓ **If your female Dachshund becomes pregnant – either by design or accident - your first step should be to consult a vet.**

The size of Dachshund litters varies, it can be as many as eight puppies, although four to six would be more typical. The number depends on factors such as bloodlines, the age of the dam and sire (young and older dogs have smaller litters), health and diet of the dam, and the size of the gene pool; the lower the genetic diversity, the smaller the litter.

False Pregnancies

Occasionally, unspayed females may display signs of a false pregnancy. Before dogs were domesticated, it was common for female dogs to have false pregnancies and to lactate (produce milk). She would then nourish puppies of the Alpha bitch or puppies who had lost their mother in the pack.

False pregnancies occur 60 to 80 days after the female was in heat - about the time she would have given birth – and are generally nothing to worry about for an owner. The exact cause is unknown; however, hormonal imbalances are thought to play an important role. Some dogs have shown symptoms within three to four days of spaying; these include:

- Making a nest

- Mothering or adopting toys and other objects

- Producing milk (lactating)

- Appetite fluctuations

- Barking or whining a lot
- Restlessness, depression or anxiety
- Swollen abdomen
- She might even appear to go into labour

Under no circumstances should you restrict your Dachshund's water supply to try and prevent her from producing milk. This is dangerous as she can become dehydrated.

One breeder added: "We usually take away the toys and reduce calorie intake to stop lactation and reduce instance of mastitis."

Some unspayed females may have a false pregnancy with each heat cycle. Spaying during a false pregnancy may actually prolong the condition, so better to wait until it is over to have her spayed.

 **False pregnancy is not a disease, but an exaggerated response to normal hormonal changes. Even if left untreated, it almost always resolves itself.**

However, if your dog appears physically ill or the behavioural changes are severe enough to worry about, visit your vet. He or she may prescribe *Galastop*, which stops milk production and quickly returns the hormones to normal. In rare cases, hormone treatment may be necessary. Generally, dogs experiencing false pregnancies do not have serious long-term problems, as the behaviour disappears when the hormones return to their normal levels in two to three weeks.

Pyometra

One exception is **Pyometra,** a serious and potentially deadly infection of the womb, caused by a hormonal abnormality. It normally follows a heat cycle in which fertilisation did not occur and the dog typically starts showing symptoms within two to four months.

Commonly referred to as *"pyo,"* there are *open* and *closed* forms of the disease. Open pyo is usually easy to identify with a smelly discharge, so prompt treatment is easy. Closed pyo is often harder to identify and you may not even notice anything until your girl becomes feverish and lethargic. When this happens, it is very serious and time is of the essence. Typically, vets will recommend immediate spaying in an effort to save her life.

Typical signs of Pyometra are excessive drinking and urination, vomiting and depression, with the female trying to lick a white discharge from her vagina. She may also have a slight temperature. If the condition becomes severe, her back legs will become weak, possibly to the point where she can no longer get up without help.

Pyometra can be fatal. It needs to be dealt with promptly by a vet, who will give the dog intravenous fluids and antibiotics for several days. In most cases this is followed by spaying.

Should I Breed From My Dachshund?

The short and very simple answer is: **NO!** Not unless you do a lot of research, and find a mentor for expert advice. The Dachshund is a breed where specialised knowledge is an advantage, as the risk of breeding puppies with health issues is very real if you don't know what you are doing.

Breeding healthy Dachshund puppies with good temperaments is an expensive, time-consuming and complex process, and should not be approached lightly.

Dachshunds are on a "watch list" in the UK of dogs which have inadvertently had genetic ailments and weaknesses bred into them.

This healthy eight-week-old pair are Hunter (Colraed Gingerbreadman) and Harry (Colraed Hobnob), bred by Pauline Cheeseman, of Colraed Miniature Dachshunds, Surrey, UK. Photo by Rob Ryan www.rsaphotography.co.uk

Today's responsible breeders are continually looking at ways of improving the health of the Dachshund through selective breeding. See **Chapter 12. Dachshund Health** for a list of recommended health tests.

 According to an in-depth UK study involving 36,000 dogs from 170 breeds published in the Journal of Small Animal Practice, over 30% of Dachshund litters were born by Caesarean, or C-Section. Typical veterinary fees for a C-section are in four figures and are not covered by normal pet insurance.

Dachshund genetics are a complicated business that cover a multitude of traits, including health, colour and coat. For example, if a male and a female Long or Smooth dapple are mated, the resulting pups are *"double dapples."* While double dapples certainly look cute, sadly they are often riddled with serious genetic health problems, such as missing eyes, micro eyes, blindness, deafness and/or skin issues. The Kennel Clubs in the UK and North America refuse to register puppies from a dapple to dapple mating.

Even then it's not always easy to tell without a DNA test; Dachshunds of different colours carry the dapple gene. Dapple is a pattern not a colour; it is also known as *merle.* Single dapples occur naturally in many litters and do not have the inherent health issues associated with double dapples, which tend to have patches of white as well as dappled markings.

 If you are attracted to dapple (merle) Dachshunds, our strong advice is to check that only ONE parent is dapple/merle and the other is tested CLEAR (mm).

Well-bred Dachshund puppies fetch four-figure sums. But despite this, many dedicated Dachshund breeders make little money from the practice, due to the high costs of veterinary fees, health screening, stud fees and expensive special nutrition and care for the female and her pups.

Responsible breeding is backed up by genetic information and screening as well as a thorough knowledge of the desired traits of the Dachshund. It is definitely not an occupation for the amateur hobbyist.

 Breeding is not just about the look or colour of the puppies; health and temperament are at least as important.

Many dog lovers do not realise that the single most important factor governing health and certain temperament traits is genetics. Top breeders have years of experience in selecting the right pair for mating after they have considered the ancestry, health, temperament, coat, size and physical characteristics of the two dogs involved.

They may travel hundreds of miles to find the right mate for their dog. Some of them also show their dogs. Anyone breeding from their Dachshund must first consider these questions:

- Did you get your Dachshund from a good, ethical breeder? Dogs sold in pet stores and on general sales websites are seldom good specimens and can be unhealthy

- Does your dog conform to the Breed Standard? Do not breed from a Dachshund that is not an excellent specimen in all respects, hoping that somehow the puppies will turn out better. They won't. Talk with experienced breeders and ask them for an honest assessment of your dog

- Do you understand COI and its implications? COI stands for Coefficient of Inbreeding. It measures the common ancestors of a dam and sire and indicates the probability of how genetically similar they are

- Do your dog and the mate both move freely with no history of IVDD?

- Have your puppy's parents been screened for Dachshund health issues that can be inherited by the offspring?

- Have you researched his or her lineage to make sure there are no problems lurking in the background? Puppies inherit traits from their grandparents and great-grandparents as well as from their mother and father

- Are you 100% sure that your dog has no temperament issues which could be inherited by the puppies?

- Are you positive that the same can be said for the dog you are planning on breeding yours with?

- Do you have the finances to keep the mother healthy through pregnancy, whelping, and care of her and the puppies after birth – even if complications occur?

- Is your female two years old or older and at least in her second heat cycle? Female Dachshunds should not be bred until they are physically mature, have had their joints screened, and are robust enough to whelp and care for a litter. Even then, not all females are suitable

- Giving birth takes a lot out of a female Dachshund - are you prepared to put yours through that?

- Some Dachshunds are poor mothers, which means that you have to look after the puppies 24/7. Even if they are not, they need daily help from the owner to rear their young

- Can you care for up to eight lively puppies if you can't find homes when they are ready to leave?

❧ Will you be able to find good homes for all the puppies? Good breeders do not let their precious puppies go to just any home. They want to be sure that the new owners will take good care of their dogs for their lifetime

❧ Would you take back, or help to rehome, one of your dogs if the owner's circumstances changes?

Having said that, experts are not born, they learn their trade over many years. Anyone who is seriously considering getting into the specialised art of breeding Dachshunds should first spend time researching the breed and its genetics.

Make sure you are going into Dachshund breeding for the right reasons and not primarily to make money - ask yourself how you intend to improve the breed. Visit dog shows and make contact with established breeders. Find yourself a mentor, somebody who is already very familiar with the breed. To find a good breeder:

✓ **In the UK**, find a member of a breed club in your area. There is a full list at: https://dachshundbreedcouncil.wordpress.com/breed-clubs Visit the Kennel Club website and find a Kennel Club *Assured Breeder* in your county.

✓ **In the USA,** look for a member of the Dachshund Club of America - search their online Breeder Directory for details of members near you at www.dachshundclubofamerica.org/dca-breeders Visit the AKC website for a *Breeder of Merit,* or one who is a member of the *Bred with H.E.A.R.T.* programme.

If you are determined to breed from your Dachshund - and breed properly - do your research. Read as much as you can; one useful resource is *"Book of the Bitch"* by J. M. Evans and Kay White.

You may have the most wonderful Dachshund in the world, but don't enter the world of canine breeding without knowledge and ethics. Don't do it for the money or the cute factor – or to show the kids "The Miracle of Birth!"

Breeding poor examples only brings heartache in the long run when health or temperament issues develop. Our strong advice is: When it comes to Dachshunds, leave it to the experts – or set out to become one yourself.

16. Dachshund Rescue

Not everyone who wants a Dachshund gets one as a puppy from a breeder. Some people prefer to give a rescue dog a second chance for a happy life.

What could be kinder and more rewarding than giving a poor, abandoned dog a loving home for the rest of his life?

Not much really; adoption saves lives and gives unfortunate dogs a second chance of happiness. The problem of homeless dogs is truly depressing. It's a big issue in Britain, but even worse in the US, where the sheer numbers in kill shelters are hard to comprehend. In *"Don't Dump The Dog,"* Randy Grim states that 1,000 dogs are being put to sleep every hour in the States.

You need patience with a Dachshund; it takes time to housetrain and obedience train one, and they can become nuisance barkers if under-exercised or unsocialised.

Although only small (Miniatures) or medium-sized (Standards), they are active dogs, and many have a strong prey drive, so teaching them to come back can be a challenge.

That gorgeous little puppy with the beautiful big eyes looked so cute. But later down the line, owners who don't put enough time and effort in can find they have a stubborn dog who ignores their commands and regularly sneaks off to pee behind the sofa.

Dachshunds, particularly Mini Smooths, have sadly become designer accessories. The internet is full of photos of Dachshunds in funny costumes and posing with their celebrity owners, like Adele and Sharon Stone. In fact, there are more than 12 million posts devoted to *#dachshund* on Instagram.

People rush out in their droves to imitate them, with scant regard to the health or nature of the Dachshund puppy they are buying.

Many expect a lapdog and realise too late that what they've actually got is a hound! By then, the dog may have become too vocal, aggressive or anxious, due to his needs not being met.

The Red Foundation Dachshund Rescue says: "We've seen a rise in dogs being given up. It's also worrying that there has been an increase in *'rare'* colour dogs, including blues. These can come with health risks, meaning many insurers won't cover them.

"Dachshunds are real characters. They can be bossy and like to rule the roost. They're not handbag dogs.

"With mental stimulation, adequate exercise, being kept at a healthy weight and being treated like dogs and not babies, they can bring lots of happiness to the right owner."

Other reasons for Dachshunds being put into rescue include:

- A change in work patterns, so the dog is left alone for long periods
- A change in family circumstance, such as divorce or a new baby
- The dog developing health issues
- Moving into smaller or rented accommodation

- 🐾 Growling or biting
- 🐾 Chewing things he shouldn't
- 🐾 Making a mess in the house
- 🐾 The dog has way too much energy and needs a lot more exercise and attention than the owner realised
- 🐾 He costs too much to keep

There is, however, a ray of sunshine for some of these dogs. Every year tens of thousands of people in the UK, North America and countries all around the world adopt a rescue dog and the story often has a happy ending.

....

The Dog's Point of View...

If you are serious about adopting a Dachshund, do so with the right motives and with your eyes wide open. If you're expecting a perfect dog, you could be in for a shock. Rescue dogs can and do become wonderful companions, but much depends on you and how much effort you are prepared to put in.

Many Dachshunds do not do well in noisy, busy, crowded rescue centres. If you can, look for a rescue organisation specialising in Dachshunds — and preferably one where the dog has been

fostered out. If a dog has bad habits, the foster parents have probably started to work on some of them.

Dachshunds are extremely loyal to their owners. Often those that end up in rescue centres are traumatised. Some may have back or other health problems.

They don't understand why they have been abandoned, neglected or badly treated by their owners and may arrive at your home with "baggage" of their own until they adjust to being part of a loving family again.

This may take time. Patience is the key to help the dog to adjust to new surroundings and family and to learn to love and trust again. Ask yourself a few questions before you take the plunge and fill in the adoption forms:

- 🐾 Are you prepared to accept and deal with any problems - such as bad behaviour, aggression, timidity, chewing, jumping up or eliminating in the house - that a rescue dog may display when initially arriving in your home?
- 🐾 Just how much time do you have to spend with your new dog to help him integrate back into normal family life?
- 🐾 Can you take time off work to be at home and help the dog settle in at the beginning?
- 🐾 Are you prepared to take on a new addition to your family that may live for another decade?
- 🐾 Will you guarantee that dog a home for life - even if he develops health issues later?

What could be worse for the unlucky dog than to be abandoned again if things don't work out between you?

Other Considerations

Adopting a rescue dog is a big commitment for all involved. It is not a cheap way of getting a Dachshund. It could cost you several hundred pounds – or dollars.

You'll have to pay adoption fees, vaccination and veterinary bills, as well as worm and flea medication and spaying or neutering. Make sure you're aware of the full cost before committing.

Many rescue dogs are older and some may have health or temperament issues. You may even have to wait a while until a suitable dog comes up. One way of finding out if you are suitable is to become a foster home for a rescue centre. Fosters offer temporary homes until a forever home comes along. It's shorter-term, but still requires commitment and patience.

And it's not just the dogs that are screened! Rescue groups make sure that prospective adopters are suitable. They also want to make the right match - placing a hyperactive Dachshund with an elderly couple, or an anxious dog in a noisy household - would be storing up trouble. It would be a tragedy for the dog if things did not work out.

Most rescue groups ask a raft of personal questions - some of which may seem intrusive. But you'll have to answer them if you are serious about adopting. Here are some typical questions:

- 🐾 Name, address, age
- 🐾 Details, including ages, of all people living in your home
- 🐾 Type of property you live in
- 🐾 Size of your garden or yard and height of the fence around it
- 🐾 Extensive details of any other pets
- 🐾 Your work hours and amount of time spent away from the home each day
- 🐾 Whether you have any previous experience with dogs or Dachshunds
- 🐾 Your reasons for wanting to adopt
- 🐾 Whether you have any experience dealing with canine behaviour or health issues
- 🐾 Details of your vet
- 🐾 If you are prepared for aggression/destructive behaviour/chewing/fear and timidity/soiling inside the house/medical issues
- 🐾 Whether you are willing to housetrain and obedience train the dog

- 🐾 Your views on dog training methods
- 🐾 Whether you are prepared for the financial costs of dog ownership
- 🐾 Where your dog will sleep at night
- 🐾 Whether you are prepared to accept a Dachshund cross
- 🐾 Two personal referees

If you go out to work, it is useful to know that UK rescue organisations will not place dogs in homes where they will be left alone for more than four to five hours at a stretch.

After you've filled in the adoption form, a chat with a representative from the charity usually follows. There will also be a home inspection visit - and even your vet may be vetted! If all goes well, you will be approved to adopt and when the right match comes along, a meeting will be arranged with all family members and the dog. You then pay the adoption fee and become the proud new owner of a Dachshund.

It might seem like a lot of red tape, but the rescue groups have to be as sure as they can that you will provide a loving, forever home for the dog. It would be terrible if things didn't work out and the dog had to be placed back in rescue again.

All rescue organisations will neuter the dog or, if he or she is too young, specify in the adoption contract that the dog must be neutered and may not be used for breeding. Some Dachshund rescue organisations have a lifetime rescue back-up policy, which means that if things don't work out, the dog must be returned to them.

Training a Rescue Dog

Some Dachshunds are in rescue because of behavioural problems, which often develop due to lack of training and attention from the previous owner.

As one rescue group put it: **"Rescue dogs are not damaged dogs; they have just been let down by humans, so take a little while to unpack their bags and get familiar with their new owners and surroundings before they settle in."**

If you approach rescue with your eyes wide open, if you're prepared to be patient and devote plenty of time to your new arrival, then rescuing a Dachshund is incredibly rewarding. They are such loving and loyal dogs, you'll have a friend for life.

Organisation with experience of Dachshunds are more likely to be able to assess the dog and give you an idea of what you might be letting yourself in for. Often, lack of socialisation and training is the root cause of any issues – but how this manifests itself varies from one dog to another.

 Ask as many questions as you can about the background of the dog, his natural temperament and any issues likely to arise. You are better having an honest appraisal than simply being told the dog is wonderful and in need of a home.

Training methods for a rescue Dachshund are similar to those for any adult Dachshund, but it may take longer as the dog first has to unlearn any bad habits.

If the dog you are interested in has a particular issue, such as indiscriminate barking or lack of housetraining, it is best to start right back at the beginning with training. Don't presume the dog knows anything and take each step slowly. See **Chapter 8. Basic Training** for more information.

Tips

- ❖ Start training the day you arrive home, not once he has settled in

- ❖ He needs your attention, but, importantly, he also needs his own space where he can chill out. Put his bed or crate in a quiet place; you want your dog to learn to relax. The more relaxed he is, the fewer hang-ups he will have

- ❖ Show him his sleeping and feeding areas, but allow him to explore these and the rest of his space in his own time

- ❖ If you have children or other animals, introduce them quietly and NEVER leave them alone with the dog for the first few months – you don't know what his triggers are

- Maintain a calm environment at home

- Never shout at the dog – even if he has made a mess in the house - it will only stress him and make things worse

- Don't give treats because you feel sorry for him. Only give him a treat when he has carried out a command. This will help him to learn quicker and you to establish leadership

- Set him up to SUCCEED and build confidence – don't ask him to do things he can't yet do

- Socialisation is extremely important – introduce him to new places and situations gradually and don't over-face him. You want him to grow in confidence, not be frightened by new things. Talk reassuringly throughout any new experience

- Mental stimulation as well as physical exercise is important for Dachshunds, so have games, toys or challenges to keep your new dog's mind occupied

- Don't introduce him to other dogs until you are confident he will behave well – and then not while he is on a lead (leash), when the *"fight or flight"* instinct might kick in

- Getting an understanding of your dog will help to train him quicker – is he by nature submissive or dominant, anxious or outgoing, fearful or bold, aggressive or timid? If he shows aggressive tendencies, such as barking, growling or even biting, he is not necessarily bold. His aggression may be rooted in fear, anxiety or lack of confidence

 The aim of training a rescue Dachshund is to have a relaxed dog, comfortable in his surroundings, who respects your authority and responds well to your positive training methods.

Rescue Organisations

Rescue organisations are usually run by volunteers who give up their time to help dogs in distress. They often have a network of foster homes, where a Dachshund is placed until a permanent new home can be found. There are also online Dachshund forums where people sometimes post information about a dog that needs a new home.

UK

Type *"Kennel Club Find a Rescue Dachshund"* into a search engine to get a list of regional Dachshund contacts. Other organisations include:

Dachshund Rescue https://dachshundrescue.org.uk

Dachshund Rescue UK www.facebook.com/DachshundRescueUK

The Red Foundation https://theredfoundation.net/adopting-a-dachshunds-uk

The Miniature Dachshund Club www.miniaturedachshundclub.co.uk/dachshund_rescue.htm

Southern Dachshund Association https://southerndachshund.wordpress.com/2020/03/20/dachshund-rescue-uk-statement

USA

Dachshund Club of America has a list of regional rescue co-ordinators at www.dachshundclubofamerica.org/rescue then click **Rescue near you.**

All American Dachshund Rescue www.facebook.com/All-American-Dachshund-Rescue-110989545588779/

Dachshund Rescue www.facebook.com/dachshund.rescueme.org

DARE To Rescue www.facebook.com/DAREtoRescue

Furever Dachshund Rescue www.facebook.com/FureverDachshundRescue

GetALong Dachshund Rescue www.getalongdachshundrescue.org

There are literally dozens of state-based Dachshund rescue groups. Type your **state** and "**Dachshund Rescue**" into Google or Facebook, many of them are Facebook-based.

....

If you visit these websites, you cannot presume that all descriptions are 100% accurate. They are given in good faith, but ideas of what constitutes a "lively" or "challenging" dog may vary.

Some dogs advertised may have other breeds in their genetic make-up. It does not mean that these are worse dogs, but if you are attracted to the Dachshund for its looks, temperament, quirky character and other assets, make sure you are looking at a Dachshund.

DON'T get a dog from eBay, Craig's List, Gumtree or any of the other general advertising websites that sell golf clubs, jewellery, old cars, washing machines, etc. You might think you are getting a bargain Dachshund, but in the long run you will pay the price.

Good breeders with healthy dogs do not advertise on these websites - or sell to pet shops. You may be storing up a whole load of trouble for yourselves in terms of health or temperament issues, due to poor genetics and/or environment.

If you haven't been put off with all of the above... **Congratulations**, you may be just the person that poor homeless Dachshund is looking for!

If you can't spare the time to adopt - and adoption means forever - you might consider fostering. Or you could help by becoming a home inspector or fundraiser to help keep these very worthy rescue groups providing such a wonderful service.

How ever you decide to get involved, Good Luck!

**Saving one dog will not change the world,
But it will change the world for one dog**

....

17. Caring for Older Dachshunds

Dachshunds live longer than many other breeds. If all goes well, you can expect your puppy to reach 12 years or more. Many of our breeders have had dogs living into their teens, and three of the 19 all-time oldest dogs verified by Guinness World Records were 20 and 21-year-old Dachshunds.

Lifespan is influenced by genetics and also by owners; how you feed, exercise and generally look after your dog will all have an impact on her life. Dachshunds can remain fit and active well into old age. But eventually all dogs – even Dachshunds – slow down.

Approaching Old Age

After having got up at the crack of dawn as a puppy, you may find that she now likes to have a lie-in in the morning. She may be even less keen to go out in the rain and snow. Physically, joints may become stiffer, and organs, such as heart or liver, may not function quite as effectively. On the mental side - just as with humans - your dog's memory, ability to learn and awareness will all start to dim.

Your faithful companion might become a bit grumpier, stubborn or a little less tolerant of lively dogs and children. You may also notice that she doesn't see or hear as well as she used to. On the other hand, your old friend might not be hard of hearing at all. She might have developed that affliction common to many older dogs of *"selective hearing."*

Our 12-year-old Max had bionic hearing when it came to the word *"Dinnertime"* whispered from 20 paces, yet seemed strangely unable to hear the commands *"Come"* or *"Down"* when we were right in front of him!

Pictured looking rather regal is 11-year-old Standard Smooth, Tootie, bred by Kristin Cihos-Williams.

You can help ease your mature dog into old age gracefully by keeping an eye on her, noticing the changes and taking action to help her as much as possible. This might involve:

- A visit to the vet for supplements and/or medications
- Modifying your dog's environment
- Slowly reducing the amount of daily exercise
- A change of diet

Much depends on the individual dog. Just as with humans, a Dachshund of ideal weight that has been active and stimulated all her life is likely to age slower than an overweight couch potato! Keeping Dachshunds at an optimum weight as they get older is very important. Their metabolisms slow down, making it even easier than normal for them to pile on the pounds. Extra weight places additional, unwanted stress on the back, joints and organs, making them all have to work harder than they should.

We normally talk about dogs being old when they reach the last third of their lives. This varies greatly from dog to dog and bloodline to bloodline. A dog is classed as a "Veteran" at seven years old in the show ring. Some Dachshunds may remain active with little sign of ageing until the day they die, others may start to show signs of ageing as they approach double figures.

Physical and Mental Signs of Ageing

Here are some signs that your Dachshund's body is feeling its age – an old dog may have a few or more of these symptoms:

- She has generally slowed down and is no longer as keen to go out on her walks, or doesn't want to go as far. She is happy pottering and sniffing - and often takes forever to inspect a single clump of grass! Some refuse to go outside in bad weather – but they still need their outdoor exercise

- She gets up from lying down and moves more slowly; all signs that joints are stiffening

- Grey hairs are appearing, particularly around the muzzle

- She has put on a bit of weight

- She may have the occasional *"accident"* (incontinence) inside the house

- She urinates more frequently

- She drinks more water

- She has bouts of constipation or diarrhoea

- She sheds more hair

- The foot pads thicken and nails may become more brittle

- One or more lumps or fatty deposits (lipomas) develop on the body. One of our old dogs developed two small bumps on top of his head aged 10 and we took him straight to the vet, who performed minor surgery to remove them. They were benign (harmless), but always get the first one(s) checked out ASAP in case they are an early form of cancer - they can also grow quite rapidly, even if benign

- She can't regulate body temperature as she used to and so feels the cold and heat more

- Hearing deteriorates

- Eyesight may also deteriorate – if her eyes appear cloudy, she may be developing cataracts, so see your vet if you notice the signs. Most older dogs live quite well with failing eyesight, particularly as Dachshunds have a highly-developed sense of smell

- Your dog has bad breath (halitosis), which could be a sign of dental or gum disease. If the bad breath persists, get her checked out by a vet

- If inactive, she may develop callouses on the elbows, especially if she lies on hard surfaces

It's not just your dog's body that deteriorates; her mind may too. Your dog may display some, all or none of these signs of *Canine Cognitive Dysfunction:*

- Sleep patterns change; an older dog may be more restless at night and sleepy during the day. She may start wandering around the house at odd times, causing you sleepless nights

- She barks more, sometimes at nothing or open spaces

- She stares at objects, such as walls, hides in a corner, or wanders aimlessly around the house or garden

- Your dog shows increased anxiety, separation anxiety or aggression

- She forgets or ignores commands or habits she once knew well, such as the Recall and sometimes toilet training

- Some dogs may become clingier and more dependent, often resulting in separation anxiety. She may seek reassurance that you are near as faculties fade and she becomes a bit less confident and independent. Others may become a bit disengaged and less interested in human contact

Understanding the changes happening to your dog and acting on them compassionately and effectively will help ease your dog's passage through her senior years.

Your dog has given you so much pleasure over the years, now she needs you to give that bit of extra care for a happy, healthy old age. You can help your Dachshund to stay mentally active by playing gentle games and getting new toys to stimulate interest.

Helping Your Dog Age Gracefully

There are many things you can do to ease your dog's passage into her declining years.

As dogs age they need fewer calories and less protein, so many owners feeding kibble switch to one specially formulated for older dogs. These are labelled *Senior, Ageing* or *Mature.* Check the labelling; some are specifically for dogs aged over eight, others may be for 10 or 12-year-olds.

If you are not sure if a senior diet is necessary for your Dachshund, talk to your vet on your next visit. Remember, if you do change brand or switch to a wet food, do it gradually over a week or so. Unlike with humans, a dog's digestive system cannot cope with sudden changes of diet.

Years of eating the same food, coupled with less sensitive taste buds can result in some dogs going off their food as they age. If you feed a dry food, try mixing a bit of gravy with it; this works well for us, as has feeding two different feeds: a morning one of kibble with gravy and the second tea-time feed of home-cooked rice and boiled chicken or fish.

Rice, white fish and chicken – all cooked – can be particularly good if your old dog has a sensitive stomach.

If you are considering a daily supplement, Omega-3 fatty acids are good for the brain and coat, and glucosamine and various other supplements help joints. Yumega Omega 3, Yumove and Joint Aid are used by lots of breeders with older dogs.

We had one dog that became very sensitive to loud noises as she got older and the lead up to Bonfire Night was a nightmare. (November 5th in the UK, when the skies are filled with fireworks and loud bangs). Some dogs may also become more stressed by grooming or trips to the vet as they get older.

 There are medications, homeopathic remedies, such as melatonin, and various DAP (dog appeasing pheromone) products that can help relieve anxiety. Check with your vet before introducing any new medicines.

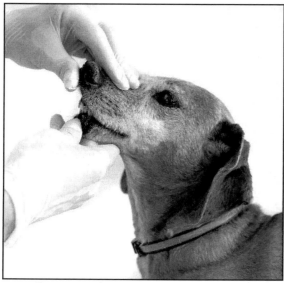

One of the most important things throughout your Dachshund's life is **dental care** - either by regular tooth brushing or feeding bones, bully sticks or antlers, etc. to gnaw on.

Not only is toothache painful and unpleasant, it can be traumatic for dogs to have teeth removed under anaesthetic after they lose weight due to being unable to eat properly.

If your old friend has started to ignore your verbal commands when out on a walk – either through *"switching off"* or deafness - try a whistle to attract her attention and then use an exaggerated hand signal for the Recall. Once your dog is looking at you, hold your arm out, palm down, at 90 degrees to your body and bring it down, keeping your arm straight, until your fingers point to your toes.

Hand signals worked very effectively with our old Max. He looked, understood ... and then decided if he was going to come or not - but at least he knew what he should be doing! More often than not he did come back, especially if the visual signal was repeated while he was still making up his mind.

Weight - no matter how old your Dachshund is, she still needs a waist! Maintaining a healthy weight with a balanced diet and regular, gentler exercise are two of the most important things you can do for your dog.

Environment - Make sure your dog has a nice soft place to rest her old bones, which may mean adding an extra blanket to her bed. This should be in a place that is not too hot or cold, as she may not be able to regulate her body temperature as well as when she was younger.

She also needs plenty of undisturbed sleep and should not be pestered and/or bullied by younger dogs, other animals or young children. If her eyesight is failing, move obstacles out of her way or use pet barriers to reduce the chance of injuries.

Going up and down stairs, jumping on and off furniture or in or out of the car should definitely NOT be allowed. It's high impact for old joints and bones. She will need a helping hand on to/into the couch, bed or car - or a ramp.

Breeder Kristin Cihos-Williams has a carpeted ramp to help her Dachshunds get on to the bed. I wish we'd thought of carpet. We bought an expensive plastic ramp for one old dog, but it proved to be a complete waste of money as she didn't like the feel of the non-slip surface on her paws. After a few tentative attempts, she steadfastly refused to set paw on it and we donated the ramp to a canine charity!

Exercise - Take the lead from your dog, if she doesn't want to walk as far, then don't. But if your dog doesn't want to go out at all, you will have to coax her out. ALL old dogs need exercise, not only to keep their joints moving, but also to keep their heart, lungs and joints exercised, and their minds engaged with different places, scents, etc.

Ears – Sometimes older dogs – particularly long-coated ones - produce more ear wax, so check inside the ears regularly. Keeping the hair under the ear flap groomed very short will allow good air circulation, reduce moisture in the ear and lessen the wax and yeast build-up. If necessary, use clean damp cotton wool to clean out the inner ear and pluck extra ear hair if it's getting waxy.

Time to Get Checked Out

If your dog is showing any of these signs, get her checked out by a vet:

- Excessive increased urination or drinking, which can be a sign of reduced liver or kidney function, Cushing's disease or diabetes

- Constipation or not urinating regularly, a possible symptom of a digestive system or organ disorder

- Incontinence, which could be a sign of a mental or physical problem

- Cloudy eyes, possibly cataracts

- Decreased appetite – often one of the first signs of an underlying problem

- Lumps or bumps on the body - often benign, but can occasionally be malignant (cancerous)

- Excessive sleeping or a lack of interest in you and her surroundings

- Diarrhoea or vomiting

- A darkening and dryness of skin that never seems to get any better, which can be a sign of hypothyroidism

- Any other out-of-the-ordinary behaviour for your dog. A change in patterns or behaviour is often your dog's way of telling you that all is not well

What the Experts Say

Kristin Cihos-Williams, Kinderteckel, California: "My Standard Smooth Dachshunds tend to start looking like seniors once they get to about 10 or 11. They rarely grey on their faces before then, especially the black and tans. I have noticed that reds tend to grey on their faces before them.

"I have eight and nine-year-old Dachshunds that run competitively in the field champion stakes at field trials. I have had Standard Smooth Dachshunds live until age 17 so, to me, an eight-year-old-dog is still in middle age.

"I don't change their diet to a senior or low-fat food. Senior foods tend to have less protein and fat. My senior dogs hunt and stay active outside so, especially in the winter months, they need fat and protein. All of my adults get salmon oil and green-lipped mussel supplements. As my dogs age, I often add joint supplements with glucosamine chondroitin and MSM. I also use Ester C (Vitamin C).

"At a certain point, closer to age 13 or 14, depending on the dog, I have noticed a form of canine dementia. As they start to progress into this stage, I notice a different tone to the bark, and the dog becomes more needy and bossy. I am not sure if this is due to neurological decline, loss of vision, etc.

"I notice some loss of muscle mass with senior dogs after about age eight or nine. If they stay active, the change is not as obvious. I have an 11-year-old Standard Smooth bitch who hunts lizards incessantly all day long! Her muscle tone feels much better to me than that of her brother, who is not an active, compulsive hunter like she is. Staying consistently active helps dogs maintain muscle mass. I do not bring senior dogs on more strenuous hikes. I let them decide when and where to self-exercise.

"Most of my dogs that stay with me for life also stay intact for life, as long as there are no compelling reasons to spay or neuter late in life. Because they are intact, they do not have *"spay coat,"* which is a curly texture of the coat that occurs after spaying or neutering changes the hormones. Without spay coat, there is only a little difference in coat between my seniors and younger adults. My seniors tend to have coarser coats, compared to the younger adults, but nothing like the difficult-to-manage spay coat.

"I bring dogs to certified canine chiropractors for routine chiropractic adjustments, but I have never tried cold laser or deep tissue massage. I have been told by families who have owned significantly aged dogs from me (over 16) that acupuncture and cold laser helped with arthritis."

Sue Seath, Sunsong Dachshunds, Buckinghamshire, England: "Dachshunds start to age at about 10 years old, although we have bred some Standard Wires that lived to 17. Typical signs are arthritis and general slowing down with movement."

Photo of Inky still enjoying life at age 11, courtesy of Sue.

"They also sleep more, are less keen to go on long walks and might be a bit grumpy due to low level pain. With the Wires, the coat quality deteriorates, with sparser, drier hair.

"We change to a Senior dry food and add Yumove joint supplement. We reduce the length of walk and eventually give up taking them walking, we just let them out in the garden to do what they like. My advice is to manage weight and levels of exercise."

Bastiaan Smit, Daxiesburrow, Aberdeenshire, Scotland: "Our Otto von Konigstannen (Standard Wire) is now 11 years young and he does not show signs of fatigue. In particular, when his girl is in heat, he is as proud as a young stag! Otto as pack leader is alert and defends his girls and, apart from a few grey hairs, he is not showing signs of ageing yet.

"We have not changed yet to a Senior diet food. We observe his weight and exercise and feed him with standard pellets (working dog) and raw tripe or mince beef. We also check his faeces, urine, coat and behaviour for signs of aging. We walk daily at least two to three kilometres, with seven to nine kilometres at intervals."

Lisa Cole, Foosayo Dachshunds, North Yorkshire; "My Ruby *(Standard Long, pictured)* is 13 years old and has slowed down a lot, but only in the last couple of years. She is drinking more, with slower walks - no rushing around - and wants to snooze a lot.

"I've kept her on the Adult diet and add any vitamins that may help her joints, skin and fur. I use CSJK9 and Billy No Mates! 325g, which is a natural flea and tick remedy. She also gets a fresh raw egg on her kibble every day.

"The older dogs are much more relaxed day-to-day, but don't tolerate youngsters! They also don't walk as far or as fast as they used to, so we adapt exercise routines and always walk to what the weakest dog can do.

"I massage all my dogs; it's very relaxing and they love it. I work across the shoulders, down the back and into all their legs. I only use vets if I have to, so worming, flea treatment, etc. I do with herbs, and arnica for knocks and bruises.

"My advice is to love them, walk them to their ability, and don't start giving human food to your old dog or they will gain weight which they will not be able to run off, so give them a good dog diet. Expect some warts, cysts, and long nails which need clipping as they don't wear them down as easily."

Melissa Sworab, Rabows (Mini Long) Dachshunds, Texas: "We had one Mini Smooth that aged very quickly – greying around the muzzle around two to three years of age, where six is usually considered a senior, but the rest of ours don't seem like seniors until well past 9 or 10.

"We usually don't change the diet unless there is a reason to - but increase fresh veggies as snacks and avoid almost all fatty foods entirely, just out of precaution. We feed kibble, raw and fresh human food, fruits and raw and cooked vegetables often. We don't usually recommend much in the way of supplements if you are feeding lots of good food, including hearts, and fresh food, fruit and vegetables. We may add additional glucosamine chondroitin if they are slowing down.

"Older dogs can be less tolerant to puppies and children, or to being harassed by another dog. They also get fussy with their food and may not eat as much OR eat everything in sight with aggression in the last weeks. Any sudden or semi-gradual change in their personality should be investigated as a sign of something not quite right.

"We pretty much let them do what they are able and not push them. We will reduce the time outside if it's hot and increase cool water access around the house. Short slow walks as tolerated. No more long strenuous walks or hikes, unless they go crazy if they don't!

"The coat will get dull and drier, sometimes fuzzy. We have found that applying a light coat oil (or cuticle oil) every two weeks, as well as using a shedding tool to remove the dry, fuzzy undercoat can bring a coat back to life in just a few weeks, if not days.

"As far as health goes, any patella issues or heart murmurs will worsen - obesity can exacerbate heart issues. Our dogs are usually great, even as oldies, albeit a little slow, right up until they aren't. So far, we haven't had any long-drawn-out age-related illnesses to contend with - and hope it stays that way. The older they get, the more we limit all scents, chemicals and non-essential vaccines. We make sure there are beds in every room, sometimes two, so they can rest between voyages around the house.

"We offer more water bowls and will on occasion add some chicken broth to be sure they stay hydrated. Moistened kibble always helps as well if dental problems are an issue, but we also feed more cooked human food versus raw, so it's easier to chew and digest.

We like to use the T-Touch (a specific massage technique) as well as chiropractic and acupuncture to help the older ones feel their best. With lifespan, 10 is a bit early to lose them, but it can happen; 12 is still too soon, but closer to expectations. 14 to 16 is phenomenal for the breed, but we have had them live to 18 without much trouble at all, right until the end."

Pauline Cheeseman, Colraed Miniature Dachshunds, Surrey, England: "I class them as senior over eight years old. They start to get the first few grey hairs and they can start to get a bit thicker round the waistline.

Photo of Pauline's Frankie looking very alert aged 11.

"I feed raw and I do give a little bit less, and not so much with bone, so four days with bone and three days without. I do give them oily fish twice a week, and turmeric made into golden paste, when they get into double figures I give green-lipped mussel extract all to help joints.

"They all get a daily once over, its vital to see if they have any lumps or bumps that need checking. Mine have had cancers. With the cancers, I've had a nasty one which looked just like a spot, I took her in and insisted on a needle biopsy.

"It came back as an aggressive melanoma, but as they knew what they were dealing with, they removed it and with a big margin to catch any spread and it has not returned so far. The others have mainly been harmless, fatty lumps, or mammary gland lumps and bad teeth, which caused an abscess into the nasal passage - something that can happen quite quickly and can be hard to heal.

"Generally, they do sleep more, but I've noticed no other changes. I don't change the exercise regime too much; the oldies usually stroll along behind us at their own speed.

"My tips for owners are: let them pace themselves on walks, watch the waistline and decrease food if they put on weight - it's better for their backs if they are leaner. Clean their teeth regularly and watch for excessive sneezing, as its often a tooth issue working its way into the nasal passage.

"When you groom, run your hands over every bit of them regularly. If a spot or lump is there for a few days, take them to the vet and get a test. Love them loads. Lift them on and off chairs if they start to struggle and you don't have a ramp, but do keep them fit and well-exercised until they can't. Then it's just lots of love and cuddles."

The Last Lap

Huge advances in veterinary science have meant that there are countless procedures and medications that can prolong the life of your dog, and this is a good thing. But there comes a time when you do have to let go.

If your dog is showing all the signs of ageing, has an ongoing medical condition from which she cannot recover, is showing signs of pain, anxiety or distress and there is no hope of improvement, then the dreaded time has come to say goodbye.

You owe it to her.

There is no point keeping an old dog alive if all the dog has ahead is pain and death. We have their lives in our hands and we can give them the gift of passing away peacefully and humanely at the end when the time is right.

Losing our beloved companion, our best friend, a member of the family, is truly heart-breaking. But one of the things we realise at the back of our minds when we got that gorgeous, lively little puppy that bounded up to meet us like we were the best person in the whole wide world is the pain that comes with it. We know we will live longer than them and that we'll probably have to make this most painful of decisions at some time in the future.

It's the worst thing about being a dog owner.

If your Dachshund has had a long and happy life, then you could not have done any more. You were a great owner and your dog was lucky to have you. Remember all the good times you had together.

Try not to rush out and buy another dog straight away. Assess your current life and lifestyle and, if your situation is right, only then consider getting another dog and all that that entails in terms of time, commitment and expense over the next 12 to 15 years.

Whatever you decide to do, put the dog first.

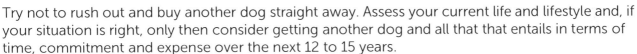

Contributing Breeders

UK

Sue and Ian Seath, Sunsong Dachshunds, (Standard Wires and Miniature Smooths), Buckinghamshire http://www.sunsong.co.uk

Stefanie and Steve Millington, CunAnnun Long-Haired Miniature Dachshunds, Norfolk

Lisa Lindfield, Zabannah Dachshunds, (all three types of Miniature), Lincolnshire
www.facebook.com/lisa.zabannah

Judith Carruthers, Stanegate Wirehaired Dachshunds, Cumbria
email: knxhll@aol.com

Bastiaan Smit and Judith Smit Haffmans, Daxiesburrow (Standard Wires), Aberdeenshire
www.facebook.com/DaxiesBurrow-Wirehaired-Dachshund-1663098473993243

Sandra and Karl Robertson, Hartlebury Miniature (Smooth) Dachshunds, Worcester

Hannah Norton, Jacksondax, (Standard and Miniature Smooths), South Devon
www.facebook.com/groups/1946129145508137

Lisa Cole, Foosayo Dachshunds, (Standard Long-Haired), North Yorkshire
https://m.facebook.com/foosayo

Pauline Cheeseman, Colraed Miniature Dachshunds, (Miniature Smooths), Surrey
www.facebook.com/groups/745598998969275

USA

Kristin Cihos-Williams, Kinderteckel Standard Smooth Dachshunds, California
kinderteckel@aol.com www.facebook.com/kinderteckel.smoothstandarddachshunds
https://schoolhousedachshunds.com/kinderteckel-smooths

Brenna Carlisle and Laura Potash, Heritage Hounds, (Long-Haired), Ragland, Alabama
www.heritagehounds.net

Marianne McCullough, Kenmar Hounds, (Miniature Long-Haired) Coconut Creek, Florida
www.Kenmarhounds.com

Pame Bates, Doxies Treasures (Miniature Long-Haired) Westwood, California
www.doxiestreasures.com

Melissa and Mark Sworab, Rabows Dachshunds, (Miniature Long-Haired), Houston, Texas
http://www.rabows.com

and

Dr Sara Skiwski, Western Dragon holistic veterinary practice, San Jose, California
www.thewesterndragon.com

Useful Contacts

UK

Dachshund Breed Council for health information and a full list of UK Dachshund clubs
https://dachshundbreedcouncil.wordpress.com

Dachshund Club www.dachshundclub.co.uk

Kennel Club (UK) Assured Breeders
www.thekennelclub.org.uk/search/find-an-assured-breeder

KC Good Citizen Scheme www.thekennelclub.org.uk/training/good-citizen-dog-training-scheme

RSPCA Puppy Contract https://puppycontract.rspca.org.uk/home

Association of Pet Dog Trainers UK www.apdt.co.uk

All About Dog Food www.allaboutdogfood.co.uk

USA

AKC (American Kennel Club) www.akc.org/dog-breeds/dachshund

AKC Preparing a Puppy Contract www.akc.org/expert-advice/dog-breeding/preparing-a-contract-for-puppy-buyers

AKC Canine Good Citizen www.akc.org/products-services/training-programs/canine-good-citizen

Helps find lost or stolen dogs, register your dog's microchip www.akcreunite.org

Useful info on dog foods (US) www.dogfoodadvisor.com

Association of Pet Dog Trainers US www.apdt.com

Canadian Association of Professional Pet Dog Trainers www.cappdt.ca

Dachshund internet forums and Facebook groups are also a good source of information from other owners.

Copyright

Disclaimer

This book has been written to provide helpful information on Dachshunds. It is not meant to be used, nor should it be used, to diagnose or treat any medical condition. For diagnosis or treatment of any animal medical problem, consult a qualified veterinarian.

The author is not responsible for any specific health or allergy conditions that may require medical supervision and is not liable for any damages or negative consequences from any treatment, action, application or preparation, to any animal or to any person reading or following the information in this book.

The views expressed by contributors to this book are solely personal and do not necessarily represent those of the author. References are provided for informational purposes only and do not constitute endorsement of any websites or other sources.

Vet's Name: _ _ _ _ _ _ _ _ _ _ _ _ _   Groomer's Name: _ _ _ _ _ _ _ _ _ _ _ _

Vet's Phone: _ _ _ _ _ _ _ _ _ _ _   Groomer's Phone: _ _ _ _ _ _ _ _ _ _ _

Day Care: _ _ _ _ _ _ _ _ _ _ _ _   Holiday Sitter: _ _ _ _ _ _ _ _ _ _ _ _

Pet's Name	Date	Vet Visit	Groomer	NOTES

Printed in Great Britain
by Amazon

11929311R10140